Triumph at Imphal-Kohima

Triumph at Imphal-Kohima

How the Indian Army Finally Stopped the Japanese Juggernaut

Raymond Callahan

University Press of Kansas

© 2017 by the University Press of Kansas
All rights reserved

Published by the University Press of Kansas (Lawrence, Kansas 66045), which
was organized by the Kansas Board of Regents and is operated and funded by
Emporia State University, Fort Hays State University, Kansas State University,
Pittsburg State University, the University of Kansas, and Wichita State
University.

Library of Congress Cataloging-in-Publication Data
Names: Callahan, Raymond, author.
Title: Triumph at Imphal-Kohima : how the Indian Army finally stopped the
Japanese juggernaut / Raymond Callahan.
Description: Lawrence, Kansas : University Press of Kansas, 2017. | Series:
Modern war studies | Includes bibliographical references and index.
Identifiers: LCCN 2016047596| ISBN 9780700624270 (cloth : alk. paper) |
ISBN 9780700624287 (ebook)
Subjects: LCSH: World War, 1939–1945—Campaigns—India. | Imphal, Battle
of, Imphal, India, 1944. | Kohima, Battle of, Kohima, India, 1944. | India.
Army—History—World War, 1939–1945. | Great Britain. Army. British Indian
Army—History—World War, 1939–1945. | Japan. Rikugun—History—World
War, 1939–1945. | World War, 1939–1945—Participation, East Indian. |
India—History, Military—20th century.
Classification: LCC D767.6 .C293 2017 | DDC 940.54/29—dc23
LC record available at https://lccn.loc.gov/2016047596.

British Library Cataloguing-in-Publication Data is available.

Printed in the United States of America

10 9 8 7 6 5 4 3 2 1

The paper used in this publication is recycled and contains 30 percent
postconsumer waste. It is acid free and meets the minimum requirements of
the American National Standard for Permanence of Paper for Printed Library
Materials Z39.48–1992.

To the memory of my beloved wife
Mary Helen McPeek Callahan,
1942–2012

. . . and in gratitude to our wonderful daughter, Sarah,
who helped me carry on.

Contents

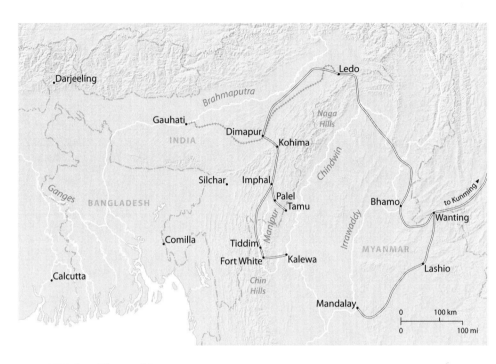

XIV Army Theater of Operations, 1943–1944

Preface and Acknowledgments

The battle of Imphal . . . is not easy to follow.
—Field Marshal Sir William Slim, 1956

This is a very considerable understatement, as anyone who has studied the battle can attest.[1] It was fought over a period of some ten months—most of 1944—from the preliminary Japanese operations in February until the conclusion of the "monsoon pursuit" in the autumn. It pitted Lieutenant General William Slim's British XIV Army (in fact largely Indian, Gurkha, and African) against the Japanese *Fifteenth Army*. It was fought on an enormous battlefield—more than three hundred miles from north to south, far larger than any European battlefield, except those of the Eastern Front. When it was over, Slim's XIV Army had inflicted on the Japanese the worst military defeat in modern Japanese history, virtually destroying *Fifteenth Army* and opening the way to the campaign in which Slim would reconquer Burma the following year, destroying the entire Japanese *Burma Area Army* (the equivalent of a British army group) in the process. Slim's victory was overshadowed in Britain at the time by war news from closer to home—the grinding struggles at Cassino and in the Anzio beachhead, the looming cross-channel invasion, and the beginnings of the "V" weapon assault. Later it would be largely ignored in Churchill's war memoirs and overshadowed in British historical writing by the generation-long fascination with the desert war against Rommel. Only in recent years have Slim's campaigns been recognized for what they are: brilliant exercises in leadership by the finest British army commander since Wellington.

Slim's 1944 victory, often called "Imphal-Kohima," was fought in a landscape some of which had not been mapped, and sustained by a highly precarious supply system. Slim was additionally burdened by a nominal

American subordinate whose agenda did not include wholehearted co-operation with British allies, and also a British military eccentric who had, as a result of Churchill's patronage, a large private army whose separate (and largely irrelevant) operations Slim had nonetheless to support. Then, of course, there was the Imperial Japanese Army, which, despite considerable shortcomings in areas like supply and operational direction, was a ferocious and unyielding opponent, whose rank and file could be depended on to fight and die where they stood rather than accept defeat.

The fact that Slim won a total victory, despite the many handicaps, suggests that Imphal should receive more attention than it has. One explanation for this comparative neglect amid the libraries of books on World War II is the nature of the army Slim commanded.[2] Officially "British," it was in fact largely drawn, like Slim himself, from Britain's other army: the Indian Army. Long one of the props of imperial Britain, the Indian Army had fared ill in the opening stages of the war against Japan, largely for reasons beyond its control. Then during 1943, in a remarkable exercise in military transformation, it remade itself. Slim's victories of 1944 were the capstone on that process of regeneration. But when Imphal was won, the Indian Army of the British Raj had only three years to live—ahead lay independence, the partition of the subcontinent, and the division of the army between India and Pakistan.

Despite Slim's remarkable personal account, *Defeat Into Victory*, one of the best military memoirs in the language, the Indian Army and its achievements in the last war it would fight under the British flag faded from the consciousness of a Britain rapidly becoming postimperial. Much of the writing on the battle focused on one of its most dramatic episodes, the siege of Kohima, where a small garrison made a heroic stand to hold a key point against huge odds. The comparative neglect of the Imphal battle is understandable—up to a point. British national strategy during the war focused intently on the European theater. Afterward, historical attention followed wartime strategic focus. This European bias was given a powerful nudge by Winston Churchill, who had always disliked and distrusted the Indian Army and who, in *Closing the Ring*, gave Imphal barely a page—and mentioned neither Slim nor XIV Army by name.

Churchill had swept Imphal and XIV Army's entire campaign to the margins of his narrative, yet they did not attain even that position in the American telling. American interest in the war against Japan had, of course, always centered on the exploits of the fast carrier task forces and the Marine Corps combat epics that carried US forces across the vast reaches of the Pacific. The Forgotten Army, as XIV Army was known during the war, became the "overlooked" army as the narrative of Britain's war took shape afterward and the "unknown" army in the United States. Lately historical attention has begun to focus on what Slim and the Indian Army accomplished in Burma and so an account centered on Imphal when that accomplishment first became manifest seems timely.

Because this book is written with a general readership in mind, it begins with the backstory, a brief account of the most remarkable institution created by the British Empire, the Indian Army, as well as the early career of William Joseph Slim, the last—and greatest—of what Napoleon once called the "sepoy generals" produced by that army. Napoleon did not intend his remark—made about Wellington—to be flattering. Many British Army officers were similarly dismissive of their Indian Army counterparts. Wellington of course won—so did Slim, the greatest British army commander since the Iron Duke, leading his service to a sunset moment of victory.

This is a work of synthesis, the result of years of reading and thinking about the subject, since my interest in it was first kindled by reading Slim's *Defeat Into Victory* as an undergraduate. During the decades since, I have accumulated numerous debts, to students, colleagues, libraries, and archives, a list too long to enumerate. I am very grateful to them all. I would, however, like to acknowledge two friends and fellow historians in particular: Alan Jeffreys of the Imperial War Museum, and Professor Daniel Marston of the Australian National University—both outstanding historians of the Indian Army of the Raj. Their impeccable scholarship has illuminated my own understanding of that fascinating institution and conversation with them has been very helpful as I finished this book. I would also like to thank Jennifer Ferris, who turned my handwriting into usable text.

Finally, my thanks to Mike Briggs of the University Press of Kansas, who, over many years, has encouraged and supported me, doing far more than an editor's job description required.

The greatest of my debts is acknowledged in the dedication. I began thinking about this book shortly before my wife was diagnosed with Stage IV cancer. From time to time during the years of treatment that followed, encouraged by her, I would jot down some ideas, even whole paragraphs (some of which in my handwritten first draft contain her editorial corrections). After her death I put it all away. When I eventually retrieved it from a drawer, several years later, I remembered that Mary Helen always told me that historians wrote too much for one another and not enough for a wider readership. I hope she would have approved of this effort to heed that advice, and that my daughter, Sarah, will see it as the fruit of the loving support she has unfailingly given me.

—Raymond Callahan
Newark, Delaware
September 2016

Triumph at
Imphal-Kohima

1

Monsoon, 1942

On a May morning during Burma's 1942 monsoon season, a deeply tired acting lieutenant general stood beside a "track"—a rough unsurfaced road—on the edge of the Imphal Plain in eastern India, close to India's border with Burma. For two months he had led "Burcorps" (Burma Corps) as, under continuous Japanese pressure, it withdrew from Burma. Now that withdrawal—the longest retreat in British military history—was over.[1] What was left of Burcorps was trudging up the muddy track from the Chindwin River, where, lacking the ability to ferry them across, the last of their wheeled and tracked vehicles, together with artillery, had been wrecked and abandoned. As they marched, they passed the pathetic human wreckage left by the columns of mostly Indian refugees who had trudged out of India before and beside them, falling victim all too often to hostile Burmese or dying by the roadside of disease and exhaustion.

As he stood there, the general was conscious that he had made mistakes, some quite costly, during the retreat. He also knew that, while now safe from Japanese pursuit, the rest and recuperation that his troops so badly needed and so richly deserved did not await them at Imphal. The formation holding what was now the front line against the Japanese, the 23rd Indian Division, was dangling at the very end of the war's most precarious line of communication. On short rations itself, there was little it could do for the decimated and tattered ranks of Burcorps. The army commander responsible for Imphal disliked the general and seemed both indifferent to the plight of the Burcorps remnants and disdainful of both them and their commander.

As he stood watching his men file past, looking like scarecrows but still behaving like soldiers, a grim determination formed in the mind of this formidable-looking man. He would fix what was wrong, eliminate the mistakes, including his own, that had led to defeat—and then redeem that defeat with victory. Two years later, Lieutenant General William Slim of the Indian Army's 6th Gurkha Rifles would do just that—at Imphal. The best way to begin an account of how that transformation and the victory that followed came about is with a look at the service to which Slim and most of Burcorps belonged—the Indian Army of the British Raj.

2

The Indian Army

The Indian Army was created by a trading company, and the shadow of its origins hovered over it until the end, affecting in important ways even the Burma campaign (at which point the Indian Army was some two centuries old). The East India Company began operations in India early in the seventeenth century (roughly coeval with English settlement at Jamestown). Almost from the beginning, it had employed Indians as guards and watchmen for its "factories," as trading stations were known. The principal factories became cities and regional Company headquarters, known as "Presidency towns"—Bombay, Madras, Calcutta (today Mumbai, Chennai, and Koalkata)—as the Company's wealth and penetration of the subcontinent increased. In the mid-eighteenth century, in response to both the threats and opportunities offered by the decline of the Mughal Empire, as well as the challenge posed by an aggressive rival, the French East India Company, the Company's factory guards morphed into three small Presidency armies. Armies, however, require officers, and here a problem arose.

The British Army, whose continuous institutional history begins with the 1660 Restoration of the Stuart monarchy at the end of Britain's civil wars, was officered in a way that reflected not only the structure of British society but one of the key lessons learned by the monarchy and the British governing class from those wars. The Royalists had been defeated, Charles I beheaded, and Britain ruled for a dozen years by a professional army, the New Model Army, and its commander, Lieutenant General Oliver Cromwell. The New Model was officered, in part at least, by base-born men (working-class or lower-middle-class in our categorization), not at all the sort who had traditionally provided military and political leadership in Britain. When Cromwell's death (1658) and fissures in the New Model's unity opened the way for the Restoration and the end of Britain's only experience with military rule, steps were taken to see that it was never repeated. Officers henceforth purchased their commissions and every subsequent step in rank up to colonel. They were not only the King's officers but also drawn from that strata of British society whose ability to purchase commissions meant they had a strong vested interest in the existing social and political structure. There would never again be an army officered by outsiders to threaten British society's natural rulers. In 1688, in a coda to the civil wars, the Glorious Revolution asserted—among many other things—the supremacy of the landed governing class in parliament over the King's army but did nothing to change the social base of the officer corps (which can not unfairly be described for the next two centuries as the landed governing class in uniform). Purchase, although often criticized, endured until 1870. Even when, in the teeth of bitter resistance, purchase was ended, the officer corps of the British Army preserved its peculiar recruitment policies in a slightly different way. An officer's pay was low, but his expenses were not. The gap was covered by private means—that is, personal and family wealth. By 1870, wealth derived from sources other than land was increasingly dominant in Britain, but that was largely screened out of the officer corps by the filter of the regimental system. The Crown bestowed a commission, but it was the officers of the regiment who decided whether to accept a new member. Thus wealth of the wrong sort, or someone from an unacceptable background, however wealthy, could be barred unofficially but effectively from the officer corps. This variant on purchase lasted until World War II. Bernard Fergusson, who fought in Burma, joined a Highland regiment, the Black Watch, in the mid-1930s. The private means necessary to join the officers' mess of the Black Watch was greater than the annual income of most Britons at that date—one of Fergusson's fellow subalterns even brought his butler with him. This system did not prevent men of ability from becoming officers and rising to the top (and the British Army's gunners and sappers—artillery and engineers—were always a partial exception), but its class basis, and class outlook, stood in total contrast to the army the East India Company created in the second half of the eighteenth century.

The Company did not have to concern itself with controlling any threat by its standing army to the existing British social and political order (it did, however, decide at an early date not to officer its armies with Indians). It simply wanted an army that would be effective and as cheap as possible. The former proved surprisingly easy to attain; the latter would prove very elusive. The effectiveness of the Company's armies had little to do with the Company itself. It was the product of exporting the end result of Europe's two-centuries-long Military Revolution and putting it to work in a setting where there was nothing comparable.[1] The disciplined firepower developed by carefully trained infantry in linear formation, supported by artillery that had genuine battlefield mobility, is the most obvious component of this style of warfare. As important, however, were the crucial underpinnings of battlefield performance: the organizational skills that raised, equipped, trained, moved, and supplied soldiers, and the financial strength to pay them while they served and to reward them when discharged. The Indian soldiers (known as "sepoys") who conquered India for the Company were, by and large, little different in background from the armies of the Indian rulers they defeated. The crucial difference was that they were operating within a structure that maximized the impact of their battlefield courage.

The Military Revolution was brought to India by the officers the Company found for its armies. If the Company had little to do with the tactical ideas and organizational norms that shaped those armies, it had a decisive impact on the structure of its officer corps. The Company's charter conferred sovereign powers on it—but only in India. Officers commissioned by the Company were officers only east of the Cape of Good Hope. The Company initially offered neither paid leaves nor pensions (and pay was not particularly generous). To hold down costs it had no ranks above colonel (and very few of them) as well as fewer officers per unit than the average British battalion, even though its battalions were a third larger than comparable British army units. Promotion could be very rapid in the British Army, driven as it was by purchase. The Company's armies, in contrast, promoted by strict seniority, something the officers strongly supported, as it gave everyone a theoretically equal shot at the few senior positions—even though the very high death rate, largely the result of climate and disease, meant very few would survive the thirty-year climb to colonel. Given all this, the obvious question is: Why did anyone choose to enter the Company's service? The answer is that India was an opportunity, albeit a very dangerous one, for young men whose family background, connections, and resources (compendiously known in the eighteenth century as "interest") were insufficient for a gentleman's career at home. The British officers of the Indian Army were always more middle class than their British Army counterparts, or, as a group of them put it in the late eighteenth century, "we are men without interest."

Having taken the gamble of Indian service, the Company's officers quickly elaborated for themselves a bewildering array of allowances and perquisites in lieu of high salaries. Growing more ample as one rose in rank, they could make extremely rich men of the small number who survived to fill the few lieutenant colonel's and colonel's slots available. By the late eighteenth century, the Company's armies had made "John Company" the most formidable force in the subcontinent (and the remaining "country powers," as the Company's local rivals were known, were scrambling desperately to refashion their armies on similar lines). Into this situation, the presence of regular British Army units introduced, as far as the Company's officers were concerned, serious and unwelcome complications. British officers were the King's officers; the Company's, the servants of a merchant corporation. Every British regular automatically outranked every Company officer of the same grade. Purchase meant a British Army captain could be in late adolescence; an Indian Army captain might have waited a decade and more for that rank. Moreover, when a British officer displaced a Company's officer from a position by virtue of automatically outranking him, that Company officer often lost the financial perquisites attached to the position. (King's officers never took command of sepoy battalions, but lucrative command of large formations often fell to them.) This affront to pride and pocketbook was only an occasional irritation until the 1770s, when, in recognition of the increasing importance of India to Britain's wealth and power, the British Army became a permanent presence there. The result was a crisis that shaped the future of the Indian Army in ways still visible in the Burma campaign 150 years later.

An ill-judged and clumsily managed attempt by Lord Cornwallis (governor general, 1786–1793), backed by the government in London, to nationalize the Company's armies produced a furious reaction by the officers of the largest of them, the Bengal Army, who displayed a formidable ability to organize and fight in defense of the perquisites that made Indian exile worthwhile to them and equally adept at forcing the concession of an improved status for themselves. They funded a committee in London to lobby on their behalf, published some remarkably frank pamphlets arguing their case, and walked right up to the edge of mutiny against Cornwallis's successor, Sir John Shore, to enforce their demands. They won across the board because the sepoy army they led was indispensable to the Company's power (London compensated itself by sacking Shore). The Company's armies remained a separate service; their officers got the right to paid leave and pensions (neither on very generous terms) and eligibility for general officer rank. They were also granted concurrent royal commissions. This meant that a Company officer held a royal commission in the same rank as his Company commission. This solved the worst problems of supersession of Company by royal officers (but, of course, did nothing to make promotions faster in the Company's service, which meant veteran Indian officers could still be bumped by much younger but higher-ranking British Army officers). Finally the financial web of perquisites and allowances, the basis for Company officers' hopes of amassing a so-called competency before retirement, remained intact.

Although rarely remarked upon by historians, this episode had enormous and long-lasting consequences. The first was the institutional separateness of the Company's armies. After the crisis of the 1790s, with its revelation of both how determined the Company's officers were and how impossible they were to replace without disrupting the vital sepoy army, London never again challenged them. But neither did the regular British Army change its view of them. Cornwallis (a Guards officer) held a low view of their "smartness"—he dismissed the parade-ground performance of the sepoys as "dancing about . . . to jig tunes," apparently oblivious to the fact that the sepoy army had won for the Company its dominant position in India. The Company's officers were, the British Army held, social inferiors, and, professionally, well, they led "black" troops, didn't they? This sense of personal and professional superiority would never disappear. Officers of the Indian Army, under the Company and later the Crown, would always remain a group apart—semipermanent exiles whose services might be valuable but who were simply not quite equals. There was another factor as well, both in their lives in India and in the assessment of them by the British Army. Service in India soon became, for both civilians (i.e., administrators) and soldiers, a family affair—and many of those families came to have Indian blood in their veins. Until well into the nineteenth century, it was not uncommon for officers to have Indian mistresses. Some of the children of those liaisons—depending on complexion, among other variables—found their way into their fathers' profession. In Victorian and Edwardian years, this "touch of the tarbrush," known or suspected, was another factor in the condescending attitude toward Indian service officers all too often displayed by British regulars.

If the lineaments of the officer corps of the Company's armies and their relationship with the regular British Army was complete by the end of the eighteenth century, the nature of the sepoy units they led was not—that would undergo a dramatic transformation in the mid-nineteenth

century. The sepoys of the Company's armies reflected the recruiting
grounds available to them. The oldest, the Bombay Army, whose Presidency controlled little territory until the early nineteenth century, took
any recruits it could get, while the Madras Army (sometimes called in its
early days the "Coast Army" from the Coromandel Coast where Madras
was located) recruited largely from those groups in South Indian society
who had traditionally soldiered for local rulers. The pattern of the Bengal
Army was very different. The largest of the Company's armies—and the
one whose officers had faced down both the governor general and London—was able to tap the richest military manpower market in India, and
it had the financial resources to do so. Bengal sepoys came to be drawn,
almost exclusively, from either the client kingdom of Oudh (Awadh) or
the territories stretching northwest along the Ganges Valley from there
to Delhi (the Company's North-West Provinces, later the United Provinces and now Uttar Pradesh). Recruits from this area were abundant
and rather taller and fairer than the short, dark Madras sepoys—thus presenting, to British eyes, a better parade-ground appearance (although,
as noted, not good enough to impress a Guards officer like Cornwallis).
They were also, by and large, high-caste Hindus. Both the recruitment
area and the caste basis of the Bengal Army gave it a homogeneity that
would pose a danger if either discontent swept the villages from which
they came or the sepoys felt their caste under threat. By 1820, when the
Company's armies had made it India's "Paramount Power" at the conclusion of a series of wars that broke the remaining independent Indian
states, changes in the tone and activities of both the Company's administration and the Bengal officer corps had begun to do just that. Company
policy, after its rule was secure, was to reform and rationalize the administration of its territories in the interest of both revenue and what would
now be called "modernization." What seemed reform to the Company,
however, looked like an onslaught on custom, tradition, and faith itself
to many Indians. Indian rulers and landowners saw rights, privileges, and
incomes abridged (and in the case of Indian rulers, now reduced to Company clients, there were often abridgements of territory as well). Peasant
farmers, on whose shoulders the whole structure of Indian rulership had
always rested, were often facing higher rates of tax, more rigorously collected, and new forms of land tenure. Company prohibitions on such
practices as *suttee*, prohibitions that were reasonable and, indeed, necessary from a British perspective, seemed to some Indians an assault on their
faith.[2] Ripples of unease began to spread across the Bengal Presidency.

This might not have mattered but for the fact that the sepoys of the Bengal Army were, simultaneously, becoming uneasy and estranged from their officers.

Exactly when the Bengal Army began to deteriorate is a point on which historians differ, but it is clear that problems were appearing as early as the 1820s. It was not only that the problems affecting their villages and fears about caste unsettled the sepoys; there were also growing problems specific to the army. The nature of the Bengal officer corps was changing, as were the uses to which the army was put. Generational change brought young officers out from Britain with new ideas and assumptions—British rule in India was a given, and in the triumphalist mood engendered by victory over Napoleon its continuation was taken for granted—as was sepoy loyalty. The seniority system, sacred to the officer corps, had pushed energetic and ambitious young officers, looking at a decades-long wait to reach field grade, to opt to leave their regiments to serve in a variety of other Company positions where promotion, responsibility, and enhanced income were easier to attain. (One favorite was "secondment"—transfer—to the Political Service, whose officers supervised Indian client states, served as diplomatic representatives to independent rulers in the Company's now huge South Asian sphere, and often organized and governed newly acquired territories.) There is evidence that those officers who remained with units were less engaged with their sepoys than in the past—fewer really in command of their men's language, fewer interested in their customs and traditions. This lessening of understanding and sympathy occurred as new issues arose that made those qualities in officers increasingly important.

The Company's armies were now seen as not only the safeguard of the Company Raj but also the strategic reserve for the growing British position all around the rim of the Indian Ocean. Madras sepoys had served in the expedition that took Spanish Manila during the Seven Years' War and continued to serve overseas with no difficulty (as did Bombay sepoys). But to the high-caste soldiers of the Bengal Army, crossing the "black water" was a serious matter, a deadly threat to caste. Orders to proceed to Burma (albeit overland) produced a bloody mutiny by a Bengal regiment in 1824, and foreign service was a major problem for Bengal sepoys thereafter. Then came the blows to the prestige of the Company's arms represented by the disasters of the First Afghan War (1839–1841) and the near defeat by the Sikhs, the last significant Indian power (whose kingdom was based in the Punjab), in the two wars that expensively conquered them in the 1840s. In the aftermath of the annexation of the Sikh kingdom, the Company's "Politicals" (nearly all drawn from the Bengal officer corps) began enlisting former soldiers from the Sikh forces (Sikhs as well as Punjabi Muslims) in a new force of irregulars to patrol the newly acquired and still turbulent territories. A very clever move to employ men who might otherwise have proved a threat to the Company's control of the Punjab, it was seen by Bengal sepoys as a threat of a different kind: the new irregular units were cheaper, made up of groups hostile to them on religious and cultural grounds, and might well signal a British plan to dispense with them. As if to validate those fears, in the aftermath of the Sikh wars came a series of cost-cutting measures that ended certain bonuses (known as *batta*, traditionally paid to Bengal sepoys at varying rates) and, finally, the General Enlistment Act of 1855. Intended to end the problem of refusals of overseas service by Bengal units, it seemed a breach of faith to the sepoys, who in many cases expected their sons to follow them into regiments that they regarded as "theirs," offering an honorable career with distinct financial advantages, various perquisites on retirement, and prestige in their villages. Now they would have to face either loss of caste or loss of a career they had expected to pass on to their sons.

The result of this accumulation of slights, neglects, and grievances was an eruption in May 1857 at Meerut near Delhi, one of the Company's major military stations. The Great Sepoy Mutiny, as the British would remember it, came, amazingly, as a complete surprise to many Bengal Army officers. The trigger for the outbreak was the greased cartridge, to be used with the new Enfield rifle with which the Company's armies were being reequipped. A rumor spread that the grease on the cartridges was a mixture of pork and beef fat, thus offending the religious sensibilities of Hindu and Muslim sepoys alike. The Company's denials—in fact largely accurate—in the atmosphere of toxic suspicion that now gripped the sepoys were simply disbelieved. Fearing ritual pollution and loss of caste (followed by forcible Christianization), the overwhelmingly Hindu Bengal Army exploded. It was the greatest challenge British rule had yet faced. The revolt of the Bengal Army set off, in turn, peasant uprisings up and down the Ganges Valley. Various Indian rulers saw an opportunity to reclaim the power and status stripped from them by the Company. Within a month the mutineers were in control of Delhi and restored the Mughal Empire in the form of the aged Mughal ruler Bahadur Shah II, long a Company pensioner. Company authority had evaporated over large areas of northern India.

British power nevertheless survived. Victorian Britons saw the putting down of the Mutiny as an epic of British courage, determination, and leadership over treacherous and savage adversaries who greatly outnumbered them. Courage, determination, and leadership were certainly on display (as was sheer ferocity, something the Victorians airbrushed out), but so were a number of other factors without which those traits would have been of little avail. The Madras and Bombay armies were unaffected, insulated by their very different recruiting patterns and perhaps as well by officers who had not drifted as far from their sepoys as those in the Bengal Army. The British had a better command and control apparatus and never relinquished either their grip on key communications or their clarity of purpose. The mutineers, aroused peasants, and rebellious princes, in contrast, had no overall leadership or clear objectives; once having seized Delhi, they relinquished the initiative. Finally a crucial part of northern India remained in British hands—the newly conquered Punjab, the old Sikh kingdom. New units, raised there in the decade since the Company's victory over the Sikhs, remained loyal. In some cases this was a personal loyalty to a charismatic Company officer. In others, it was the lure of loot and the chance for revenge against the high-caste Hindu sepoys of the Company's army. To these Punjab units, whose number rapidly expanded during the course of the Mutiny, were added soldiers from the Company's Nepalese client state—the famous Gurkhas. Of course, British seapower allowed prompt reinforcement of the 40,000 British troops in India by units summoned from China, South Africa, and Britain itself. Despite the focus in many contemporary and later accounts on the redoubtable British infantry, however, the majority of the troops who broke the Mutiny were Indian: Bombay and Madras sepoys, the loyal remnant (about a third) of the Bengal Army, Punjabi Muslims and Sikhs, and of course Gurkhas (who, if not exactly Indian, were certainly not British). Within six months, Delhi had been retaken (by a force two-thirds of which was Indian) and the backbone of the Mutiny broken, although the final embers were not stamped out for over a year.

As the Mutiny sputtered out, British attention turned to the future governance of India and the structure of its armies. The Company, long an anomaly, was wound up, and the Crown took over direct management of the Indian Empire the Company had built. The Company's administrative and military services, however, continued their separate existence, since the day-to-day management of India and its armies was recognized as a specialist occupation requiring career-long semi-exile in India. In any case, the British Army had no interest in absorbing the Company's large officer corps. Indian Army officers, hitherto trained at the Company's "military seminary" at Addiscombe, would now be Sandhurst graduates and would have exactly the same royal commission as their British Army counterparts. (And even though many of the financial perquisites of the Company era disappeared, Indian service remained well paid.) Newly commissioned officers would then spend a year attached to a British Army unit in India before joining their Indian regiment. This requirement seems to have been based on nothing more substantial than the British Army's cherished belief that Indian Army officers ought to see real soldiering before going off to command natives. The continuing existence of two armies and two officer corps meant that the rivalry and tension that had marked the relationship of Crown and Company officers would persist as long as British rule in India lasted.

The most obvious change in the Indian Army was in sepoy recruitment. The three separate armies were retained, not least because the loyalty of the Bombay and Madras armies during the 1857 Mutiny suggested that the armies could act as counterbalances to one another. The Bombay and Madras armies retained their customary recruitment patterns but entered a long period of decline, a development largely driven by the post-Mutiny trajectory of the Bengal Army. Much of that army had been destroyed by the Mutiny—units had either revolted or been preemptively disbanded. British analysis fastened on the recruitment of the pre-1857 Bengal Army and found an explanation of its behavior in its homogeneous, high-caste Hindu composition. The Bengal Army kept its name and some of its Hindu units, but its rebuilt regiments were largely drawn not from the Ganges Valley, but from the Punjab. Sikhs and Punjabi Muslims, embodied in irregular corps raised by the Punjab administration (itself a quasi-autonomous unit of the Bengal Presidency), had made up a large part of the force that had retaken Delhi in September 1857 and thereafter made up a steadily rising percentage of the reconstituted Bengal Army. To them were added a growing number of Gurkha units. British recruitment of Gurkhas had begun in the aftermath of the Company's war with Nepal (1814–1816)—an expensive victory that left a lasting impression of Gurkha martial prowess on the minds of British officers.[3] It was the Mutiny, however, and in particular the Gurkha record during the siege and storming of Delhi, that began the love affair between the British and these tough mountaineers that still endures. Ultimately the Gurkha Rifles units, and their British officers, came to regard themselves as the Indian

Army's elite, its equivalent of the British Army's Household Brigade. The new structure of the Bengal Army was underpinned by the elaboration of a theory: the "martial races" hypothesis. It was further strengthened by new concerns about the security of the Indian Empire focusing on its North-West Frontier. The man whose career embodies the post-Mutiny transformation in India, Frederick Sleigh Roberts, Kipling's "Bobs Bahadur," was deeply involved in both these developments.

Initially, the new Sikh and Punjabi units represented a pragmatic reaction to the 1857 emergency. They were available and remained loyal (although that loyalty was based at least as much on hostility to the Hindu sepoys of the Bengal Army who had conquered the Punjab for the Company over a decade before as on affection for their new British rulers). Soon enough, however, where expediency led, codifying dogma followed. The idea (which had both pre-Mutiny roots and links with wider currents of thought on "race" and "natural selection") that some Indian groups were "natural" soldiers—toughened by a harsh environment, uncorrupted by modernity, enthusiastic for combat—took root and began to affect how the Indian Army looked for recruits. A quarter of its intake was from the Punjab by 1875 and over half by 1900, while the Gurkha Rifles grew apace. Roberts, the son of a major general in the Bengal Army, began his career in the Bengal Artillery, won a Victoria Cross (VC) in the Mutiny (something he set out to do), and rose steadily thereafter, aided by political and media manipulation skills as considerable as his more narrow military gifts. He ended his career as Field Marshal Lord Roberts of Kandahar and commander in chief of the British Army, one of only two Indian service officers ever to reach the professional summit of the British Army (Sir William Slim, a Gurkha Rifles officer, became Chief of the Imperial General Staff in 1948, after the end of the Raj and the division of its army between India and Pakistan). Roberts believed in a racial hierarchy of fighting men. Nothing, of course, could compare to the indomitable British soldier, but the right sort of Indian soldier, with good British officers, could come close, and the right sort of Indians came from the Punjab and its mountainous northern fringes as well as from beyond the frontiers of the Raj: Gurkhas and Pathan tribesmen from the Raj's North-West Frontier Province and Afghanistan (now commonly called Pashtuns). As for the older armies, the Madras Army (which Roberts commanded prior to becoming Commander-in-Chief, India), was recruited from "races" that had once been martial but, softened by long years of peace, had now lost their fighting edge (Roberts was similarly dismissive of the Bombay Army's recruiting pool). Under the influence of these beliefs the Madras Army's southern regiments were steadily reduced in number and replaced by more martial-races regiments. Eventually, in 1895, the old Bombay and Madras armies fell victim to Roberts's prejudices, and the three armies were fused into a single Indian Army, where southern and western units were few and in which the dominance of the northern martial races was clearly established—a situation that would endure for the rest of the British period. The transformation of the army after 1857, however, was driven not just by the martial races theory but by the new tasks envisioned for the army by its own hierarchy, the Government of India and London. Here too Roberts played a crucial role.

The conquest of the Sikh kingdom not only filled out the Company's domains but also brought its frontiers up against the mountainous borderlands of Afghanistan and the ferocious tribesmen who lived there. Thereafter, the problem of "the Frontier"—where exactly it should be fixed and how the tribesmen should be controlled—was to be a permanent preoccupation. This was strongly reinforced by the perception of a new and serious external threat to the Raj: the looming menace of Russia. The roots of this fear went back to the Napoleonic Wars and the Emperor's success in persuading Tsar Paul to mount an invasion of the Company's domains by an army of Cossacks. Cut short by Paul's assassination and a reorientation of Russian policy before distance, terrain, and tribal resistance had a chance to reveal the fatuity of the idea, it nevertheless threw a considerable scare into policy makers in both London and India. This episode marked the beginning of a century-long concern with the northwestern frontiers of British India. The best-known manifestation of this concern is the intelligence-gathering enterprise known as the "Great Game." Lesser known, but of critical importance to the post-Mutiny development of the Indian Army, is the way in which the fear of a Russian threat to India (and Russia's eastern frontier was much closer to India in 1860 than it had been in 1800) tied into the martial-races preoccupations of Roberts and his acolytes. If the Russians were to emerge from the Khyber and Bolan Passes, the Indian troops who, alongside the British Army's Indian garrison, would face them would have to be extremely able, not only in training and equipment but in morale and will to combat, in order to meet European opponents. This, the Roberts school held, made it doubly important to rebuild the army around the taller, fairer, sturdier, and more warlike "races" found in the Punjab, the northern mountains, and on (and across) the Frontier.

Watch and ward on the Frontier had another advantage as well. It would keep the army in fighting trim, avoiding the deterioration that long years of peace had caused in the Madras and Bombay armies. By jousting with the tribesmen and preparing to confront a Russian army, the quality of the army would be kept at a higher level than could be attained by garrison duty in the now tranquil interior of the Raj. The Indian Army that Kipling depicted was now an army for which Frontier soldiering was central. That kind of nearly continuous small-unit action spawned both an impressive body of small-wars doctrine and a formidable degree of tactical skill at levels up to brigade. But both the doctrine and the skills would prove minimally relevant to the war to which the King-Emperor's Indian Empire was committed in 1914.

The Indian Army went to war about 159,000 strong (of whom only 2,300 were British officers). It was not built for a long, grinding war of attrition (it had only forty-seven reserve officers). There were only twelve British officers in a battalion, and Indian units would experience serious problems as the prewar British regulars, who spoke the sepoys' language, became casualties.[4] The army's medical and supply arrangements, stunted by financial parsimony and, in any case, designed for the North-West Frontier's small wars, collapsed when the army was committed to large-scale campaigning in Mesopotamia (now Iraq) in 1915. Better than half the army came from the Punjab, which continued to provide a disproportionate share of recruits throughout the war (nearly half of the Indian Army's 65,000 war dead came from that province). But as the army grew, the Punjab would begin to run dry.

Despite the handicaps from which it suffered in mobilizing, expanding, and fighting a very different war in very different settings from anything foreseen before 1914, the Indian Army made a major contribution to the British war effort. Brushing aside prewar worries about involving Indian troops in "white man's wars," two infantry divisions and a cavalry division went to France in September 1914. The two infantry divisions—the Indian Corps—remained for over a year on the Western Front, suffering casualties that amounted to better than 100 percent of the Indian battalions' mobilization strength. Indian cavalry divisions served in France until nearly war's end.[5] But the principal theater for the Indian Army was the Middle East. By 1918, thirteen of the seventeen "British" divisions in Mesopotamia and Palestine were Indian Army formations. The Mesopotamia campaign, which began disastrously in 1915, ended with the Indian Army in Mosul; two Indian cavalry divisions were prominent in General

Sir Edmund Allenby's final, victorious offensive in Palestine, which carried him on to Damascus and Aleppo. By the Armistice, just under a million Indian troops were serving abroad (and many would remain abroad for years more garrisoning the Middle East). Eleven Indian soldiers had won the Victoria Cross (for which Indians had become eligible in 1911).

Despite the scale of India's war effort, few Indian Army officers rose to senior commands. William Birdwood and Claude Jacob were exceptions, but Birdwood was a protégé of Lord Kitchener, the British Army regular who had been a prewar Commander-in-Chief, India, and who, as secretary of state for war, was one of the dominant figures in the British government in 1914–1915. Jacob, who had begun his career with twenty unbroken years on the Frontier (and would end it a field marshal and Commander-in-Chief, India), went to France with the Indian Corps in 1914 and remained there, becoming one of the more successful corps commanders in the British Expeditionary Force (BEF), noted for the care with which he prepared operations. (Lloyd George felt he would make a better commander for the BEF than Haig, although even the "Welsh Wizard" realized that replacing a Guardsman with royal connections with an Indian Army officer was a nonstarter.) The underrepresentation of Indian Army officers in senior commands reflected the longstanding British Army undervaluation of Indian service and would resurface again in 1939–1943.

Other problems also foreshadowed issues that would arise during World War II. The demand for troops strained the demographic resources of the so-called martial races (and forced recruiters to look outside customary groups). Although there was no conscription in India, the pressures on local officials in 1917–1918 to fill quotas of recruits produced enlistments that were far from voluntary, causing serious discontent. The scale of India's war effort produced rising Indian expectations for postwar political concessions, something the British government appeared to meet with its August 1917 declaration that the *progressive realization of responsible government* would be the future direction of British policy in India. Political advance would certainly bring with it Indian demands for the "Indianization" of the Indian administration—and the officer corps of the army.

When World War I ended, the Indian Army, over a million strong, was spread from China to France. In its recruiting grounds, nearly stripped of military manpower, there was exhaustion and some resentment. There was also price inflation and influenza to add to the distress. Political India was poised to claim what it felt was only its due after India's contribution

to British victory. At this moment of difficult transition from war to uneasy peace, a young officer twice wounded in action and decorated for
valor transferred into 6th Gurkha Rifles. Twenty-five years later, William
Joseph Slim would lead the Indian Army of the Raj to its greatest—and
final—victory.[6]

3

Slim

The British officers of the Indian Army were quite different, in their social class origins, from the regular officers of the British Army. William Joseph Slim was different, in turn, from most Indian Army officers. Since the post-Mutiny reorganization, most Indian Army officers had been Sandhurst graduates. Sandhurst, however, was not free, and its fees put it beyond the reach of Slim's family resources. His father was a moderately successful shopkeeper who, after a business failure in Bristol, rebuilt his (modest) fortunes in the great industrial city of Birmingham, where Slim attended a local grammar school. (In the complex world of English secondary education, these were schools, often giving excellent education, that catered to the children of families whose status and means precluded attendance at the socially desirable, and expensive, public schools.) Slim wanted a military career and was a member of the Officer Training Corps (OTC) at his school. After graduating and beginning work as a teacher, he managed to attach himself to the OTC at Birmingham University, but for someone of his background and income, a commission was out of the question. He was, in fact, about to begin an overseas career with Shell Oil when the lights went out all over Europe in August 1914. For Slim the war opened a door. As the British Army grew exponentially in the early months of the war (while the prewar regular army suffered massive casualties in France), the need for officers was desperate. Slim's prewar OTC qualifications—and determination—got him a "hostilities only" commission in the Royal Warwickshire Regiment in September 1914.

World War I shaped Slim's military career, as it did that of every British senior officer of World War II. Slim's war, however, was not the Western Front that so indelibly imprinted itself upon the imagination of posterity but two "sideshows"—Gallipoli, best remembered now for the shadow it cast over Winston Churchill's career, and Mesopotamia (now Iraq), a campaign barely remembered at all. Slim's battalion, the 9th Royal War-wicks, was part of the 13th Division, a New Army division, made up of the enthusiastic volunteers who had mobbed recruiting stations in the early months of the war. Committed briefly to the British beachhead at Cape Helles on the tip of the Gallipoli Peninsula, Slim's battalion lost four officers and 510 men killed and wounded while merely holding the line (at this stage of the war British battalions were nearly 1,000 strong). Then the battalion was committed to a major offensive to break the stalemate that had turned the Cape Helles beachhead into a mini Western Front. Known as the Battle of Sari Bair, it saw every officer of the battalion killed or wounded and only 175 men left to answer the roll call. Among the wounded was Slim, who was lucky to survive and was evacuated to Brit-ain, where he was told he would lose the use of an arm and was finished with soldiering. As the army medical establishment would discover, it was never a useful exercise to stand between Slim and his objective. Pro-nounced unfit for active service, Slim was posted to the Royal Warwicks reinforcement depot, where newly trained soldiers were held pending dispatch overseas to one of the regiment's active service battalions. While whiling away time there, Slim, still determined to have a military career despite the verdict of the Royal Army Medical Corps doctors, found a path to a regular commission, despite his lack of private means. He ex-changed his temporary commission in the Royal Warwicks for a regular commission in the West India Regiment, perhaps the least prestigious regiment on the Army List and, crucially, one that required neither family connections nor private wealth. Now a regular, Slim was given a draft of replacements to accompany to the Royal Warwicks battalion on active service with the Mesopotamia Expeditionary Force (MEF). The assump-tion was that, as an unfit officer, he would deliver his draft and then re-turn. What happened, however, was that, having delivered the draft, he then got himself attached again to the 9th Royal Warwicks, participated in several battles as the MEF pushed the Turks steadily back, won a Military Cross for gallantry—and sustained a second serious wound. (This caused some consternation at the War Office, which had him listed as unfit for active service and therefore, presumably, not at the front.) Evacuated to India for convalescence, he was then posted to Indian Army Headquarters in Delhi (officially known as "Army Headquarters, India"), where war's end found him an acting major in a staff appointment. Peacetime in the West Indies held no charms for an ambitious soldier, and Slim therefore made another move—this time to the Indian Army. The India Office in

London, which had to approve the transfer, was initially reluctant—they were swamped with transfer requests from hostilities-only officers seeking a permanent billet. What tipped the scales in Slim's favor was the personal support of the Commander-in-Chief, India, General Sir Charles Monro. Clearly Slim had made an impression, and the India Office subsided, grumbling. Slim moved onto the Indian Army List and from there to the regiment that would henceforth be his army home, 6th Gurkha Rifles, whose 1st Battalion he joined in March 1920. He had met the 1/6 before—on the shell-blasted slopes of Sari Bair, where these formidable soldiers had made a lasting impression.[1]

It is useful to pause on Slim's World War I record. Many junior officers could match his combat service and decorations, but few could match the determination with which he seized (or created) opportunities to move toward the realization of his objective: a military career.[2] Even fewer demonstrated his remarkable skill in working the system (and flouting it when necessary). A fellow Gurkha officer said of him many years later that he knew exactly when to be disobedient. The combination of implacable determination and canniness would discomfit a number of enemies in the future, not all of them on the other side of the battle line.

One other point about the young Slim is worth noting. He saw a battered, depressed army turned into a victorious fighting force. The MEF had suffered a series of setbacks culminating in the April 1916 surrender of an entire Indian division, cut off and besieged by the Turks at Kut-al-Amara (or Al Kut), southeast of Baghdad. The MEF had been committed to an ill-conceived campaign; it was neither well commanded nor properly supported—its logistics were precarious and its medical services, in a very unhealthy climate, shamefully bad. In the aftermath of the disaster at Kut, the whole command structure was shaken up, both in Mesopotamia and in India (which supplied most of the troops and bore responsibility for supporting the MEF). A new commander, Lieutenant General Stanley Maude, took over and revitalized the command structure, the supply system, and the medical arrangements. Slim's time with the MEF coincided with this transformation, which led to the capture of Baghdad and the steady advance toward Mosul during which Slim was wounded (and had good reason to appreciate the improved medical services). It was a lesson in how effectively an army could be turned around when given vigorous, intelligent leadership.[3]

Army command, or anything like it, seemed far away in the 1920s. The Indian Army was readjusting to a peacetime routine. It was coming to grips as well with the major changes brought by the war to India. In August 1917, the secretary of state for India, Edwin Montagu, had proclaimed "responsible government" as Britain's objective in India. This proclamation, a commitment to ultimate "dominion status" (i.e., self-government), was prompted both by India's massive contribution to Britain's war effort and the conviction that, if Indian hopes for movement toward self-government were disappointed, there would be serious unrest. As it turned out, by the time Montagu's promise had been given statutory form (the 1919 Government of India Act), there had been very serious unrest, especially in the Indian Army's Punjab homeland (culminating at Amritsar in 1919, when the exceedingly bad judgment, to put it no higher, of Brigadier Reginald Dyer led to the death of nearly 400 demonstrators—an event that prompted Mohandas Gandhi's first major campaign of protest against the Raj). Thereafter, a rising tempo of political agitation and protest, accompanied by a growing incidence of communal (i.e., Hindu-Muslim) clashes, meant that "aid to the civil"—deployment of troops to support the police in averting, containing, or suppressing unrest—became as constant a feature of the Indian Army's life as tours of frontier duty. Slim, of course, experienced both—and left well-written accounts of what they were like for a young officer.[4]

The Indian Army also faced another major adjustment in the interwar years: Indianization. The Indian Civil Service had begun to accept Indian recruits before World War I, and the pace increased after 1919 as Indian nationalist opinion pressed for more Indian participation in the country's governance. The Army, however, presented special issues. After a brief experiment at Madras in the mid-eighteenth century when Indian troops were commanded by Indian officers, the Company had decided that command should be kept in European hands, and there it had remained. Periodically the issue of commissioning Indians would be raised, only to be met with nearly universal opposition. A very tentative experiment—the "Imperial Cadet Corps," involving the sons of Indian rulers—was as far as the idea had gotten by 1919. The Government of India Act, however, meant that the issue had finally to be faced. Its implications were numerous and, to many British soldiers and officials, alarming. The Indian Army was the praetorian guard of the Raj—as well as London's cost-free strategic reserve. Would it be as reliable in both roles once its officer corps was no longer entirely British? Could Indians show the leadership skills that British officers believed had been their unique contribution to the Indian Army? How would British officers react to coming under the command of Indians, as would inevitably happen when Indians began to rise in rank, and would that make an Indian Army career less attractive to Britons? How, finally, would rank-and-file British soldiers react to "black" officers who would, at minimum, require a salute from them and might well eventually have command authority over them? These, and a great many other questions (or excuses), meant that the pace at which Indians received the King's commission in the interwar years was glacial, and the first generation of Indians to hold that commission faced all too often considerable suspicion and in some cases racist hostility. Confronting German or Japanese enemies must have seemed to many of them no more daunting than first walking into the mess, newly commissioned officers whose appearance signaled to many of their British fellow officers the impending end of "their" army. The Gurkhas, whose units were raised under the terms of a treaty with the client state of Nepal, were not subject to Indianization, so Slim would not have had to deal with the issue directly. But two decades on, XIV Army under his command would demonstrate that the changing pigmentation of the Indian Army's officer corps made no difference to its formidable fighting qualities.[5]

Alongside the routine of regimental life, Slim's increasingly obvious professional skills brought him a series of appointments that honed his military thinking. He attended the Indian Army's Staff College at Quetta in 1926 (one of the instructors was Percy Hobart, among the British Army's most prominent "apostles of mobility" who believed in the tank as the future of warfare). From his time at Quetta—where one of his fellow students described him as future commander in chief—comes a story that signposts Slim's evolving approach to battle. Commenting on his solution to a tactical problem, an instructor observed that he had used a pile driver to crush a walnut. "Sir, have you ever seen a walnut that has been crushed by a pile driver?" was the response.[6] For all the discussion of the role of armored formations in a future war, the British Army's doctrine in the interwar years was based on the tactical successes of 1917–1918 with their emphasis on the combination of well-handled artillery and infantry to make limited advances at an acceptable cost. These would be the tactics that Bernard "Monty" Montgomery would make the British Army standard in 1942–1945. Slim would approach his battles differently. The destruction of the opposing army, not merely its retreat, was his objective. How that would be done would depend on circumstances.

That flexibility of approach got Slim into some difficulty on his next posting—a staff position at India Army Headquarters in Delhi. There he began investigating the possibilities of air supply—a subject that would be crucial to his success in Burma. He approached the staff of Air Headquarters, India, about arranging a joint exercise. Given the distant and frosty relationship between the Royal Air Force (RAF) and the other services, this was an unauthorized crossing of a clearly marked and heavily defended frontier for which Slim received a magisterial rebuke from the Commander-in-Chief, India. Fortunately the trajectory of his career was not disturbed. He would become successively Indian Army member of the Directing Staff at the British Army's Staff College at Camberley and then a student at the newly created Imperial Defence College, where promising officers from all the services and some rising civil servants spent a year as graduate students. Slim made an impression on those he had encountered, as he had at Quetta, as someone who could go far. However, in 1937, when he finished his year at the Imperial Defence College, he had been away from regimental service for some time and was rather elderly for his rank. The promotion board that, in 1937, advanced him to lieutenant colonel almost passed him over on grounds of age and decided in his favor by only one vote. Upon returning to India he took command, briefly, of a Gurkha battalion and then moved on to the Indian Army's Senior Officers School as commandant. There, at Belgaum, an acting brigadier, war found him.[7]

The mobilization of the Indian Army in 1914 had been a largely ad hoc affair, and preparations to support the prolonged deployment of large numbers of Indian units overseas were quickly revealed as quite inadequate. In the war's aftermath there was systematic planning for the mobilization and deployment of the Indian Army "next time." The army would double its size, and Indian units would deploy to the Middle East and Singapore. When Viceroy Lord Linlithgow announced that the King-Emperor's declaration of war on 3 September 1939 committed the Indian Empire to war, army expansion therefore began automatically, as did a flow of Indian troops overseas. In May–June 1940, however, the tempo of the Indian war effort accelerated dramatically as Germany's stunning victories in Western Europe knocked France out of the war and left Britain alone (apart from the dominions, India, and the colonial empire) facing the most formidable war machine on the planet in the worst strategic circumstances in modern British history. Despite Britain's precarious situation, Churchill decided to maintain Britain's position in the Middle East, and that became the focus of the Indian war effort for the next two years. Controlled expansion was abandoned in favor of an open-ended effort to raise the largest possible Indian Army in the shortest time. That rapidly growing force was destined for the Middle East, and its training and equipment were designed with only that theater in mind. The flood of Indian units surging into the Middle East carried Slim, now a brigade commander, with it.

The next eighteen months were Slim's apprenticeship for high command. He took his brigade into action at Gallabat on the frontier between the Sudan and Italian-occupied Ethiopia in November 1940. The operation failed, and Slim was again wounded. Reflecting on the battle, Slim decided that he had made a mistake: "I had not chosen, as a good commander should, the bolder" course of action.[8] Slim never had to learn a lesson twice. One particular episode of the Gallabat battle would, however, come back to haunt him. After the 1857 Mutiny it became established practice for every Indian infantry brigade to contain a British battalion as an insurance policy to ensure sepoy loyalty, as well as—in some British minds—an example to Indian troops of proper soldiering. The British battalion in Slim's brigade belonged to the Essex Regiment and performed very poorly at Gallabat, with parts of it, unnerved by Italian bombing, dissolving into panicky retreat. Slim promptly sacked the Essex's commanding officer. While this action was correct, he was an Indian Army officer and the episode would be noticed and remembered by a British regular, also of the Essex Regiment, who a few years later would be Slim's superior.

Failure in the field could mark the end of an officer's career, or at least relegation to second-tier commands, but the Commander-in-Chief, India, General Sir Claude Auchinleck, aware of Slim's record and the impression he left on those who encountered him, did not allow Gallabat to affect his judgment. In May 1941, Slim took over the 10th Indian Division, deployed in Iraq. The 10th was a new division and, when Slim took it over, not a particularly happy one—the divisional commander he was replacing had been removed because he had "lost the confidence of his officers." Slim quickly pulled the division into shape, leading it through the brief campaign to suppress a pro-Axis revolt by the army of Britain's Iraqi client state and then the much more serious campaign to occupy Vichy-controlled Syria. That operation had barely concluded when the 10th was committed to the occupation of Persia (as the British still called Iran), whose ruler had unacceptably pro-German leanings. Although the Shah's forces put up only token resistance, the mission involved collaboration with the Red Army, which had also moved into the country to secure the vital Persian Corridor rail link to Basra, the Persian Gulf port through which desperately needed Anglo-American supplies reached the Soviet Union. The difficulties encountered in dealing with the suspicious and opaque Soviets were an introduction to the complexities of coalition war, something he was about to encounter on a much larger scale. In late February 1942, he was summoned to the telephone by Lieutenant General E. P. Quinan, the Indian Army officer who commanded the largely Indian X Army responsible for Syria, Iraq, and Persia, and told he was leaving his division to become a corps commander in Burma.

Burma, when Slim arrived in March 1942, was a stage on which was displayed all the flaws in British planning for the defense of its Asian empire as well as all the problems caused by the much too rapid expansion of the Indian Army. Annexed piecemeal to the Indian Empire in three wars over the course of the nineteenth century, Burma had never been seen as at risk of serious attack and had a correspondingly low priority for everything. Far East Command, based in Singapore, was responsible for its defense from 1940 on (despite the fact that support for Burma would have to come from India, something pointed out fruitlessly to London). Far East Command, underresourced and with much else on its plate, almost predictably ignored Burma. When Japan struck, Burma was immediately transferred back to India, which then had to reinforce the completely inadequate garrison at a time when it was already scraping the bottom of the barrel for even half-trained units. The single Indian brigade in Burma and the local forces—grandly called the 1st Burma Division (even though it was largely without equipment and made up of newly raised, nearly untrained, and often dubiously reliable Burma Rifles units, and very far from a functioning division)—was joined by the headquarters and a single brigade of the new 17th Indian Division. That formation, originally destined for the Middle East and deemed unfit for battle without considerable additional training, had already lost two of its brigades rushed into Singapore. The divisional commander, Major General J. G. Smyth, had won a Victoria Cross on the Somme in 1916, but in early 1942 he was a sick man unfit for active service who had successfully concealed his condition in order to accompany his division into the field. Not surprisingly, when the Japanese opened their attack on Burma in January, aiming for Rangoon, there ensued a doleful tale of miscues, defeats, and almost immediate retreat. The Burma Division simply fell apart, its Burmese soldiers deserting (although units recruited from Burma's ethnically distinct "hill tribes" remained loyal). The raw Indian troops of the 17th Division performed better than anyone had a right to expect but, without either air support or combat experience, were forced steadily back. At the last major obstacle before Rangoon, the broad Sittang River, the division was nearly destroyed when poor communications led to the premature destruction of the bridge that was the division's line of retreat—with two-thirds of the force still on the wrong side of the river. Rangoon soon fell, severing Burma's connection with its source of supplies and reinforcements and opening the way for Japanese units to pour in. The badly tattered remnants of the Burma garrison, now two nominal divisions about to be constituted into Burcorps (Burma Corps), retired up the Irrawaddy Valley, the first stage of a long trek back to India. At this point Slim arrived from Iraq to take command.

Slim was to be the solution to a command problem that had bedeviled the campaign from the beginning. The General Officer Commanding (GOC) in Burma held a static administrative position—and in a backwater of empire. As such it was considered an undemanding final posting for someone headed for retirement. Even the approach of war had not led to the upgrading of the position. When the Japanese attacked Malaya, and Churchill moved Burma back to India Command, General Sir Archibald Wavell, Commander-in-Chief, India, flew to Rangoon, evaluated the incumbent GOC, and promptly sacked him. He then made a decision over his replacement, however, that created a new set of problems. Lieutenant General Thomas Hutton had been Wavell's chief of staff in India and was primarily a staff officer. Wavell put him in Rangoon with orders to hold that vital port, thus creating a situation in which Hutton had to press Smyth to hold as long as possible each of the positions to which the Japanese successively forced back the 17th Indian Division. Smyth knew that his weakening division needed to retreat farther and faster if it was to survive, thus putting him into conflict with Hutton. Meanwhile, Wavell had been transferred from Delhi to Java as head of American-British-Dutch-Australian (ABDA) Command, the Allies' first integrated command created by Churchill and Franklin Roosevelt at the Arcadia meeting held in Washington after Pearl Harbor. ABDA was given the hopeless task of holding Malaya, Singapore, the Netherlands East Indies, and Burma, which was once again moved from India Command to a headquarters that had neither the time, staff, nor communications to control it effectively. Hutton, realizing that he could not both manage overall command in Burma and at the same time control formations actively engaged, asked at this point for a corps headquarters. Almost simultaneously, Wavell's acting successor as Commander-in-Chief, India,

General Sir Alan Hartley, and Viceroy Lord Linlithgow decided that the Indian troops in Burma would fight better under a more inspirational commander than Hutton (thus blaming him for all the failings of raw, underequipped, inadequately trained troops). Out of all this came both Slim's appointment and the shape of the command structure within which he would operate. Hutton was replaced by Lieutenant General Sir Harold Alexander, chosen by Churchill and the Chief of the Imperial General Staff, General Sir Alan Brooke, in London. "Alex" (brave and charismatic and destined to become Churchill's favorite general) was, however, a Guardsman, not an Indian Army officer. Hutton stayed on as his chief of staff. And Slim, marked by Wavell (as he had been by Auchinleck) as capable of high command, took over operational control of the 17th Indian and 1st Burma Divisions. Finally Wavell, back in Delhi again after the inevitable demise of ABDA, descended again on Burma shortly before Slim's arrival and sacked Smyth.

Slim had under his command in Burcorps an overwhelmingly Indian force. There were six battalions of British infantry, all understrength. His gunners and sappers were Indian, as were the fifteen battalions, many badly under strength, that made up most of the fighting element of his two divisions (1st Burma Division at this point comprised the remnants of the Burma Rifles units—mostly hill tribesmen—and two Indian battalions). The loss of Rangoon meant that there could be neither reinforcement nor resupply, but Hutton and his chief supply officer, Major General Eric Goddard, had the foresight to backload supplies from Rangoon to central and northern Burma (today referred to as Upper Burma) so that Burcorps could sustain itself (barely) during its long fighting retreat over the next two months.

Slim had some other assets as well. Smyth's successor in command of 17th Indian Division was Major General D. T. "Punch" Cowan, who, like Slim, came from 6th Gurkha Rifles. Cowan was a flexible and forward-looking officer who would command the division for the rest of the war. The 1st Burma Division was commanded by Major General J. Bruce Scott, another 6th Gurkha. Slim and his two key subordinates all came from the same regimental family, had known one another a long time, and worked smoothly together—an invaluable asset in a precarious situation. Alexander, who had little to do with the handling of Burcorps, had in addition to his charm and courage one character trait that was of great value to Slim: he could recognize an able and determined subordinate and had the sense to sustain and not interfere (it was to be the basis of his later successful partnership with Montgomery). Finally, Slim had the 7th Armoured Brigade. The original "Desert Rats," they had been among the reinforcements flung into Rangoon at the last minute. In an army of mostly raw troops, the armored brigade provided an invaluable veteran presence. It also, in an army deficient in signals, gave Slim a reliable communications network. But perhaps the greatest of Burcorps's assets was Slim himself—tough, clear-sighted, indomitable. Many years later, he wrote a short essay on generalship, which included this striking pen portrait, obviously based on his memories of Burcorps:

> [The general] is short of sleep, he is tired, he is probably wet, his nose is running and a sodden map is flapping about in his hands. Before him stand, in a rather forlorn group, some of his staff, a couple of subordinate commanders convinced that whatever eventuates, they will have the dirty work to do, and most embarrassing of all, an ally or two, oozing suspicion. If the military situation is bad—and the odds are it will be—they will just stand looking at him, their eyes all asking the same mute question "what do we do now?" . . . They want an answer and they want it now. He knows, and they know that unless something pretty brisk and decisive is done quickly neither he nor they will be there in a week's time.[9]

Acting boldly and decisively would never be a problem for Slim—the need to do so was the lesson he had learned from his experience at Gallabat. The suspicious allies he remembered were factors not entirely under his control. There were two in Burma—the Chinese and the Americans—and the complications they caused would plague Slim until 1945.

Americans generally—and the Roosevelt administration in particular—disapproved of the British Empire. A quite small but disproportionately influential group of Americans—known as the "China Lobby"—were, however, strong supporters of the Chinese Nationalist government of Generalissimo Chiang Kai-shek, seeing China as a future diplomatic partner (and a huge potential market). The United States was Chiang's principal foreign backer and supplier, pouring into Rangoon supplies that reached China by a rail and road connection (the Burma Road), linking Lashio in northeastern Burma with Kunming in the southwestern Chinese province of Yunnan. By the time Slim arrived on the scene, Rangoon had already fallen, severing the supply line. US policy for the balance of the war would be focused relentlessly on reopening overland communications with China (meanwhile, an air bridge—the famous Hump airlift—was improvised to carry supplies from airfields in northeastern Assam in India over some of the most forbidding terrain in the world to Kunming). The symbol of that US determination to sustain China was Lieutenant General Joseph Stilwell, already in place as both commanding general of the US Army's newly created China-Burma-India (CBI) theater and, at least notionally, chief of staff to the generalissimo in the latter's capacity as commander in chief of the Allies' China theater. Much of this was political theater. Stilwell and Chiang hated each other, and there was no Allied China theater—only the vast but ill-organized Chinese armies, badly equipped, poorly trained, and often indifferently led, which Stilwell was supposed to energize with US supplies, advice, and training. However fanciful American views of China may have been, Stilwell's appointment, and what it symbolized, had real and serious consequences for the British, and especially for Slim, for the next two and a half years. At this point, the British really did not yet have a strategy for their new war—they were focused on stemming the tide of disaster and improvising a defense for India's eastern frontier, never before considered a danger point. The Americans had a clear (if misconceived) objective: sustain China with airborne supplies and then reconquer Burma, or enough of it to connect the old Burma Road to a new road from Ledo in Assam to Lashio and on to Kunming. Supplies formerly landed at Rangoon could then arrive at Bombay or Calcutta and ultimately China by rail, river, and road. The Americans also suspected (correctly) that the British shared neither their enthusiasm for China nor their commitment to push supplies to the Chinese, regardless of cost. Stilwell was the personification of US policy and suspicions. He had some talent as a combat commander but little for high command and absolutely none for coalition warfare. Tactless, closed-minded, and profane, he affected a "plain American tough guy" persona and nourished as well a deep, irrational Anglophobia ("pig fuckers" was one of his more colorful descriptions of the British). There was, however, method to the apparent madness of his appointment by George Marshall, the US Army Chief of Staff. In Europe, where there was an agreed aim (if not a completely agreed strategy) and Anglo-American cooperation was vital, Marshall would appoint the charming, emollient Dwight Eisenhower. In the Asian war, where there was no agreement about goals or strategies (and serious US doubts about British willingness to sustain China), Stilwell's brief was to see that US aims were never sidelined and US resources devoted solely to achieving those aims. Slim's description of an ally oozing suspicion was a considerable understatement where Stilwell was concerned.

During the two-month retreat, the burden of dealing with Stilwell and the Chinese (whose troops had entered Burma early in the campaign to assist in the defense of their vital link to the outside world) fell mostly to Alexander. His charm and tact made him more successful with Americans than most senior British officers and had a limited impact even on Stilwell. Slim's interactions with Stilwell (both were, in effect, corps commanders under Alexander) were relatively limited, but there was certainly enough for him to take the measure of Stilwell: "He was two people, one when he had an audience, and quite a different person when talking to you alone. . . . He was not a great soldier in the highest sense, but he was a real leader in the field."[10] Their relations were eased by Slim's recognition of Stilwell's qualities as a fighter, as well as his acknowledgment that the Chinese troops under Stilwell's somewhat nominal command (Chinese commanders checked with the generalissimo before carrying out their American superior's orders) could be, if properly led and equipped, effective fighters. Perhaps what eased his relations with Stilwell most, however, was the fact that he was clearly not cut from the same cloth as most British senior officers, and his voice and manner did not ignite Stilwell's perpetually simmering Anglophobia. During the retreat from Burma, however, Stilwell was far from the most important of Slim's worries.

That retreat was a close-run thing, teetering several times on the edge of disaster. Despite the foresight of Hutton and Goddard, supplies were scarce and equipment almost impossible to replace; replacing casualties was totally impossible. The sky belonged to the Japanese, the RAF, what there was left of it, having been driven out of Burma. The countryside was hostile, the civil government disintegrating, and ahead of and alongside the withdrawing troops was a horde of refugees, frightened and often sick—the Indian population of Burma, established there under the auspices of the British Raj and now fleeing both the Japanese and the hostility of the Burmese, who saw them as the Raj's collaborators. Three things brought Burcorps through: Slim's determination and leadership, the mobile firepower and communications of the armored brigade, and the surprising resilience of his Indian and Gurkha battalions. Newly raised units with prewar regulars spread very thin and already having endured a long withdrawal and multiple, occasionally disastrous engagements prior to Slim's arrival, his Indian Army formations pulled themselves together repeatedly and fought well enough, often enough, to make a coherent retreat possible. Burcorps marched into the Imphal Plain, in the Indian border state of Manipur, in May 1942, having destroyed their remaining guns and vehicles, which they could not get across the Chindwin River, the last barrier before they reached India. Their performance gave Slim not only some consolation for defeat but also hope for a future when he might lead an army, better trained and equipped, back into Burma.[11]

Before that could happen, however, there were many obstacles to surmount. The first of those was Lieutenant General Noel Irwin, the commander of IV Corps, the formation responsible for the defense of India's eastern frontier, suddenly the front line in Britain's war with Japan. Irwin in fact had been born in Assam, the sprawling province of northeastern India, where his father had been a tea planter, but his career path was very different from Slim's. He was a British Army officer, from the Essex Regiment. A battalion of that regiment had been a part of Slim's 10th Indian Infantry Brigade and had, as noted, failed at Gallabat, leading Slim to sack the commanding officer, a personal friend of Irwin's, who felt that Slim had cast a shadow on his regiment's reputation. When Burcorps reached Imphal no arrangements had been made to accommodate or refit its formations. Medical arrangements were primitive, and there were no plans to give the troops much-needed leave. To some extent this was explicable in terms of the state of communications to Imphal, which dangled at the very end of a highly precarious supply line. Since the Indo-Burma frontier had never been regarded as under threat, communications to it were correspondingly underdeveloped. In fact, the rough track up which Burcorps had retreated from the Chindwin River to Imphal had only just been completed by hastily impressed labor gathered from the tea plantations. If there is some excuse for the primitive arrangements awaiting Burcorps at Imphal, there is none for Irwin's behavior. He made it plain that he thought Burcorps were poor soldiers and Slim himself responsible for the loss of Burma. He flatly rejected Slim's request for some leave for Burcorps's regiments. Slim and Irwin—who had a very bad temper—had a sharp confrontation in which Slim told Irwin that he was out of touch with what had happened in Burma and added that Irwin's behavior to Burcorps was rude. Irwin's reply will rank high in the annals of fatuous utterance: "I can't be rude, I'm senior!" His command now dissolved, Slim, exhausted, went on leave. He had been defeated in the field in his first independent command, and his immediate superior had made it plain that he had little regard for Slim as a soldier. When he handed over Burcorps and left Imphal, his tattered soldiers cheered him. Neither Burma, nor Irwin, had seen the last of Slim.

4

Marking Time

Fifteen months passed between the time Slim handed over Burcorps and the moment he assumed command of XIV Army. During that time there was prolonged disagreement between the United States and Britain over the purpose of the war against Japan in South Asia, leading to a nearly dysfunctional alliance on the ground. Driven largely by the dynamics of this sputtering alliance, there was a premature offensive into Burma by an unready Indian Army, producing a debacle exceeding anything that happened during the 1942 retreat and giving the Imperial Japanese Army its last victory in Burma. That defeat (known as the First Arakan Campaign) also convinced Winston Churchill, never an admirer of the Indian Army, that it was useless and that his purposes would best be accomplished by restructuring the theater command to remove control of the war in Burma from Indian Army Headquarters in Delhi while entrusting operations in Burma to the highly unorthodox, but charismatic, Brigadier Orde Wingate. Wingate's unconventional tactics—known as "Long Range Penetration" (LRP)—employed on a raid into Burma simultaneous with the Arakan fiasco had yielded at least the appearance of success. The upshot of all these developments was that, when Slim took command of XIV Army in October 1943, he would operate within a byzantine command structure and have to deal with the consequences of an ambiguous theater strategy as well as the presence of the war's largest "private army," Wingate's corps-sized Special Force—all of it the result of the fact that the British and the Americans were fighting two separate wars in South Asia, wars that continually reacted on one another in jarring and unexpected ways.

By the time Slim became army commander, however, something else had dramatically changed: there had been a quiet but thorough revolution in the nature of the Indian Army and an equally remarkable transformation in the structure that supported and supplied its war in Burma. Theater strategy and command structure shaped much of what Slim and the Indian Army would do in Burma; the revolution in that army's training and doctrine, as well as in its medical and logistic support, is what made it all possible.

When Japan attacked, the Commander-in-Chief, India, was General Sir Archibald Wavell, a British Army officer whose regiment was the Black Watch. Wavell had been Commander-in-Chief, Middle East, from 1939 to 1941 and had gradually exhausted his credit with Churchill, who relieved him in June 1941 after the failure of the first major British offensive against Erwin Rommel (Operation Battleax), replacing him with the Commander-in-Chief, India, General Sir Claude Auchinleck.[1] Wavell, by his own admission, was at that point a tired man. Churchill did not, however, want him back in London where, the prime minister feared, he would sit about in his club, disgruntled, and become a focus for complaints about the management of the war. So Churchill dispatched Wavell to India to "sit under the pagoda tree," in his striking if inapt phrase. Wavell thus became responsible for the frantic Indian Army expansion program in an equipment-starved environment (something he pointed out to London but could do nothing to remedy). He also pointed out the error of detaching Burma from India Command, its source of supplies and reinforcements, and putting it under Far East Command in Singapore, which gave no attention to it. This, like his complaints about raising armored divisions without tanks, was ignored. The Commander-in-Chief, India, was also a member of the Viceroy's Executive Council, an important and demanding position that inevitably absorbed much time and energy. Then came the Japanese attack. Churchill's immediate response was to tell Wavell to "look East" and to hand Burma back to India Command to become yet another claimant on India's new, half-trained formations. Soon enough, Wavell himself was pulled out of India and named Supreme Allied Commander of the newly formed ABDA Command. Wavell took with him to his new headquarters in Java operational responsibility for Burma, leaving administrative support (i.e., supplies and reinforcements) to India Command, now temporarily under General Sir Alan Hartley. This clumsy arrangement lasted only until ABDA's inevitable disintegration. By March, Wavell was back in Delhi, where responsibility for Burma also returned.

Wavell had been tired when he left Cairo. By the time he returned to Delhi in the early spring of 1942, he had had nearly a year of further heavy responsibility for Indian Army expansion (plus the additional burden of membership of the Viceroy's Executive Council at a moment when all of India's resources were being mobilized for war and internal political tensions were rising fast). Then came theater command in a doomed enterprise (and a serious accident while on a visit to Singapore shortly before its fall). Wavell was well past his best by the time he grappled with the consequences of the fall of Burma and the arrival of the Japanese on India's eastern frontiers. But his greatest deficiency may not have been fatigue but the assessment he had formed of the Japanese.

Remarkably, Wavell underestimated them and would continue to do so (something he candidly admitted, after the war, in a casual conversation on a golf course). Despite Japanese battlefield performance in Malaya and Burma, Wavell thought them overrated, perhaps because he did not have a high opinion of the British commander in Malaya, the unfortunate Lieutenant General Arthur Percival. He also was critical of British leadership in Burma prior to Slim's arrival (despite having appointed Hutton). Wavell was convinced that, given an offensive-minded approach by British troops and commanders, the Japanese could be beaten. That ignored the actual state of the "British" troops available, who were, overwhelmingly, raw Indian units—a very curious mistake by someone who had already been Commander-in-Chief, India, for a year. Wavell was as determined a believer in the efficacy of the offensive spirit as the prime minister with whom he never quite got on. Slim's Burcorps was barely out of Burma when Wavell was laying plans for a counteroffensive, telling his chief of staff (like him a British Army officer) that he had a "hunch" that the Imperial Japanese Army might not be very good on the defensive. Wavell's misreading of the Japanese and his failure to grasp the frailty of his own formations were compounded by Churchill, who, for reasons of alliance politics, began to press Wavell hard for a counteroffensive into Burma.

In a message to Wavell shortly after returning from the Arcadia Conference, Churchill told him that, if he were to summarize what he had learned in Washington, he could do so in one word: China. That country, or more correctly the United States' obsession with it, would cast a long shadow over the Burma campaign—indeed it would be the raison d'être of the longest single land campaign the British would wage during the war. Without the US commitment to China the Burma campaign would never have taken the shape it did.

Wavell, basing himself on his dangerous underestimation of the Japanese, had actually begun thinking of a counteroffensive into Burma even before Burcorps withdrew from it. His target was Rangoon, which would cut off the Japanese forces in Burma the same way its British defenders had been when it fell to the Japanese in March 1942. As a preliminary move, Akyab Island, lying just off Burma's Arakan Coast, would be seized. Airfields there would provide cover for the assault on Rangoon. Wavell's ideas, at this point, harmonized with the prime minister's, who then and later sought an amphibious strategy in the theater, aimed ultimately at the recovery of Singapore and the restoration of imperial prestige he expected that to bring. Both Wavell and Churchill knew that the recovery of Rangoon, with its promise of reopening overland communications with China, would satisfy US objectives (and, Churchill must have calculated, make them easier to deal with over issues much closer to his heart, like alliance strategy in the European war). Meanwhile, the Americans, basing themselves in northeastern India, were pursuing on a small scale their project of an Americanized Chinese Army, reequipping and retraining those Chinese units that had withdrawn from Burma into the Indian province of Assam. They were also developing the trans-Himalayan airlift to fly into China some of the supplies that could no longer reach Chiang overland. (The returning transport aircraft were ferrying back Chinese soldiers to bring up to strength Chinese divisions Stilwell was training.) The restoration of the overland route was taking shape as a project to push a road from the railhead at Ledo in Assam south into Burma, its construction covered by Stilwell's Chinese divisions, to link up with the old Burma Road. All of this, of course, added immensely to the weight on the already inadequate and desperately overburdened lines of communication to northeastern India. A host of problems could be solved, at theater and alliance level, by a counteroffensive that retook Rangoon. This was the starting point of a process that would produce the 1942–1943 Arakan offensive—the low point in the Indian Army's war that became the starting point of a change in that army, as well as in Slim's fortunes. The road to victory at Imphal begins with the debacle in the Arakan.[2]

The advantages of seizing Akyab and going on to Rangoon were clear to everyone. The problem was doing it. The RAF was not able as yet to secure air superiority over the battlefield—the doughty Hawker

Hurricane, its mainstay, had no clear advantage over Japanese fighter air-craft. The Royal Navy's Eastern Fleet, forced to abandon its bases in Ceylon in the face of an incursion into the Indian Ocean in April by the same Japanese carrier task force that had struck Pearl Harbor, was now based in East Africa and could not yet contest Japanese maritime supremacy in the Bay of Bengal. Amphibious trooplift was unavailable (the Allied descent on French North Africa, Operation Torch, for which Churchill had argued relentlessly, was the priority operation). The state of communications to northeastern India (now supporting, in addition to IV Corps at Imphal, Stilwell's various enterprises) was so precarious that IV Corps's forward divisions were on reduced rations and living in absolutely spartan circumstances. No offensive moves based on Imphal or Ledo were possible. Finally, the 1942 monsoon (May–September) was unusually severe and was playing havoc with such roads and railways as were there. Since something had to be done and the desirable course of action was impossible, the only option left, an overland advance through the Arakan, became the "dry season" (October–April) choice for 1942–1943. It was a disastrous decision.

The Indian Army was simply not yet ready to confront the Imperial Japanese Army. Still in the full throes of open-ended expansion, with pre-war regulars spread ever thinner and training still largely focused on the needs of the Middle East theater, its available formations were simply too new and inexperienced for the task about to be set before them.[3] More-over, to training deficits and the shakiness of the lines of communication were added very serious medical problems. The Arakan was malarial (as, for that matter, was all of India's North-East Frontier). The sickness rates in 1942 ran as high as 1,850 per thousand per annum—nearly every mem-ber of a battalion could have two bouts of malaria in a year. Malaria treat-ment—whose dramatic improvement over the next two years would be crucial to Slim's success—was at this point totally inadequate.[4]

All these factors taken together might well have given Wavell pause. But they were far from the sum of the Indian Army's problems in the summer and autumn of 1942. The fall of Singapore and the loss of Burma (with a flood of Indian refugees pouring back into India) were major blows to British prestige. Indian politics had been tense even before Japan attacked. When war came in 1939 most of India's provinces were gov-erned by Indian administrations based on elections held in 1937 under the terms of the 1935 India Act (which Churchill had fought so doggedly). The Congress Party provincial governments had, however, resigned to protest the Viceroy's unilateral declaration of war on India's behalf. Muslim League provincial ministries remained in office, but at its 1940 annual meeting, held at Lahore in the Punjab, the Indian Army's principal recruiting ground, the League had committed itself to the goal of a separate Muslim state: Pakistan. After Churchill arrived at 10 Downing Street, attempts to coax the Congress Party back into, if not office, at least a supporting posture for India's war effort were not pursued with any urgency. When a series of calamitous defeats brought the war to India's eastern frontiers (and a panic induced by the presence of the Japanese fleet in the Bay of Bengal temporarily reduced southern India to near chaos) it is not therefore surprising that Gandhi and the Congress Party leadership thought the moment had come to extract major concessions.[5] Churchill, they knew, was under great pressure, not only from Roosevelt but also from the Labour Party members of his Coalition government to make concessions to Indian nationalism. He had already agreed to offer what to his mind were major concessions: a postwar constituent assembly to revise the 1935 India Act and prepare for "dominion status" (i.e., independence) in return for full support for the war effort. This offer was carried to India in April 1942 by Sir Stafford Cripps, a Labour member of the War Cabinet personally sympathetic to the Congress Party (and a friend of Jawaharlal Nehru, the Congress Party's second-ranking member). The "Cripps Mission" failed, the negotiations foundering over Churchill's insistence, supported by his War Cabinet, on retaining control of the Indian war effort while Congress insisted, equally strongly, on some share in its direction. It is hard to believe that Churchill was disappointed. He had warded off US interference and defended British control of India's military effort. At this point Gandhi, believing the Raj was tottering, overplayed his hand and gave Churchill an even more considerable victory.[6]

The Quit India movement, and the associated Congress Revolt of August 1942, proved that in fact the British Raj had a surprising amount of residual strength that, for the last time, it exercised decisively. The Indian Civil Service—the "steel framework" of the Raj—now more than half Indian, still functioned at British command, as for the most part did the police. Most important, the Indian Army did not waver. Its numbers were vastly swollen, and it was now accepting recruits from groups either never recruited before or not recruited for a very long time (like Madrassis from southern India). Its officer corps was now filling with growing numbers of Indians. The army might have seemed ripe for serious unrest. In the event, however, it remained responsive to its (still almost entirely British) chain of command. Fifty-seven battalions were deployed in "aid to the civil" duties, the sort of deployment where troops are often used in small units under junior officers (many now Indian) and Non-Commissioned Officers (NCOs—themselves new and inexperienced). There is no doubt that had there been serious unrest in the army at this juncture the British would have faced a desperate situation. In all of India there was only one complete British division, the 70th, part of Slim's new command, XV Corps, based at Ranchi in Bihar—one of the most disturbed provinces—and training for jungle warfare. Scattered over the rest of India's vastness were other British battalions on "internal security" duties, but they were often composed of men considered too old (or otherwise unfit) for service in frontline combat units and, by themselves, unlikely to prevail against serious unrest. The reliability of the Indian Army was crucial to the ability of the Raj to weather the disasters of 1942—a fact Churchill would never acknowledge, then or later. But a high price was extracted for this staunchness, because training cycles were seriously disrupted by the Congress Revolt—between six and eight weeks were lost, a serious matter for raw recruits. Despite the fact that all the evidence indicated the need for delay in resuming the offensive in Burma, the imperatives of alliance politics and Wavell's own hunch-based optimism about what could be accomplished prevailed. In September 1942, Major General Wilfred Lloyd's 14th Indian Division began to inch its way into the Arakan.[7]

The 14th Indian Division could well have been the poster child for the state of the Indian Army at the end of the calamitous year 1942 (when, in addition to its heavy losses in Malaya and Burma, the equivalent of over a division was lost in the desert fighting against Rommel). The division was part of the 1941 expansion program and was in the early stages of its training when one of its brigades was sent to Burma. Brought up to strength again by troops moved from the North-West Frontier and others culled from units on internal security, it was moved to the eastern frontier of Bengal, bordering the Burmese Arakan. Yet more of its brigades were detached as the relentless expansion program and the reshuffling of formations to meet the emerging threat to India's eastern frontiers (as well as the heightened demand for internal security troops) kept the army in a perpetual churn. At one point 14th Division was a one-brigade division. When it was again brought up to strength, one of the brigades it received, detached from 23rd Indian Division in Assam, arrived riddled with malaria. When it finally moved forward into the Arakan, it had become a top-heavy four-brigade division. Two of its brigades were composed entirely of Indian battalions, breaching the rule established after the 1857 Mutiny that all Indian brigades must include a British battalion. As the Indian Army continued to grow, however, while British manpower became ever more thinly stretched, there was no choice.[8] Moreover, like all Indian Army divisions, the 14th lacked some of its equipment. (On the eve of the Japanese attack, the Indian Army had received only 36 percent of its allotment of field guns *for the original 1940 expansion program*, and signals equipment, crucial to command and control, was in particularly short supply.)[9]

To all their deficits and problems, Lloyd and his division had to add one more—one that, in the end, would prove decisive. The command structure controlling their advance was very badly flawed. After the withdrawal from Burma, the defense of India's eastern frontiers was the responsibility of Eastern Army, one of the territorial commands into which India was divided. Eastern Army was commanded by Lieutenant General Sir Charles Broad, a British Army gunner officer, who, in the interwar arguments over the proper role for armor, had been accounted as a "progressive" (his nickname was "the Brain"). War Office infighting had sidetracked his career, rerouting it to India, and Eastern Army was his final stop. Under him were IV Corps in Assam, commanded by Irwin, and XV Corps at the historic Barrackpore military station outside Calcutta, which Slim now commanded, after a brief leave. Normally, Slim would have been responsible for the Arakan offensive since Lloyd's division was part of his corps. On Broad's retirement, however, Irwin moved up to Eastern Army and quickly sidelined Slim. Electing to control the Arakan offensive directly from his headquarters, Irwin switched its location to Barrackpore, sending Slim and XV Corps to Ranchi in Bihar, hundreds of miles from the front. Irwin had made clear when he met Slim at Imphal that he had little regard for either Burcorps's performance or that of its commander. Like many British Army regular officers, he may have been rather dismissive of Indian Army officers in general. He certainly felt Slim had cast a slur on his regiment when he sacked its commanding officer at Gallabat. One of his first actions was to discard the preliminary planning Slim—the only lieutenant general in India who had commanded in the field against the Japanese—had done with Lloyd. Irwin had, temporarily, marginalized Slim. The price would be paid by 14th Indian Division.

When considering an offensive, Slim had been struck by the problem of a frontal attack into the very inhospitable terrain of the Arakan's Mayu Peninsula. Some ninety miles long, it tapers to a point—aptly named Foul

Point—across a channel from Akyab Island, the objective of the offensive. However, the peninsula itself is bisected by the Mayu Range—steep, jungle-clad hills that run north-south down its middle, making lateral communications between troops on either side virtually impossible. Furthermore, the numerous watercourses flowing west into the Bay of Bengal or (on the eastern side of the dividing hills) into the Mayu River provide ready-made defensive positions. Wavell may have believed that the Japanese had never fought defensively and might not be good at it, but Slim knew better. He therefore planned to supplement an advance overland with short seaborne hooks behind Japanese positions using, in the absence of proper amphibious craft, an improvised flotilla of miscellaneous vessels. He also thought of using a new unconventional raiding formation, being assembled and trained by Brigadier Orde Wingate, to swing widely around the other Japanese flank. This multipronged offense, which respected the tenacity of the Japanese in defense, using every available asset (and resembling the tactics the Japanese had used against him in Burma), was immediately discarded by Irwin in favor of a straightforward frontal attack down the peninsula. Although Lloyd began probing forward in September, supply problems delayed 14th Indian Division's main effort until December, by which time, of course, the Japanese were well aware of British intentions. Lloyd's four brigades heavily outnumbered the two defending Japanese battalions, which slowly gave way before them. By New Year's 1943, 14th Indian Division's twin advances on either side of the central range had almost reached the tip of the peninsula. There the Japanese stood—and Lloyd's problems began.

The Japanese were dug in, using the bunkers that were to become a depressingly familiar feature of the Burma campaign. Heavily walled and roofed with timber covered with up to five feet of dirt, carefully camouflaged, manned by anywhere from five to twenty men with machine guns and ample ammunition, and sited in mutually supporting groupings, they were proof against even heavy bombardment and a formidable challenge for inadequately trained troops—the only type available to Lloyd. With each failure by Lloyd's division to crack the Japanese defenses, Irwin, under pressure from Wavell, pushed more troops forward. Lloyd would ultimately control nine brigades, the infantry strength of an army corps—an unworkable arrangement.[10] The obvious solution was to put a corps headquarters in charge, but the corps headquarters available was Slim's, and Irwin stubbornly refused to utilize it. Slim did have to supply a squadron of tanks from his 50th Armoured Brigade. Both Slim himself and his armored brigade commander felt that tanks should be employed in much larger numbers to knock out the bunker complexes that were frustrating 14th Indian Division. Slim told Irwin so and was ignored. The tanks, employed in "penny packets," failed. Irwin then ordered Slim to visit Lloyd's headquarters, but only as an observer without any command authority. Quite what this was supposed to accomplish is unclear. Irwin and Wavell had made almost every conceivable mistake, for which 14th Indian Division was now about to pay dearly.

The Japanese had had ample time to reinforce the Arakan with their entire *55th Division*. The bunker complexes at the tip of the peninsula were held by three battalions while the Japanese commander planned to swing around the inland flank of Lloyd's force east of the Mayu Range (the maneuver Slim's original plan for the offensive had proposed in reverse). Lieutenant General Koga Takeshi aimed to get astride 14th Indian Division's communications and force it into the same disorderly retreat that similar Japanese tactics had produced in Malaya and Burma the previous year. The Japanese offensive against Lloyd's inland flank opened on 1 March, as 14th Indian Division was about to launch its sixth frontal attack on the Japanese bunker line. The attack would be made by the 6th Brigade of the newly arrived British 2nd Division, placed under Lloyd because Irwin and Wavell felt fresh British troops would succeed where tired, and increasingly dispirited, Indian troops had repeatedly failed. On 18–19 March the 6th Brigade failed as well, the change in the ethnicity of the attacking force not compensating for the faultiness of Irwin's design. By this time, as the Japanese counteroffensive developed, the whole British position in the Arakan was at risk. After his rather pointless tour earlier in the month, Slim had gone to Delhi for a conference and then snatched a few days' leave. On the train back to Ranchi, he was awakened at a stop to take a call in the stationmaster's office. His brigadier, general staff (basically a corps chief of staff), was on the line to tell him "the woodcock are flighting," code for the movement of XV Corps headquarters to the Arakan. At the eleventh hour, Slim was going back into action.

Or so it seemed. But Irwin was not quite ready to hand over control to Slim. In the aftermath of the 6th Brigade failure Irwin had decided to try again, after swapping Lloyd's tired 14th Indian Division headquarters for Major General Cyril Lomax's fresh 26th Indian Division headquarters (without changing the arrangement whereby a division headquarters controlled, or tried to, a corps-size force). After telling Slim to bring with him only the operations side of his headquarters since he proposed to retain administrative (i.e., logistic) control, Irwin kept XV Corps at Chittagong in eastern Bengal, the supply base for Arakan operations and well to the rear, until 14 April. By that time the situation was beyond saving—worse than Slim had faced when he took over Burcorps—and all he could do was supervise a withdrawal to a position he felt the battered and demoralized troops could hold during the now imminent monsoon. Irwin had prescribed a line that Slim felt was impracticable. Slim told him so, persuaded Irwin into accepting his recommendation, and then pulled his troops back into his preferred—and tactically and logistically sounder—position. The Arakan offensive was over and so, it soon appeared, was Slim's career. On 26 May Irwin sacked him, by telegram, criticizing his conduct of the battle (which of course he had taken over only after a successful conclusion was beyond anyone's reach). Slim's fruitless familiarization tour in March, and the summoning forward of a truncated XV Corps headquarters in early April only to keep it marking time in the rear until the situation was past saving, all look like nothing so much as an attempt to have a scapegoat handy if failure in the Arakan put Irwin himself at risk. Slim, however, would prove as hard to defeat as the enemy.[11]

Wavell was no longer in Delhi.[12] Summoned home by Churchill for "consultations" (so often the euphemism for sacking), he had been added to the prime minister's entourage for the Anglo-American summit in Washington in May (the Trident Conference). Churchill made it abundantly plain to Wavell during the voyage across the Atlantic that he had totally lost patience with the Indian Army; indeed the whole Indian administration was dismissed as a "welter of lassitude and inefficiency."[13] Privately he had decided to replace Wavell as commander in chief with General Sir Claude Auchinleck, who had succeeded Wavell in Cairo in 1941 and been unemployed since Churchill sacked him in August 1942 after yet more defeats at Rommel's hands. "The Auk" was an Indian Army officer and had been Commander-in-Chief, India, before being summoned to the Middle East. His appointment was part of a tsunami of change in India, propelled by the Arakan fiasco, that would produce, in a remarkably short time, an astonishing military transformation. Meanwhile, in his waning days as Commander-in-Chief, India, Wavell, who knew perfectly well who had shaped and controlled the Arakan operations (and who, at ABDA, had his own experience of being handed a hopeless task), decided to replace Irwin. The telegram informing Irwin of his removal reached him shortly after he had sent Slim his dismissal. In the only grace note of his tenure Irwin promptly telegraphed Slim, "You're not sacked; I am."[14]

Irwin's replacement at Eastern Army was a soldier of a totally different type. General Sir George Giffard, a British Army officer, came to India from the post of General Officer Commanding, West Africa, where he had presided over the very rapid expansion (from an even smaller base) of the colonial military establishments there. Slim would later pay tribute to him (and simultaneously deliver a stinging indictment of Irwin, whose attempt to scapegoat him for the Arakan fiasco he never mentioned in his memoir): "He understood the fundamentals of war—that soldiers must train before they can fight, be fed before they can march, and be relieved before they are worn out. . . . *The* quality which showed through him was integrity, and that was the quality as much as any other, we wanted in our Army Commander."[15] Yet Giffard's appointment was only the first installment of the major overhaul of the Indian war effort precipitated by the third consecutive British defeat by the Imperial Japanese Army.

The prime minister, embarrassed before his US allies by what he saw as the hopeless ineptitude of Delhi and its army, was set on transforming the command structure for Britain's war against Japan—and the methods by which that war would be fought. The former would take form in an Allied theater command modeled on the one created first for Wavell's doomed ABDA Command and then for Operation Torch and subsequent Mediterranean campaigns. Slowly fleshed out after Trident and approved at the next Allied summit (the Quadrant Conference at Quebec in September), the new South East Asia Command (SEAC) would take control of operations from India Command. A Supreme Allied Commander (Vice Admiral Lord Louis Mountbatten) with three service commanders under him would, subject to the strategic guidance of the Anglo-American Combined Chiefs of Staff, run Britain's war against Japan. India would continue to raise and train troops—and of course provide the base area and the logistic support for SEAC. But the new command was plagued from the beginning both by its abundance of discordant personalities and by the divergent aims of its creators. To the Americans, the purpose of SEAC was to constrain the British to make a major effort to reconquer northern Burma in the interest of reopening overland communications with China. To see that the British never forgot that *this* was SEAC's mission, Stilwell was built into the command structure as deputy supreme commander (while retaining his positions as commanding general, CBI, allied chief of staff to Chiang, and commander of the Northern

Combat Area Command, the US-trained Chinese force based on Ledo that had begun to advance slowly south into Burma, covering Stilwell's road builders). Stilwell, as abrasive and Anglophobic as ever, guaranteed that SEAC would never forget US priorities—or work smoothly.[16] An additional massive complication was that Churchill had a very different vision of SEAC's destiny. The prime minister wanted it to design and execute an amphibious strategy that would, ultimately, reclaim Singapore and, with it, the imperial prestige shredded by the defeats of 1941–1943. This was, given the increasing poverty of British resources, an unrealistic aim, as time would show. Churchill did realize, however, that he would have to satisfy the Americans about northern Burma or face serious complications in alliance politics. He planned to do this, freeing SEAC to follow his preferred strategy, by changing the operational approach to the problem of Burma, thereby eliminating the India Army from all but a minor role. This would be done by embracing the unorthodox ideas of Brigadier Orde Wingate.

Controversial during his lifetime, Wingate remains difficult to assess.[17] A British Army gunner officer, he came from an army family (and was distantly related to T. E. Lawrence). He had discovered a taste and talent for irregular warfare in Palestine during the 1936–1937 Arab Revolt against the British Mandate, when he ran a counterterrorism operation whose tactics and conduct at times skirted the boundaries of legality. He attracted the attention and patronage of Wavell, then a lieutenant general and in command in Palestine. Wavell would subsequently use him to train and lead Ethiopian guerrillas against the Italian occupiers (Wingate and Slim first met during the East Africa campaign). Wavell brought him to India in the spring of 1942, hoping to use him against the Japanese in Burma. The speed of the collapse in Burma precluded that, but Wingate did have time to make a reconnaissance of the country. He then persuaded Wavell to give him a brigade to train in his newly devised tactics and lead into Burma. 77th Indian Infantry Brigade (the force's cover name) was intended to operate in conjunction with an advance by IV Corps from Imphal across the Chindwin River into Burma. When logistics doomed that plan, Wingate persuaded Wavell to allow him to lead the "Chindits" into Burma to test their new tactics.[18] Wavell agreed, and in February 1943, as the Arakan offensive was stalling, Wingate crossed the Chindwin in what Slim later described as the equivalent of a cavalry raid.

Wingate had serious weaknesses as a military commander. Brave and charismatic—at least to some—he was a fanatical believer in his tactic of long-range penetration and utterly intolerant of those who disagreed with him. Adept at finding patrons—his cousin General Sir Reginald Wingate early in his career, then Wavell—he had been able to survive what in a less well-protected officer would have been career-ending behavior, including a suicide attempt in Cairo in 1941. When his ideas were scrutinized by skeptical staff officers (often rendered hostile because of Wingate's attitude toward them), his high-level backing negated their reservations. Wingate took the standard infantry battalion and broke it into "columns," each basically an infantry rifle company with some attached personnel. Filtering past the widely separated Japanese posts on the Chindwin, these columns, coordinated by radio and supplied by air, were to attack Japanese communications in Burma. The Chindits remained in Burma for three months, did some easily repaired damage to rail lines west of the Irrawaddy, and then, partly due to Wingate's mistakes (notably crossing that river), were cornered on the eastern bank. Breaking into small "dispersal groups," the Chindits dribbled back into India with a loss of a third of the 3,000-man brigade and nearly all of its equipment. As Slim later wrote (and many of Wingate's officers felt at the time), it was an "expensive failure." Even considered as a military experiment, Slim concluded, "if anything was learnt . . . it was a costly schooling."[19] But, as Napoleon once pointed out, luck is a major factor in any general's career. Wingate emerged from Burma not to be written off as another failed effort to confront the dual challenges of the Japanese and the jungle but to face and seize the opportunity that circumstances offered to make himself, briefly, a key element in Churchill's strategy for SEAC.

When the Arakan offensive began in the autumn of 1942, it did so to considerable fanfare. The British Raj needed a victory after calamitous defeats in Malaya and Burma and serious unrest in India itself. Although an operation with strictly limited objectives, it was billed as the beginning of a major counteroffensive. When it collapsed ignominiously, the disappointment and deflation were correspondingly sharp. Slim later argued that the publicity buildup was a mistake and that victory (if achieved) would have spoken for itself. While true, it is very easy to see why the authorities in Delhi took the opposite course. When it boomeranged on them, a window of opportunity opened for Wingate that he exploited to the fullest. Once again acting as commander in chief in Wavell's absence, General Sir Alan Hartley gave maximum publicity to Wingate's raid. After all, the Chindits had gone into Burma, engaged the Japanese, and returned. However minor the damage inflicted and however high the price paid for doing so, Wingate's raid could at least be represented as a success, offsetting the dismal conclusion of the Arakan operation. One of those persuaded by the media blitz about the "Clive of Burma" was the prime minister. Facing serious arguments with the Americans over Mediterranean operations and US dissatisfaction with British failure to reopen their road to China—dissatisfaction fed by Stilwell's complaints about British unwillingness to fight in Burma—Churchill avidly seized on what seemed to be a striking success. He speculated about putting Lieutenant General Sir Oliver Lesse, a second-rate general at best but one of Monty's favorite subordinates, in overall charge of the Burma campaign, with Wingate in command of operations. He also ordered Wingate home for consultations. Wingate himself had already sent a copy of his report, written to argue for much wider application of LRP tactics by a vastly expanded Chindit force, through backchannels to another of his well-placed patrons in London. Since his time in Palestine he had been an ardent and militant Zionist. This had won him the patronage of Leo Amery, the secretary of state for India and Burma in Churchill's cabinet and himself a strong "gentile Zionist." Wingate's report (and advertisement) was, thanks to this characteristic act of insubordination, circulating in London before Indian Army Headquarters in Delhi had a chance to weigh in on the actual merits of his ideas.

What followed was, even in seven decades' retrospect, one of the most remarkable series of actions and decisions that Churchill took during the entire course of the war. Wingate arrived in London, a lieutenant colonel with a distinctly checkered career, the leadership of one costly raid into Burma to his credit, and an enticing theory, whose feasibility was far from certain, for reconquering Burma. The prime minister (whom Wingate had met once before at a dinner party in November 1938) saw him at dinner at 10 Downing Street on the eve of departing for the Quadrant Conference and decided on the spot to take him to Quebec and there present him to the Americans as proof that the British were serious about Burma: the charismatic Wingate and his new tactics, proven by the recent Chindit sally into Burma, would clear the way for Stilwell's road builders. The Americans were as impressed as Churchill. (Wingate was always at his best when presenting his ideas to those whose support he needed.) Wingate emerged from Quadrant an acting major general with commitments for an increase in LRP units to the infantry strength of an army corps and, courtesy of the Americans, a dedicated air component (Number One Air Commando). His LRP units would spearhead the 1943–1944 dry season campaign in northern Burma, levering the Japanese out and opening the way for the linkup of the "Stilwell Road" from Ledo with the old Burma Road.

Churchill left Quebec with considerable success in hand: he had turned US skepticism about Britain's commitment to the reconquest of Burma into enthusiastic support for a British initiative there—and, of course, avoided the danger that US irritation and impatience over the situation in northern Burma would affect the argument over Allied strategy in Europe, something vastly more important to the prime minister. The Chief of the Imperial General Staff, General Sir Alan Brooke, watching this performance with some detachment, understood exactly what Churchill had done: he had produced someone who would dazzle the Americans, dissipate their suspicions of British bona fides in Burma—and allow him to refocus on the Mediterranean.[20]

All of this, of course, was done without much reference to India. At this point, there was something of a vacuum in Delhi. Viceroy Lord Linlithgow was giving way to Wavell (named because no first-rank British political figure was willing to occupy the position) while Auchinleck was just resuming the commander-in-chief's job. General Giffard was new at Eastern Army. Amery was not at Quebec and was in any case almost routinely ignored by Churchill. The Indian Army had no defenders and a number of enemies (one of them Wingate) at Quadrant. The prime minister had always had reservations about it, clearly harboring doubts about its loyalty.[21] Wingate openly derided it, referring to it as a system of "outdoor relief" (i.e., a welfare scheme), a phrase the prime minister would make his own. Wingate wanted nothing to do with Indian Army units (with the exception of the Gurkha battalions). In his conception of 1943–1944 operations in Burma, his LRP brigades would clear the way, with the second-class Indian Army units following behind as a mop-up and occupation force. Before SEAC took over control of the Burma campaign in November, the centerpiece of the next dry season operations had been put in place, and the Indian Army was assigned the marginal role that, in Churchill's view, it was suited for.

In the early autumn of 1943 a great reshuffle of players took place in India. Wavell settled into Viceregal Lodge and the Auk had the Indian Army's reins in his hands again. The new Supreme Allied Commander, Vice Admiral Lord Louis Mountbatten—handsome, confident, charismatic, and related to the royal family (or, according to his many enemies, sly, manipulative, of modest abilities, and badly overpromoted)—was assembling what would prove to be one of the war's largest headquarters in Delhi and preparing for the mid-November activation of SEAC. Giffard, slated to become SEAC's land forces commander as head of 11th Army Group, was leaving Barrackpore for Delhi. To replace him at Eastern Army (now renamed XIV Army), Slim was summoned from XV Corps. As he sat in the staff car taking him from the airfield at Calcutta to his new headquarters, he looked at the army commander's flag fluttering on its bonnet and "wondered where I was really going."[22]

5

The Quiet Revolution

The vehicle that would carry Slim on his journey toward victory was the Indian Army. That force, which in 1939 still resembled the army Kipling had known, was in the midst of an enormous change, one of the two remarkable military transformations seen during World War II (the other being the rebirth of the Red Army comprehensively beaten by the Germans in 1941–1942, which turned itself into the force that remorselessly ground the Wehrmacht to pieces in 1943–1945). The Indian Army's transformation, however, had a more than military significance. As it transformed into a modern army, and with a very large number of Indian officers for the first time in its history, the life expectancy of the Raj, already shortened by interwar political developments, shrank ever faster. Moreover, behind the changes in the Indian Army another equally dramatic process was occurring—in a final convulsive exertion, the machinery of the Raj wrung out of India a truly remarkable war effort. That effort both sustained the Indian Army (and ultimately Slim's campaign) and wrought major changes in the subcontinent, but not without imposing very high costs on it. These two interrelated changes—the growth and modernization of the army and the mobilization of India to sustain an imperial war effort—have only recently drawn the attention they deserve from historians, but without considering them it is impossible to understand how the great victories to which Slim led the XIV Army were made possible.

The Indian Army's wartime journey really began not in September 1939 but in May 1940 when, with catastrophic defeat staring Britain in the face, Churchill's government ordered the Indian Army expanded as fast as possible, largely to sustain the imperial position in the Middle East. This posed huge problems. Where were the officers for this much expanded

army to come from? For that matter, how were the ranks to be filled? For
an army carefully constructed to be "reliable" (i.e., insulated from nationalist politics) and heavily dependent on the Punjab, rapid expansion meant
that when the Punjab ran dry (as it had in World War I) the recruiters
would have to range far more widely, bringing in men from "nonmar-
tial" backgrounds. And what would be the impact of this on the army's
reliability? Even if officers and men could be found, where would equipment come from? And then, what doctrine would inform the training
of the growing army—and control the sort of equipment it would have?
All these questions, and many more, would crowd upon Indian Army
Headquarters in Delhi. The answers given were not always complete, and
time would show that some were quite unsatisfactory. Unlike Britain,
which had a highly developed governmental machine, not to mention a
powerful modern economy and several years of prewar planning to draw
on, the Raj was largely improvising a total war effort with a governmental
structure never designed to do so. The remarkable thing was how effectively it was all done.

First, the matter of officers.[1] The 1939 Indian Army was still officered
overwhelmingly by men from Britain. Many, like John Masters, whose
two volumes of memoirs are an oft-cited portrait of that army in its last
decades, came from families that had served in India generation after generation (and some of those families, like Masters's, had, as a legacy of
Company days, a family tree with an Indian branch).[2] India was for them
a career and, for some, a place for which they had great affection. In 1940,
it was simply impossible to multiply their numbers, local knowledge, and
language skills quickly. British men of appropriate age (and background)
working in India could be commissioned; some British NCOs could
morph into officers and there was a flow of officer cadets from the UK
throughout the war. Processed through several officer training centers in
India, these men became Emergency Commissioned Officers (ECOs).[3]
Lacking the Indian experience—and language skills—of the regulars, their
relationship with their soldiers was different from that of the pre-1939
army. Above all, they had no commitment to the Raj and an Indian
career—the war was an interruption in the lives and careers they wanted,
and although for the most part they did their job very well (aided by the
indispensable Viceroy Commissioned Officers [VCOs]) their aim was a
speedy return home after the war was won. There was, however, another
category of officer, whose numbers could grow as much as required, who
had local knowledge and languages and for whom India was home and

the army a long-term career. These were Indian officers, either regulars or Emergency Commissioned Indian Officers (ECIOs).

The Indian regulars were the products of the cautious Indianization program that had begun after World War I (and, in 1939, was producing a third of the annual officer intake). The ECIOs, like their British counterparts, had the social and educational qualifications to become officers for the duration (although probably a higher percentage of them hoped for a postwar military career). However, Indian officers, critical from 1940 on since the patchwork of expedients cobbled together to find British officers for the expanding Indian Army was never going to identify enough of them, raised pressing questions that had hitherto been fudged—or completely evaded.

From the earliest discussions (which began before 1914) of commissioning Indians, there had hovered over the whole issue the concern that doing so would inevitably mean that Indians would exercise command authority over British officers and, even more problematic, British Other Ranks (BORs), as rank-and-file soldiers were called then. The War Office in London was adamant that this must not be allowed to happen—BORs must not be placed under the orders of Indians. This thinking was clearly based on both a sense of racial superiority and a fear of what the reaction of British troops might be. These concerns were reflected in the early Indianization plans. Eight units were chosen for Indianization, and when Indian officers were posted to these units no further postings of British officers to them would be made. The units would slowly acquire an all-Indian officers' mess from the bottom up. This scheme, which was meant to ensure that no serving British officer ever came under Indian command, reflected all too well the mixed feelings and hesitations with which the whole question of commissioning Indians was being approached. The Military Revolution of 1940 ended this incrementalism. Auchinleck had always been a supporter of Indianization and recognized that the thinly veiled discrimination of the eight-units scheme had to go.[4] When he became Commander-in-Chief, India, for the first time in 1941 Indian officers became eligible to be posted to any unit, which meant that, in some cases, they would be commanding British officers. Pay anomalies—British officers were paid at a higher rate than Indian on the grounds that they were serving overseas while Indian officers were serving in their homeland—were also tackled by Auchinleck, although it took much of the war to be settled. Indian officers received equal command rights over BORs (which, as it turned out, caused scarcely a ripple), but power of punishment (i.e., the right to sit on court-martials of British soldiers) was withheld until 1943, when Auchinleck, as Commander-in-Chief, India, for the second time pushed that through as well, in the teeth of opposition from London. It was Claude Auchinleck who made a reality of Indianization, enabled to do so by the enormous pressures generated by the war. London wanted the largest possible Indian Army raised, and raised quickly. Only large numbers of Indian officers would make that possible, and Auchinleck was clear that they would have to be officers in every sense: "equal treatment regardless of colour." While prewar attitudes certainly did not vanish, they were much attenuated in the army by the example Auchinleck set and by the fact that the new British ECOs flooding into the Indian Army had no Indian experience and therefore few, if any, of the attitudes and fears that had handicapped the Indianization process before the war—and Auchinleck's ascendancy. Accepting orders from superiors who happened to be Indian held few terrors—after all, it was for a British ECO only a temporary situation.

If officering the expanding army meant confronting and solving one set of problems, rank-and-file recruitment posed another. Of course, as the Indian Army began to expand, the traditional sources were tapped, but as expansion continued with no end in sight and it grew beyond its World War I size (which it had by the end of 1941) the "family circle" of the martial races simply could not supply enough men. Shortages appeared as early as 1941, and by 1943 the supply of men from traditional sources was exhausted. New pools of manpower had to be found and exploited. The old Madras Presidency had supplied many of the soldiers who had established the Company's power. Then, scorned by Roberts and his disciples as having lost their martial qualities, South Indians had been edged out of the Indian Army in the last quarter of the nineteenth century. Now the recruiters rediscovered them, and they returned in strength (as did men from groups never before recruited). Moreover, as the Indian Army became a modern fighting force, its technical branches expanded even more rapidly than its combatant (or "teeth") arms. Field artillery units, abolished after Indian gunners had proved all too proficient during the Mutiny, were reestablished in 1935. Indian cavalry regiments, all horsed in 1939, were transformed into armored units. Signals, vital to battlefield command and control; transport units; support and supply units to service the combat units; and very large numbers of units to work ports, base areas, and lines of communication—all these proliferated. Many of these units required men with some education (not often found in martial-races recruits). All of them required not only officers but also VCOs and NCOs; and many VCOs and NCOs, coming from martial-race backgrounds, had the same problems as British ECOs—lack of familiarity with the language and culture of the men they now commanded. Finally, as the army ceased to be drawn exclusively from rural backgrounds, recruits with urban backgrounds and at least some education brought with them into the army (as well as the Royal Indian Air Force and the Royal Indian Navy) levels of political awareness hitherto lacking among the rank and file. To expand the army vastly in 1940–1943 presented an unparalleled range of challenges. The surprising thing is not that there were numerous problems by 1942–1943, but that the institution continued to function at all, and that it remained a reliable instrument in the hands of the Raj. To ensure that it did so required careful management. The army closely monitored opinion in heavily recruited areas, as it was received wisdom that unhappiness in the sepoys' home villages had been a major contributory cause of the 1857 Mutiny. "Welfare arrangements" for World War II's *jawan*s (a word replacing the venerable "sepoy")—matters of pay, leave, and medical care—were also a priority, especially for Auchinleck in his second tour as Commander-in-Chief, India. The Raj in its twilight, like the Company in its heyday, took the best care it could of its soldiers because, in the last instance, not only its war effort but its survival rested on them.[5]

Finding competent officers to lead and soldiers to fill the ranks, maintaining the *jawan*s' continuing loyalty as the Raj faced defeat abroad, rebellion at home, and catastrophes like the 1943 Bengal Famine were only part of the problem.[6] Equipping and training the expanding army were major challenges as well. The equipment problems in the first stages of expansion were dire. Auchinleck raised them personally with Churchill only to have them brushed aside in one of the prime minister's most offensive comments of the war about the Indian Army: he asked Auchinleck whether he was sure that, with modern weapons in their hands, Indian soldiers would point them in the right direction. Wavell, taking up the cudgels when he and Auchinleck swapped jobs in mid-1941, reminded Churchill that India was raising armored units despite the total absence of modern tanks in the subcontinent. In January 1941—before Auchinleck's departure—one new unit's problems with equipment could have been replicated across the army. The 1st Sikh Light Infantry began training with "unit transport" that consisted of the adjutant's car, bicycles, camels, and some requisitioned civilian buses. When sniper training was undertaken, it was with air rifles purchased in the local bazaar. The first battalion exercise saw the unit "armed" with the bamboo poles that usually supported mosquito netting.[7] Many British Home Guard units were far better equipped. This farcical situation only slowly improved. By 1942, London had not yet delivered the full quota of field guns for the units raised under the 1940 expansion program, even though two more expansion programs had been undertaken by then.[8] When Slim took over XIV Army in the autumn of 1943, the corner had been turned, aided by both the flow of supplies from the United States and the reopening of the Mediterranean route to India, which vastly improved the productivity of shipping by shortening the turnaround time between Britain and India. Slim's army, however, would remain, to the end, masters of improvisation because the lavish levels of support that Britain's 8th Army in Italy and 2nd Army in Northwest Europe took as a matter of course would never be available to the Indian Army.

Shortages—or, on occasion, the total absence—of equipment compounded the problems of training but were not in fact at the heart of the training dilemma the Indian Army faced from the moment expansion began: For what sort of war, and against what enemies, was the Indian Army expanding? Since the post-Mutiny reconstruction of the Indian Army, its focus had been on the North-West Frontier. After 1918, like a compass needle swinging north, the Indian Army went back to the Frontier, where units spent two years of every six. The interwar years saw a number of sharp frontier campaigns, notably in Waziristan in 1937–1938. Although the old Russian Empire was under new management, the specter of the Soviet Union still loomed as large in the imaginations of the defenders of the Raj as the intentions of czarist Russia had in the minds of their nineteenth-century predecessors. In fact, the North-West Frontier (and Russia) remained a preoccupation for the army until 1943, one reinforced by the Hitler-Stalin pact, which conjured up the specter that German agents and gold, infiltrated into Afghanistan with Russian connivance, would stir up the Frontier tribesmen (and perhaps their Afghan cousins) and spark a major war there. Then, in 1941–1942, the concern shifted to the possible arrival of the Wehrmacht itself, which seemed on the verge of smashing the Soviet Union, as it had everything else in its path since 1939. It is easy today to label these fears as exaggerated and the large numbers of troops kept on the Frontier as a waste of resources (as late as 1943, the Frontier absorbed fifty-seven infantry battalions). At the time, however, it seemed an all too real possibility against which provision needed to be made (as was the case with the Northern Front in the Middle East). Despite continuing concerns about the Frontier, however, from the beginning of Indian Army expansion in 1940 the principal focus was the Middle East. This conditioned everything else—equipment, training, even the location of the army's intelligence school (Karachi, a major port of embarkation for the Middle East) and its focus on the German and Italian armies. The simplicity of concentrating on one enemy and one theater obviously had a strong appeal at a time when rapid expansion was posing so many other problems. The scale of the Indian commitment to the Middle East has never been fully recognized (largely because Churchill never acknowledged it in his war memoirs). Ultimately India would send about seven divisions there. In addition to combat units there were also very large numbers of support troops and labor units servicing both the huge Egyptian base and the base complex at Basra through which Lend-Lease supplies began their rail journey north to Russia. Indian troops had put down the Iraqi revolt in 1941 and a few months later occupied Persia. When Churchill decided in August 1942 to sharpen the focus of Middle East Command by removing from its responsibilities Persia and Iraq (still at that date thought at risk if the German offensive in southern Russia succeeded), the new command created to oversee the area—christened "Paiforce" (for Persia and Iraq Force)—was dependent on Indian troops as occupation forces for the remainder of the war.[9] All in all, given the reality of breakneck expansion and London's preoccupation with the Middle East and the desert war, the Indian Army's focus on the area is understandable. The unreadiness of Indian Army units to confront the Japanese in Malaya and Burma in 1941–1942 is usually ascribed to these two factors: excessively rapid expansion (in an equipment-starved environment), and exclusive focus on the Middle East in training. As a generalization this is true, but it is not the case that the challenges of fighting in the very different climate and terrain to the east of the Raj were totally ignored. The Army's Training Directorate produced pamphlets and memoranda on "forest warfare" that provided valuable guidance, although the degree to which they affected the training of units in Malaya and Burma is unclear. The Middle East was an active theater and the pressure to prepare units for it intense; Malaya was not a war zone and not expected to become one, and a Japanese assault on Burma seemed very unlikely. The Indian Army divisions sent to Malaya in 1941 (9th and 11th) were new units not up to strength and composed of incompletely trained recruits who were not fully equipped and faced so many local problems that specialized training for jungle warfare simply went by the board. The units hastily flung into Burma after the Japanese attacked were recognized by the Directorate of Military Training as unfit for combat. However, the need was urgent and they were all that was available.

In the aftermath of six months of unrelieved disaster in Malaya (where the Indian Army lost the equivalent of three divisions) and in Burma, the renaissance that would produce XIV Army began. A few officers had escaped from the Malayan debacle—and others had been ordered back to India to ensure that the "lessons learned" from that campaign would be passed along. Burcorps retired, attenuated but intact, into India, bringing with it a great deal of hard-won knowledge about the Imperial Japanese Army. The new division defending the North-East Frontier in Assam, the 23rd, was commanded by Major General Reginald Savory, who with the three Burcorps generals (Slim, "Punch" Cowan of 17th Indian Division, and J. Bruce Scott of 1st Burma Division) would play crucial roles in the rebirth of the Indian Army, which has been very aptly described by the leading historian of the process as a phoenix arising from its own ashes. Slim, whose next posting was to XV Corps, began to work out his own answers to the problems of confronting the Japanese, answers that came down to rigorous retraining and new tactical doctrine. Cowan, who as deputy director of military training had assessed 17th Indian Division prior to its departure for Burma as unfit for combat, took over the division in the aftermath of its near destruction at the Sittang River in February 1942. He would remain with it for the rest of the Burma campaign, rebuilding and retraining it into one of XIV Army's elite formations (the division's symbol was a black cat; unofficially it christened itself "God's Own Division"). Scott had had the thankless task of commanding 1st Burma Division, barely a functioning formation at the campaign's beginning, which disintegrated rapidly as its raw Burmese troops deserted (and by the retreat's end was composed of Indian units and a few Burmese hill tribesmen). He went next to the crucial staff posting of director of infantry, a position to which Savory, who had immediately begun to retrain 23rd Division to incorporate Burcorps's experience, would succeed in 1943. Scott was too tired to make much of an impact, but his task was not eased by the continuing expansion of the army with its accompanying churn of personnel and units. Nonetheless there was a beginning: Army Headquarters produced Army in India Training Memoranda (known as "AITMs") and Military Training Pamphlets ("MTPs") incorporating the lessons learned from Malaya and, more important, Burcorps's experiences. Some divisions, like Major General Wilfred Lloyd's 14th Indian Division, formed their own jungle warfare schools. It was, however, not yet a coordinated, army-wide effort: one vigorous corps commander, several division commanders, and a very tired staff director at Army Headquarters were not enough to revitalize the army. It took the 1942–1943 Arakan disaster and the subsequent command upheavals to bring that about and put Slim on the road to high command. The disaster in the Arakan both revealed just how much open-ended expansion had degraded the fighting qualities of the army ("a rather unwilling band of raw levies" was the unflattering description by one of Slim's staff officers of some of the new units flung into the Arakan) and precipitated a major command upheaval—the biggest of the war in any British theater, in fact. Churchill was enraged by the failure. The Americans wanted a strong British effort in Burma. The Arakan fiasco certainly did not look like such an effort. Stilwell's continuing denigration of British courage, competence, and good faith heightened both the impact of defeat and the pressure on Churchill. (This led to the sweeping changes described in chapter 4.) For the future of the Indian Army none was as important as Auchinleck's return as Commander-in-Chief, India. Without this appointment, the transformation of the Indian Army would have been, at best, partial. As he left the Commander-in-Chief's job, however, Wavell did two things that helped jumpstart that change: he sacked Noel Irwin, which cleared the way for Slim to move from corps command to Eastern Army, soon to morph into XIV Army. He also appointed a committee, the Infantry Committee, to review the recent fighting and make recommendations for improving the fighting quality of the army.

Little of this was on Churchill's radar. He did not want to fight the Japanese in Burma, which he likened to going into the water to fight a shark. He envisioned an amphibious strategy for SEAC, symbolized by the appointment of an admiral to command it (albeit an admiral with a long record of mishandling the ships he commanded).[10] He hoped for operations aimed at the northern tip of Sumatra, moving on to retake Singapore—the one operation that, in his view, would restore the Empire's badly battered prestige in South Asia. As to Burma, the Americans, of course, with their obsession about China, would have to be satisfied, but he had decided on a solution that would require only minimum dependence on the Indian Army (which, in one tirade to Wavell, he roundly denounced for failings going back to the 1857 Mutiny). But while Churchill dreamed of an amphibious strategy (for which there were no resources) and placating the Americans with Wingate's schemes for retaking Burma, Auchinleck at Army Headquarters, Slim at Barrackpore, and the work of the Infantry Committee were preparing a different future for both the Indian Army and the war in Burma.

At the root of most of the Indian Army's problems by 1943 was over-expansion and the concomitant "milking" of units to provide cadre on which to build yet more new formations. This had produced an army that in Malaya and Burma in 1941–1942 and in the Arakan in 1943 fielded raw soldiers led by equally inexperienced officers, VCOs, and NCOs. Moreover, the continuing shortfalls in equipment were aggravated by the ongoing expansion program. Available equipment was spread over more and more units until ludicrous situations (like that facing the Sikh Light Infantry when first raised) became the norm. No overhaul of doctrine would have a fighting chance of having an impact on training and, thus, of producing a more battle-worthy army until the core issue of open-ended expansion was confronted. In the spring of 1943 it finally was. Ironically, the Indian Army's ability to tackle what all its senior officers had long recognized as the crucial problem it faced received powerful reinforcement from an unlikely source: the prime minister's simmering prejudices against that army.

In his fury at the failure of the Arakan offensive, Churchill fastened onto not only Wavell but also the Indian Army. The prime minister had long distrusted it, as he had made abundantly clear to Auchinleck in August 1941. He now regarded it as too big, too lacking in fighting quality—and of dubious reliability. Of course, this ignored the role his own policies had played in committing the Indian Army to open-ended expansion in 1940. It also, and quite incredibly, ignored the fact that the disasters of 1942, even when reinforced by Gandhi's Quit India campaign, had produced no disaffection in the army. The prime minister's hostility and suspicion, however, provided an opening to bring the expansion program under control. On 20 May 1943, with Clement Attlee presiding (Churchill was at sea, on his way to an Anglo-American Trident Conference in Washington), the War Cabinet decided, on Amery's recommendation, to fix the size of the Indian Army at thirteen infantry and two armored divisions. Without this key change, Wavell's decision in the twilight of his tenure as Commander-in-Chief, India, to replace Irwin with Slim

and appoint a committee to recommend what needed to be done to improve combat efficiency would not have produced the dramatic results
that followed.

The Infantry Committee met for two weeks in June 1943. Chaired
by Major General Roland Richardson, deputy chief of the General Staff
at Army Headquarters, it was made up of four major generals and two
brigadiers. One of the major generals was "Taffy" Davies, who had been
Slim's chief of staff during Burcorps's long retreat (another was about to
become inspector of training centers). The committee's conclusions were
no surprise: any milking should stop (something that the War Cabinet's
cap on expansion made possible); recruits should receive longer, sounder
basic training followed by specialized training focusing on jungle warfare;
two divisions should be converted to training divisions; and every unit,
British and Indian, should pass through those divisions for advanced jungle warfare instruction before commitment to operations. Furthermore,
doctrine for jungle warfare should be standardized army-wide. A week after the Infantry Committee finished work, Claude Auchinleck returned as
Commander-in-Chief, India. Shortly thereafter, Savory was summoned
from 23rd Indian Division to be inspector of infantry (soon upgraded to
director) and the Indian Army's transformation moved into high gear.

In essentials that transformation came down to producing well-trained,
confident infantry able to take on the Imperial Japanese Army in the
daunting environment of the Arakan or in Assam's jungle-clad hills and
mountains. Slim, reflecting on the lessons of the 1942 withdrawal from
Burma, had realized that what was needed was hard, realistic training,
allied to a doctrine for dealing with the Japanese and the jungle. When
he assumed command of XV Corps, he had a chance to both shape the
training of a large formation and create his own doctrine to guide that
training. The training regime was so intense that even the *babus*—the
Indian noncombatant clerks who had been a feature of the Indian Army
since Company days—were required to do physical training. "It had been
impressed on me during the Retreat from Burma that in the jungle there
are no non-combatants," Slim later wrote.[11] Similarly, Slim insisted on
the inculcation of a tactical doctrine that was clear, simple, comprehensive, and infused with his own core belief: "If the Japanese are allowed
to hold the initiative they are formidable. When we have it they are
confused and easy to kill."[12] Slim meant his soldiers to be able to go anywhere and do anything. In June 1943, the Infantry Committee in effect
made Slim's approach to preparing troops the army's norm. Auchinleck's

arrival that same month ensured that there would be no deviations from that norm. In 1940, the Directorate of Military Training had produced the first edition of Military Training Pamphlet (India) No. 9, titled "Forest Warfare." The fourth edition, known as the "Jungle Book," came out in September 1943 and became the Indian Army's jungle warfare bible (as well as the basis for several manuals issued by the War Office in London to the British Army). Essentially, its prescriptions were the same as those issued by Slim to XV Corps. As better basic training took hold, followed by advanced instruction at the hands of the training divisions, another reform added a capstone. The reinforcement camps where replacements were held pending their posting to units had become sloughs of despond. No useful training was being carried out; the officers assigned to the camps were inadequate in numbers and often devoid of recent combat experience. Discipline was lax, and the camps had been the reverse of what the final stage of preparation for combat ought to be. All this was now vigorously taken in hand: more officers with front-line experience were posted to them, discipline tightened, and relevant training imposed. Auchinleck added to this better pay and improved welfare arrangements for the troops. The army's improving medical arrangements were beginning to turn the corner in the battle against malaria. In the seven months that separated the convening of the Infantry Committee and Auchinleck's reappointment from XIV Army's first great test in February 1944, a new army was forged.[13]

Yet even the revitalization of the Indian Army would not have had the battlefield impact it did if it could not have been adequately supplied for an extended period in an area where no one had ever envisioned major combat operations prior to 1942. That in turn depended on the mobilization of India's resources to sustain not only a war effort in the Middle East but also a major campaign in Burma (overlaid by the US airlift of supplies to China). Ultimately, Slim's war in Burma rested on the development of the massive Indian base as well as a supply line more precarious than anything seen in any other theater.

It is a historical commonplace in discussions of both world wars that they required the total mobilization of the major combatants: population, economy, finances, and emotions—and, it is increasingly recognized, of dependent empires as well. Of none was this more true than of the Indian Empire.[14] In 1939, India was still overwhelmingly an agricultural society, although industrialization, begun in the nineteenth century and pushed forward by the Great War, was significant both around Calcutta and in western India near Bombay. No one in 1939, however, expected India to support a huge war effort stretching from the Middle East to Burma. In 1939–1940, as the Indian Army grew at a modest rate and troops deployed to Egypt, Aden, and Singapore, the existing infrastructure of cantonments, railroads, and local suppliers was adequate to the effort. Then came the events of May–June 1940. Army expansion moved into high gear. The Mediterranean was closed by the Italian declaration of war in June 1940 and would remain shut as a route to India for three years. Now the voyage from the United Kingdom to India was again, as it had been for the East India Company, a long slog around the Cape of Good Hope. This increased the turnaround time, sharply cutting into the productivity of shipping. Suddenly, every effort was required to save on shipping space by producing as much as possible locally. In December 1940, the Government of India took the lead in setting up the Eastern Group Supply Council in Delhi. Its objective was to coordinate production efforts from East Africa to Australia in the interest of saving on shipping space by making the area as self-sufficient as possible while also supporting the war effort in the Middle East, to which more and more of India's expanding army was being committed.

As the tempo of mobilization increased, and the conflict in the Middle East deepened, not only were men and material flowing westward out of India; some of India's infrastructure was moved to the Middle East as well. Locomotives and rolling stock from Indian railways were taken to improve the carrying capacity of the Persian corridor route to Russia. Similarly, river shipping was redeployed to Iraq's Tigris and Euphrates Rivers. Indian workshops could make some railway equipment, but locomotives still came from Britain, and replacements for those shipped to the Middle East were as slow to arrive as was heavy equipment for the expanding army. Then, when Japan attacked, with India's North-East Frontier becoming an active theater of operations, a whole new set of stresses was imposed on an already overworked transportation structure. The Imperial Japanese Navy's incursion into the Indian Ocean in April 1942 meant that shipping once destined for Calcutta had to be unloaded at Bombay or Karachi and cargoes shifted a thousand miles and more across India by rail—on a system already short of locomotives and rolling stock. The US decision to replace the lost overland link with China by a trans-Himalayan airlift added greatly to the tonnage arriving in Indian ports and needing carriage on Indian railways and rivers (the Hump airlift would carry 650,000 tons of cargo during its three-year life). Of course, there was also the added burden of supporting the growing number of US service personnel in India, and US servicemen required more lavish supplies than the British, who in turn needed far more than the Indian *jawans*. By 1943, the mobilization of Indian resources in support of the imperial war effort was enormous, straining the structure of the Raj to the breaking point. (India was building base facilities for sixteen divisions, twelve of them Indian, plus the equivalent of fifteen more in independent brigades.) Some fourteen million people were either serving in the military and its noncombatant supporting services, working on the railways, in the war industry, or in construction (some 200 airfields were being built, many dedicated to supporting the US airlift). India was producing more war material than Australia, New Zealand, and South Africa combined—only Britain itself and Canada were producing more. It was this strained system that now had as well to support a war effort on its eastern frontier that would first equal, and then exceed, the Indian effort in the Middle East and do it, moreover, in an area where climate and terrain were daunting and communications were both complex and primitive.

The thrust of British expansion in India had been to the northwest. The province of Assam, part of India's North-East Frontier, was added in a piecemeal fashion by the East India Company to its Raj, mostly to buttress its eastern boundary with Burma. Much of Assam was mountainous and heavily forested. As late as World War II, some of its remote tracts were not fully mapped (unfortunately, those areas would be the scene of active operations in 1944). In 1941, its principal export was tea, grown in the "tea gardens" that dotted the hillsides around Darjeeling and Shillong. Tea was a labor-intensive business, and the labor force mustered by the Assam Tea Planters Association would play a critical role in the development of communications in 1942–1943. Prewar roads and railways were few and, unlike communications to the North-West Frontier, had never been designed with strategic considerations in mind. The roads with few exceptions were not all-weather, which meant that most rapidly became unfit for use during the monsoon, and even the all-weather roads could be blocked by monsoon-induced landslides. There was no road link of any sort between Assam and Burma. There were two principal means of moving men and supplies: by river steamer and barge on the unbridged Brahmaputra River, from which much of the shipping had been sent to the Middle East (and which had a turnaround time of over a month for the remaining steamers); or the narrow-gage railway, of strictly limited capacity, which had been built to serve the tea estates, not sustain a major land campaign, much less the US airlift to China. When Japan attacked and it became apparent that Burma would become an active theater, Wavell, in December 1941, ordered the road from the Dimapur, on the railroad in the Brahmaputra Valley, to Imphal, the capital of the princely state of Manipur (which was all-weather, albeit single-lane) extended to the Burmese frontier to link with Burma's road system. An army of Tea Association laborers completed a fair-weather track on 28 April 1942—just in time for Burcorps to stagger up it to Imphal. The Dimapur-Imphal Road, however, immediately began to disintegrate under the impact of unaccustomed traffic and the monsoon. Savory's 23rd Indian Division, based at Imphal, had to be put on half-rations, as did the convalescent formations of Burcorps, simply because the Assam line of communications could not carry enough. (In August 1942, only seventy-two truckloads of supplies made it through from Dimapur to Imphal.) From this point on, the history of the campaign is as much logistical (the British phrase at the time was "administrative") as operational. The first question to be answered about India's new war was: Could India find the personnel, equipment, and technical expertise to fashion and sustain communications that would support a full-scale campaign by a modern army and air force based in Assam for operations into Burma? Not the least of the successes of the Raj and its army in World War II was that they managed to do so.

The complexity of supporting what became Slim's XIV Army in October 1943 was several orders of magnitude greater than the effort required to sustain Eisenhower's armies from Normandy to VE Day. First, the sheer distances involved were staggering. An artillery piece unloaded in Bombay and destined for a unit in Assam first had to travel 1,130 miles to one of the base areas (at Benares or Calcutta) that supported the war on India's eastern frontier. Then onward it went to the Brahmaputra. There it was unloaded—India's railroads were mostly broad gage, Assam's narrow gage. Ferried across the river and reloaded on smaller rolling stock, it trundled slowly onward along rail lines that were single-track with not enough rolling stock or communications to handle the traffic generated by the war. Eventually, it would be offloaded at Dimapur, the railhead for the Manipur Road to Imphal (where it would complete a journey as long as from London to Moscow). The Manipur Road was 134 miles of one-lane blacktop. Twenty miles of that road traversed a steeply sloping shale mountainside. The road was ostensibly all-weather, but the mountain was not. During the monsoon, whole sections would slide slowly downhill, taking out the road. The road then had to be closed and rebuilt, only to collapse again under the weight of heavy trucks. The only solution—and a temporary one at that—was to wait until the end of the monsoon allowed the soil (and shale) to dry out and stabilize and then reconstruct and widen the road. The two divisions of IV Corps stationed on the Imphal Plain (17th and 23rd Indian Infantry Divisions) were on half-rations for most of the 1942 monsoon because the line of communications behind them was in a perpetual state of near collapse. Before the Indian Army could effectively fight the Japanese on the Indo-Burmese frontier, it had to be supplied there. Much of 1942–1943 was devoted to making this possible.

The problems of keeping the Manipur Road open were not merely weather-related. When the artillery piece reached the railhead, it had to be towed onward, assuming the road was passable, and here another major problem presented itself. The armies of Britain—and even more those of the United States—already had drivers and mechanics available and could train more easily, aided by the literacy and familiarity with vehicles of many, if not most, of their wartime conscripts. The Indian Army had only begun the switchover from animal to mechanical transport on the very eve of the war, few of the volunteers pouring into the depots were literate, and even fewer were familiar with any kind of machinery. Yet drivers and mechanics had to be trained in large numbers, and quickly. The truck companies that ferried supplies, equipment, and personnel from Dimapur forward to Imphal were inadequate in number (in December 1942 there was a shortage of 1,600 vehicles for the road—plus a shortfall of 1,400 for the mostly US airfield construction program) and subject to a very high rate of wastage from bad driving and mechanical breakdown. The drivers were as prone to sickness—malaria and dysentery—as their vehicles were to accident, as they often had to overnight in unhealthy areas, sleeping in or under their trucks. At one point the sickness rate among them hit 75 percent. But in December 1942, as the dry season set in, the situation on the Manipur Road finally began to turn around.

Colonel R. J. Holmes, who had previously worked on keeping the Burma Road (much of which, of course, ran through British territory) operational, was put in charge of transport on the Manipur Road. He overhauled the way drivers and vehicles were handled, basing procedures for both initially on the system used by the London General Omnibus Company. As the system was further refined, accident rates and the incidence of breakdowns declined, drivers' health improved, and the amount of tonnage reaching Imphal climbed. Despite setbacks during the 1943 monsoon—which was of unusual severity, washing out roads, bridges, and sections of railroad—by October 1943 the capacity of the Assam line of communications had risen dramatically. The size of the river fleet (which in early 1942 amounted to 27,000 tons of shipping as against an estimated need of 84,000 tons) grew. River ports and the railway system were being improved, and the Manipur Road was delivering at a peak rate of 40,000 tons a month—albeit in that month there were still 313 accidents and 443 vehicles in workshops for repair and overhaul. It was, in the circumstances, a truly remarkable achievement.

Unfortunately, it was one invisible to the prime minister. When Auchinleck took over in June 1943 and confronted London with the logistic realities of the war on India's eastern frontiers, it merely reinforced Churchill's belief that the Raj was a "welter of lassitude and inefficiency." In the aftermath of the Arakan fiasco, and with the Americans openly skeptical about British ability (and willingness) to push the Japanese out of the way of their engineers and a restored overland link with China, the prime minister wanted results, not explanations about the Assam line of communications. In some ways, Churchill's attitude toward logistics is hard to understand. In his instant history of the reconquest of the Sudan, *The River War*, he had devoted a chapter to the construction of the "desert railway" that sustained Sir Herbert Kitchener's army as it moved remorselessly up the Nile toward Khartoum. It was, wrote Lieutenant Churchill, the railway that made Kitchener's victory certain.[15] Similarly, it was the infinitely more complex, slowly maturing development of the Assam line of communications that was the necessary prelude to what Slim would do in 1944–1945. But in June 1943 that was not the message Churchill wanted to hear—he needed success in Burma to placate the Americans (who, incidentally, were themselves a large part of the logistical problem). To sustain the China airlift and the effort to push a road from Ledo in Assam into Burma, Stilwell's US forces required daily deliveries of fuel and stores equal to the daily requirements of IV Corps at Imphal. Churchill's impatience with all this inconvenient administrative detail, combined with his disdain for the Indian Army and the machinery of the Raj, were significant contributions to the radical changes that he engineered between June and September 1943.

As the 1943 monsoon ended, the Indian Army was beginning to change in important ways as new training inculcated new doctrine and new steps to improve health and morale began to take effect. The ability to sustain

the front-line forces in Assam had improved dramatically. As yet, however, the Indian Army had not confronted the Imperial Japanese Army
on the battlefield and won. Slim knew that new doctrine, better training,
and sound logistics were only a means to an end. He now had to lead his
rejuvenated forces to a victory.

6

Curtain Raiser

The premature attempt to drive the Japanese from the Arakan almost put an end to Slim's career. It was therefore fitting that the first test of the new army he had done so much to forge should take place there as well. Victory in the Arakan in February 1944 not only validated the work done by Auchinleck, Slim, Savory, and many others to rebuild the Indian Army but also was the first step on a road that would take Slim to the summit of his profession—a field marshal's baton. That this took place in the Arakan, however, was not due to Slim but to his opposite number, Lieutenant General Mutaguchi Renya, commanding the Imperial Japanese Army's (IJA) *Fifteenth Army* in Burma.

The IJA was, measured by the standard of any Western army, a difficult institution to understand.[1] Forged during the turbulent years of the Meiji Restoration—the revolution in the 1860s that ended both the Tokugawa Shogunate and Japan's isolation from the world—it was an odd mixture of Western technology and organizational structure with a spirit very different from that of any Western army. The militaristic ethos that gripped Japan as the IJA tightened its hold on the country during the interwar years certainly resembled superficially the militarism associated with Prussia, but at its heart was something very different: a belief in Japanese exceptionalism allied to the cult of duty to the Emperor unto death, sedulously inculcated not only in the army but also by the educational system and by popular culture. This produced a singularly tenacious army. The IJA was perhaps the only army in modern times where the command to fight to the last man and last round was always taken literally, as the tiny prisoner totals for both the Pacific war and the fighting in Burma attest. Slim would later say that the IJA expected and got, as routine behavior, performances that in other armies would merit the highest decorations for valor. This willingness to fight to the end, regardless of the tactical situation, made the IJA unusually formidable and covered up, at least in the war's opening stages, its equally significant shortcomings.

The officer corps of the IJA was riven by a factionalism that was intense. Moreover, although Japanese officers were in general well trained, the army's ethos—a relentless commitment to the offensive and a refusal to admit any limits to what the offensive spirit by itself could achieve—deprived it of flexibility both in planning and on the battlefield. Like the German Army, which provided advisers and mentors to the IJA in its early formative years, operations were prioritized over logistics in any officer's career path. This would lead in Burma to offensives being planned not only without sound logistic support but also in defiance of logistic realities. Finally, the IJA that went to war against Britain and the United States in 1941 had major equipment deficiencies that were, by that point, past remedying.

The IJA had by the mid-1930s recognized the need for modernizing its structure and equipment in preparation for an expected future clash with the Red Army. Artillery, armor, and motorization would be necessary to fight on the open plains that characterized the borderlands between the Soviet Union and Japan's expanding empire in Asia. Instead of modernization, however, the IJA got the "China Incident." A war very largely of the IJA's own making, it proved also to be a war without end, pulling in more men and resources, postponing any comprehensive modernization program, and eventually triggering a much larger war that the IJA embarked on with equipment that was basically little different from that of 1914–1918, relatively little armor (and that mostly light tanks), and a supply system that depended as much on animal power as on the internal combustion engine. Resource constraints thereafter made this situation impossible to change. The enormous success of the IJA in 1941–1942 (and, in Burma, in 1943) seemed to validate the IJA's approach to battle and gave the Japanese a completely false idea of what they could accomplish on the basis of willpower, tactical aggressiveness, and the filling of gaps in their logistics with captured enemy supplies.

The Japanese commander whom Slim would face in 1944 embodied in acute form all the IJA's problems. Mutaguchi Renya, who took over *Fifteenth Army* in March 1943, had been linked to various factions in the officer corps since his junior officer days. His career was made, however, when he hitched his fortunes to the group led by Tojo Hideki. As a regimental commander in northern China in 1937, he orchestrated the Marco Polo Bridge Incident that sparked the Sino-Japanese War. The commander of the *Burma Area Army* in 1943, Lieutenant General Kawabe Shozo, had been his superior officer in 1937. And Tojo—Japan's prime minister by 1943—had been a major general and chief of staff of the IJA's Kwantung Army, which wanted war with China. Mutaguchi had subsequently commanded *18th Division* during the Malayan campaign. He was thus well connected in the army and owned a very successful combat record. This, his ambition, experiences in the stunning victory over the British in 1941–1942, and arrival in Burma as the Arakan offensive ended in a calamitous tactical defeat for the Indian Army all predisposed him toward a forward strategy. The only question was the form it would take.

When the conquest of Burma was complete in mid-1942 both Imperial General Headquarters in Tokyo and the theater command, *Southern Army*, suggested that a further push into Assam, perhaps as far as Dimapur, would provide a better defensive frontier than the Chindwin. The commander on the spot, confronted with the formidable terrain on the Indo-Burmese frontier, disagreed, and the suggestion was dropped. When Mutaguchi assumed command of *Fifteenth Army* in March 1943, he concurred: an offensive into Assam was not feasible. Two things then changed his mind. The first was the realization that the original suggestion had come from Imperial General Headquarters and might therefore have conveyed the Emperor's wishes. To not concur was, to an officer like Mutaguchi, virtually impious. Rather more practically, Wingate's first Chindit expedition, however devoid of concrete results, made a powerful impression on Mutaguchi. If the British, whom Mutaguchi disdained in light of his Malayan experience, could operate across the wild terrain that separated their base at Imphal from the Burmese plains, then surely Japanese units, infused with their incomparable warrior spirit, could do so as well. From this point on Mutaguchi became relentless in arguing for an offensive into Assam. It may well count as Orde Wingate's greatest contribution to victory in Burma.

The key issue, as *Fifteenth Army* began planning, was supply. Wingate's brigade of lightly equipped raiders had been supplied by air. *Fifteenth Army*, three divisions strong plus supporting troops, would be a different matter. Mutaguchi fired his chief of staff for arguing that a major offensive into Assam was logistically impractical. Other staff officers, however—beyond Mutaguchi's reach at *Southern Army* headquarters in Singapore—raised the same issue. That Mutaguchi eventually prevailed was due to two things. The *Burma Area Army* commander, Kawabe, was no more willing to rein in a subordinate about whom he had reservations but whose dynamism he found impressive than he had been in northern China in 1937. Moreover, both *Southern Army* and Imperial General Headquarters were swayed by the prospect of winning a major success that would raise the morale of a nation battered by eighteen months of bad news: the losses in the Battles of the Coral Sea and Midway; the brutal attritional struggle at Guadalcanal; rising shipping losses; and the interminable China war. The upshot was that after a final conversation with a senior staff officer from *Southern Army*, conducted while he bathed, Tojo climbed out of his tub, toweled off, and signed the order for an offensive into Assam to take Imphal and improve the defensibility of Burma—the western anchor of Japan's Co-Prosperity Sphere.

The problem of supply had not been solved (certainly not by Mutaguchi's decision, based on reading about Genghis Khan, to drive herds of cattle and goats along with his army as provisions on the hoof). It had been brushed aside. Mutaguchi had seen a Japanese offensive sustained in Malaya by "Churchill supplies"—captured British dumps. He expected the same to happen again. His men would carry three weeks' supplies with them. By the end of that period, he expected to be in possession of Imphal and the British dumps there (and of course there were always the cattle and goats).

The logistics of Operation U-Go were very shaky from the beginning. A further complication arose from the fact that the operation authorized by Imperial General Headquarters, *Southern Army*, and *Burma Area Army* was not quite the same operation Mutaguchi had in mind. While his superiors thought in terms of a morale-enhancing victory and the improvement of Burma's western defenses, Mutaguchi privately was thinking about a victory much more sweeping. Conscious of his role in triggering the war in China, he hoped to bring the whole East Asian war to a victorious conclusion. The catalyst for this fantasy was Subhas Chandra Bose, the charismatic Bengali radical (and onetime rival of Nehru and Gandhi for leadership of the Congress Party). Bose, who had fled internment in India and spent several years in Berlin trying vainly to interest Hitler in an invasion of India, had reached Southeast Asia in 1943 (via a German U-boat and then a Japanese submarine). Installed by the Japanese as head of the Free India exile government, Bose was thought of by the Japanese primarily as a propaganda asset. However, Bose had grander ambitions. He had his own army, the Indian National Army (INA), raised (largely by Japanese intelligence officers) in the aftermath of Singapore's fall from among the thousands of disoriented and disillusioned Indian troops (mostly raw recruits) taken prisoner there. It had propaganda value but little else to commend it to Japanese commanders, who had only contempt for soldiers who surrendered. Moreover, the IJA, as an institution, was as racist as any group of European colonials. By the time Bose reached Singapore, the Indian National Army was moribund. Bose revived it, increasing its numbers by recruiting from the large Indian population of Malaya and eventually forming three "divisions" (each actually about the strength of an Indian Army brigade). They were poorly equipped and morale was uneven. (Many former Indian Army soldiers had joined simply to escape Japanese POW camps, and some hoped to desert back to the Indian Army at the first opportunity.) Bose had grand ideas for his army, and it was these that caught Mutaguchi's volatile imagination. Bose was convinced that if he could unfurl his banner on Indian soil the Indian Army would desert to him in droves, leading to the collapse of the Raj. Mutaguchi in turn convinced himself that a collapse in India would take Britain out of the Asian war, thereby also discouraging the United States, which then would be forced to open negotiations with Japan. Put simply, Mutaguchi, the man whose actions had triggered the war in which Japan was mired, would be instrumental in bringing it to a glorious conclusion. The two mutually reinforcing fantasies of Mutaguchi and Bose led to a situation in which the limited offensive that had been approved in Tokyo, Singapore, and Rangoon was, in the mind of *Fifteenth Army*'s commander, the first step in a drive that would take not only Imphal but also Dimapur and penetrate into the Brahmaputra Valley, where Bose would be unleashed to bring down British India. An offensive plan whose logistics were based on wishful thinking and an army commander with a private plan very different from the officially sanctioned one would by themselves have been enough to doom U-Go, but these were not the sum total of its handicaps. There was a worse flaw yet. All the Japanese planning was based on a fundamental misconception about their opponent: the belief that the raw, undertrained, incompletely equipped, and often poorly led Indian Army of 1941–1942 was still the opponent they faced. That it was not—that a sea change in that army had taken place in a remarkably short time—was about to be dramatically revealed.[2]

When Slim moved up to XIV Army, his former command, XV Corps, remained in the Arakan under Lieutenant General A. F. P. Christison. The corps was unusually large—five Indian divisions and a West African division. It was positioning itself to resume the offensive as indications mounted that a Japanese attack was in the offing.[3] Slim's intelligence sources were multiple. There was an Indian outpost of Bletchley Park, the Wireless Experimental Center, in Delhi, which worked successfully on breaking IJA codes. There was also photo reconnaissance and, at the grassroots, V Force and the Z Patrols. V Force, set up as the British withdrew from Burma, was made up of locals, usually hill tribesmen, not formally enlisted in any military formation and commanded by former Burma police officers, British civilians with local knowledge (often former employees of the teak industry), and volunteers from the army. It was spread across the approaches to British positions in both the Arakan and Assam to gather intelligence and provide early warning of Japanese movements. Z Patrols were military units—"fighting patrols"—that worked in the immediate rear of Japanese positions and along the Japanese lines of communications. From all these sources it now became evident that a Japanese forward movement was imminent.[4] Mutaguchi's design for U-Go called for a preliminary attack (Operation Ha-Go) in the Arakan to pull in and pin down Slim's reserves. The operation would be undertaken by Lieutenant General Hanaya Tadashi's *55th Division*. The division was part of the newly formed Twenty-Eighth Army, and it is indicative of the low opinion the Japanese had of their opponents that one full-strength division was judged to be adequate for the task.

Hanaya's attack would fall on Christison's two forward divisions: 5th and 7th Indian Divisions, very different formations from the luckless 14th Indian Division routed less than a year before. For one thing, both were commanded by very experienced officers. Major General Harold Briggs, whose 5th Indian Division (on the western side of the Mayu Range) had been among the first Indian formations deployed to the Middle East, had distinguished himself in the desert war. The 7th Division (on the eastern side of the range) had not fought in the Middle East, but its commander, Major General Frank Messervy, had fought both in the reconquest of Ethiopia and against Rommel in the desert. Their divisions, like all of XIV Army, had had nearly half a year to absorb the new training norms and tactics that were the essence of the quiet revolution. Slim, when he took over XIV Army, had instructed units cut off by Japanese attacks to form an all-around defense and rely on air supply. They would then become anvils on which British reserve formations would pulverize the attacking Japanese. Hanaya's plan called for a sweep around the eastern flank of Messervy's division, aiming for the communications of the two Indian divisions positioned on either side of the mountain spine and the supply dumps that sustained them. The expected response was a rapid and disorganized British retreat—and a harvest of Churchill supplies.

On the morning of 4 February 1944, cloaked by morning fog and mist, Hanaya's striking force, a brigade-sized force named the "Sakurai Column" after its commander, swung around the left flank of Messervy's division, which was held by Brigadier Michael Roberts's 114th Indian Infantry Brigade. Despite the knowledge that a Japanese attack was likely, the Japanese advance came as a complete tactical surprise. (The official historians would later criticize both XV Corps and XIV Army for paying insufficient attention to tactical intelligence from front-line units that might have warned them of the imminence of the Japanese forward movement.)[5] The Japanese, in a column sixteen abreast, simply marched through a gap in Roberts's widely extended brigade front. Following the main body was a supply column that was caught and dispersed by Roberts's units—the impressed Arakanese porters simply dropped their loads and fled when the fighting started. This loss of supplies made the seizure of the British dumps even more vital. (In subsequent days the Sakurai Column would also lose a complete list of all the radio call signs assigned to it, which complicated command and control, and a marked map laying out its dispositions and plans—both immense boons to British commanders.) Initially, however, Sakurai's force, moving very fast, seemed set to reprise the heady days of 1941–1943. Early on 5 February, the Japanese overran Messervy's headquarters (Messervy had some experience of this in the desert, his headquarters having been overrun by Rommel's *Afrika Corps*). He survived, as did most of his staff, but a temporary loss of communications disrupted his control of the division. In Malaya, Burma, and the previous Arakan fighting this would have virtually guaranteed a Japanese victory. But this was a new army.

Christison, losing touch with Messervy, correctly assumed that his command post had been overrun and, recognizing that the corps maintenance area at Sinzweya was an obvious Japanese target, ordered Brigadier Geoffrey Evans (who had arrived to assume command of Messervy's 9th Brigade only the day before and was not yet sure exactly where Sinzweya was) to take what spare troops were available, assume command of what became known as the Admin Box, and hold it at all costs. Evans got to Sinzweya quickly enough, walking the last mile when the tracked carrier he was using became stuck in the mud. Messervy made it to the Box later that day, followed by most of his staff. Radio links were improvised using the sets of the 25th Dragoons. (In the event, two squadrons of its tanks would play a crucial role in the ensuing siege.) 7th Indian Division was back in business.[6]

Slim, who had been receiving medical injections to deal with dysentery, was far from well when the Japanese attack opened. Nonetheless, strongly supported by Giffard, he swung into action. He had already instructed XIV Army, in October 1943, that any cut-off units should stand fast and expect air supply. Major General A. H. J. "Alf" Snelling, his principal administrative staff officer, was instructed to be prepared at any time to put forward units on air supply. Snelling, in turn, beefed up both the numbers and training of the air-supply units—the packers, loaders, and dispatchers (or "kickers out"). Even before the Japanese attack, Snelling's men were working around the clock in anticipation of a major air-supply operation. They were now told that beginning 8 February Messervy's entire division would be on air supply. XIV Army had a new doctrine, a new training regimen, and a new supply system—all of which would now be tested on the battlefield. Could the hastily improvised defenses of the Admin Box, and its heterogeneous garrison of combat and support troops (including a mule company and one of truck drivers), hold in the face of the sort of ferocious assault that was the IJA's specialty?

In the aftermath of the withdrawal from Burma, Slim had recognized that secure rear areas, such as had characterized the Western Front in World War I, would be rare in the sort of fighting likely to occur in India's eastern borderlands. Thus he had insisted, while commanding XV Corps, on a program of "physical toughening" plus "weapon training for everybody."[7] The ideas Slim developed at XV Corps became the XIV Army norm. When Evans took over command of the Admin Box most of its defenders were rear-area personnel—clerks, mechanics, storemen, drivers. Formed into improvised combat units, backed by the gunners available, some tanks, and a miscellany of infantry (British, Gurkha, and Indian), amounting to about a battalion in numbers, they held their positions with determination and success. The action of the Japanese in one of their first attacks, when they overran the field hospital in the Box, slaughtering patients and staff alike (as they had done in Singapore two years earlier), stiffened rather than intimidated the defenders. Evans's improvised force held the Box firmly. Messervy's brigades, rather than falling back, stood fast. They were the anvil. The "pile driver" in this set piece would be supplied by two reserve divisions moving forward, 26th Indian and the understrength 36th, designated as an Indian division but in fact at this point made up of British units and soon to be designated as a British division—the only one in combat at this point in Slim's army. The Japanese, already short of everything due to destruction of Sakurai's supply column and deprived of the expected haul of Churchill supplies, would be increasingly pinched logistically. (When they overran the field hospital, in fact, they ransacked it for the medical supplies they themselves lacked.) Meanwhile, XIV Army's planning and preparation kept Messervy's division and the defenders of the Box fully supplied. The key to the success of XIV Army's air-supply operation was the Douglas DC-3 (whose military version was the C-47), known to the British as the Dakota. This rugged and versatile transport—well adapted to supply-dropping—would be the key to Slim's operations until the final victory in 1945.

The potentialities of air supply were obvious from World War I onward. Slim, when doing a tour at Indian Army headquarters in the mid-1920s, had, as noted, investigated the problem. Wingate's first Chindit expedition did not suddenly reveal the possibilities but was a dramatic demonstration of them—as well as very useful practice in working out the techniques. What was necessary to using air supply (and the rapid movement of troops by air) was the right aircraft in adequate numbers. The British in 1940 had decided, understandably, to concentrate on building fighters and bombers. Transport aircraft they would buy from the Americans. Once US mobilization gained momentum, however, the British were competing with the demands of the United States' own burgeoning armed services. India, of course, was at the end of the pipeline for transport aircraft (as for everything else). In September 1942, the RAF had one Dakota squadron positioned there. In June 1943, it had three transport squadrons, only two equipped with Dakotas. When SEAC became operational in November 1943 the number of RAF Dakota squadrons had inched up to three. SEAC's Troop Carrier Command (under US Brigadier General William Old) included as well two US C-47 squadrons. There were of course other C-47 squadrons in India (as well as squadrons flying the slightly larger C-46 Commando), but they were dedicated to the Hump airlift. Mountbatten had been authorized at the Sextant Conference in Cairo (the Anglo-American-Chinese summit meeting that preceded the Tehran Conference) to divert up to 1,100 tons of carrying capacity per month from the China airlift to support operations in Burma. Transport squadrons could also be borrowed from the Mediterranean theater—where in July 1943 there were twenty-nine Dakota squadrons, all under command of the US Army Air Forces (USAAF)—in an emergency. However, diverting C-47s from the Hump—or any other theaters—meant referral up to the Combined Chiefs of Staff. Slim's operations, from February 1944 on, depended crucially on the availability of Dakota squadrons, which neither he nor Mountbatten controlled. This fact would hover over XIV Army's campaign until the very end.

However, in the Arakan no major diversion from the airlift was needed. (Although Mountbatten had asked for, and the Combined Chiefs approved, a temporary switch of transport aircraft, by the time they began to arrive the crisis of the Arakan battle had passed and they were promptly returned.) Air superiority over the battlefield was, however, a necessity for daylight supply-dropping, and that the RAF had not yet quite attained. Hitherto the workhorse Hawker Hurricanes had not been able to outperform the Japanese Zero fighters. (Spitfires were another matter when they finally began to reach Southeast Asia; however, there were only three Spitfire squadrons available in the Arakan, whereas the sprawling Mediterranean theater had more than twenty.) When aerial supply was ordered for Messervy's division, the first dropping sortie was led by Brigadier General Old personally piloting a C-47. Despite this display of determination, Japanese opposition in the skies, plus the fact that accurate aerial supply required Dakotas to make their runs virtually at treetop heights—exposing them to Japanese ground fire—forced some drops to be made during nighttime. This made no difference to the operation's efficiency. Over five weeks, 714 sorties delivered 2,300 tons of not only basic supplies but also such things as the theater newspaper and spare eyeglasses and toothbrushes for Messervy's headquarters personnel, who had lost their kits when overrun by the Japanese. Amazingly, only one Dakota was lost to ground fire. With Messervy's brigades all holding their ground and the Admin Box (whose tanks and gunners could develop considerable firepower to back the improvised infantry garrison) standing fast, the Japanese, as Slim had foreseen, found that they, not 7th Indian Division, were in a precarious situation. Hanaya's troops carried little with them (complicated by the fact that Sakurai lost his supply column on the opening day). They had counted on capturing British dumps. When they did not, they nonetheless fought on, with what Slim characterized as "dull ferocity." Japanese military culture became Slim's unwitting ally as he brought forward reserve formations to pulverize the attackers against the anvil formed by 7th Indian Division: "Have you ever seen a walnut pulverized by a pile driver?" On 24 February Hanaya finally broke off his attack. XV Corps took 3,500 casualties. Hanaya lost at least 5,000 dead by British count (and probably many more lay undiscovered in the jungle).

But the significance of the battle far exceeded the casualties inflicted on the Japanese. This was the first test of Slim's rebuilt army: its doctrine, training, and fighting spirit. For the first time since December 1941 the Japanese had been beaten decisively by the Indian Army. It was the turning point of the war in Burma—the dress rehearsal for the much greater drama that opened in Assam as Hanaya's beaten troops retreated in the Arakan.[8]

The North-East Frontier of India, which became in 1942 the Assam (or Central) Front, was relatively quiet during the 1942–1943 dry-weather campaigning season, roughly October to April. To some extent this was inevitable due to its logistic issues. IV Corps, based on the Imphal Plain—about the only extensive piece of flat terrain between the frontier with Burma and the Brahmaputra Valley)—had its two divisions on short rations for months, and neither was combat ready. The 23rd, formed only in January 1942, had no combat experience. The 17th, which did, had come out of Burma with Slim severely attenuated and was recovering (a quarter of its men were down with malaria at one point) and retraining. By late 1942, however, the thoughts of the theater commander, Wavell, were turning, as in the Arakan, to the offensive. The drive on Akyab was the priority operation, but with the supply situation very slowly easing, IV Corps, now commanded by Lieutenant General Geoffrey Scoones (a Gurkha Rifles officer, like Slim, who described him as careful, thoughtful, and steady in a crisis), began to push its two divisions forward. Savory's 23rd Indian Division began to push eastward, some of its forward patrols supplied by air during the monsoon. Cowan's 17th Indian Division started southward down the valley of the Manipur River. Savory's initial objective was Tamu, sixty-four miles away on the Indo-Burmese border; Cowan's Tiddim, 164 miles south near the lonely British outpost at Fort White in the Chin Hills held by the British officered Chin Levies supported by the Chin Hills battalion of the paramilitary Burma Frontier Force. Fort White was supplied largely by air. The units based there, together with V Force, covered the frontier with Japanese-occupied Burma, gathering intelligence and functioning as a tripwire. As the divisions moved forward they spooled out behind them roads—and armies of civilian road-builders. Their ultimate objectives were to move on from Tamu and Tiddim to the Chindwin, from which point an advance into Burma could begin—someday.

There were few clashes of significance on the Assam front until the 1943 dry season began, when the forward movement of Scoones's better-trained and better-supplied divisions produced more contact with the Japanese, who were also moving forward—like the British intent on securing jumping-off points for future offensive operations.[9] During the 1943 monsoon season both divisions had continued to patrol vigorously and had begun to experience increasing success in the small-scale clashes that developed—an important landmark in the gradual rebuilding of the Indian Army. With the coming of the 1943–1944 dry season, operations in company and battalion strength became the norm as the Japanese began to push forward into the Chin Hills and 17th Division, supporting the Chin Hills Battalion, and the Chin Levies fought to maintain the British foothold there. In a series of small-scale operations the Indian units involved performed well, although the jousting for position ended, in November 1943, with the Japanese in possession of Fort White largely because the British still tended to underestimate the speed with which the Japanese moved across country. The movement down the Kabaw Valley, south of Tamu, was now in the hands of 20th Indian Division (which had been part of Slim's command at Ranchi), commanded by Major General Douglas Gracey, another Gurkha Rifles officer. The 23rd Indian Division, now led by Major General Ouvry Roberts, a British Army officer (who had, however, been on Slim's 10th Indian Division staff in Iraq), moved into corps reserve. Gracey's division continued the slow movement toward the Chindwin, mounting small-scale operations in January 1944 that took a number of Japanese outposts. These clashes revealed two things that were to become continuing features of XIV Army's campaign. As in the Arakan, Japanese bunkers presented formidable defensive obstacles. Slim's solution, urged in vain on Irwin, was close tank-infantry cooperation. Gracey's division had no tank support, and tactical air, at least on the scale available, was insufficient to overcome the bunkers. The division resorted to surrounding and besieging bunker complexes, cutting off resupply and aiming at starving out the Japanese. (In fact, the Japanese were able to successfully withdraw the defenders when their position became untenable.) These small-scale battles also highlighted something else: British infantry was a wasting asset in XIV Army. The 1st Northamptons, one of Gracey's British battalions, went into action in January 1944 with only three companies rather than four, and those companies averaged about 82 fighting men each (normal strength would have been about 130). Sickness still accounted for some of the shortfall, but India was at the end of the line for British infantry replacements as well as material; this situation would only worsen as 1944 went on. Inevitably, most of the impending struggle would be borne by the Indian Army.[10]

17th Indian Division's fight to maintain itself in the Chin Hills, and 20th Division's slow forward advance, paused in February 1944 as both IV Corps and XIV Army, convinced that a major Japanese offensive impended, began to reconfigure themselves to meet it. The performance of both divisions, however, had given strong indications that, as in the Arakan, it was a new Indian Army that Mutaguchi would encounter. It was fortunate that this was so because his attack would open with two tactical surprises, one of which put 17th Indian Division, perhaps the best in IV Corps, in a very precarious position, while the other forced two determined stands, reminiscent of Rorke's Drift, by badly outnumbered XIV Army units.[11]

As it became clear that a Japanese offensive was imminent—more new units identified, more vigorous Japanese activity, especially in the Chin Hills, more rivercraft on the Chindwin, even the herds of cattle and goats collecting east of the river—Scoones's headquarters issued on 3 February a new "appreciation" (i.e., analysis and orders). Gracey's 20th Indian Division in the Kabaw Valley was felt to be principally at risk. Scoones felt that the Japanese would cross the Chindwin two divisions strong north of Gracey's division and detach a brigade-sized force to take Kohima (thus blocking the Dimapur-Imphal Road), while the bulk of the attacking force swung around 20th Indian aiming at the Imphal Plain. His plan to meet this attack was to pull Gracey's division back to Tamu, where it would make a defensive stand. One brigade from Scoones's reserve division, 23rd Indian, would be positioned to block a Japanese thrust at Kohima. The rest of the division plus IV Corps's armor, 254th Indian Tank Brigade (one British and one Indian tank battalion equipped with obsolete US tanks), would be held available to support Gracey. By the end of February, however, Scoones (and Slim) had rethought this plan and made fundamental changes.

The position of IV Corps's two forward divisions, 17th and 20th, was the end result of nearly two years of cautious forward movement, covering road building by civilian laborers working with a minimum of equipment (heavy road-building equipment, like everything else, had been scarce in India in 1942–1943). The goal was to position IV Corps to cross the Chindwin and maintain itself there whatever the ultimate shape of the theater strategy. Elements of two Japanese divisions had held

the Chindwin line for much of 1942–1943. By late February 1944, however, there were three Japanese divisions (plus supporting troops) poised
to attack. 17th Indian Division was dangling at the end of a 300-mile
supply line from Dimapur, only half of which was all-weather (and in
monsoon-induced landslide season, "all-weather" was largely notional).
20th Indian Division was 213 miles from Dimapur while the road distance between the two divisions was 250 miles. This clearly risked defeat
in detail by a concentrated Japanese force. Scoones's revised plan, issued
on 29 February, called for 17th Indian Division to withdraw north to the
southern edge of the Imphal Plain the minute the Japanese attack opened.
It would leave a brigade to block the southern entrance to the plain and
join 23rd Indian Division in corps reserve. 20th Division would also fall
back, abandoning Tamu and taking its stand on the eastern edge of the
plain, where the painfully constructed road climbed from Imphal into the
hills. On the perimeter of the plain, where air power and artillery could be
used to maximum effect, IV Corps would make its stand. Slim approved
Scoones's plan but added that, as it withdrew from Tamu, Gracey's division should hold a series of intermediate positions formed by brigade
"boxes" (like those against which the Japanese had dashed themselves in
vain during the Arakan fighting). These would blunt the Japanese attack
and inflict casualties. When 20th Division had fallen back to Shenam,
where the road from Tamu begins its descent into the plain, it was to
stand firm.[12]

The decision to move from preparations for an offensive to a defensive
stand anchored on the Imphal Plain carried with it a radical change in
the administrative structure supporting IV Corps. First, the army of engineers and laborers (some 60,000–70,000, Slim estimated) engaged in road
building, and maintenance behind 17th and 20th Indian Divisions had to
be pulled back and much of their work prepared for demolition. Then the
base area on the Imphal Plain had to be reorganized, the sprawling establishment of dumps, camps, and depots concentrated into fortified boxes
covering the two all-weather airfields at Imphal and Palel, whose reten-
tion in operating condition would be crucial to the success of Slim's design. This was to let the invariable Japanese commitment to the offensive
destroy Mutaguchi's army, as, on a smaller scale, it had decimated Hanaya's force in the Arakan. However, everything depended on the skill and
success of Gracey and, above all, Cowan in carrying out what is widely regarded as one of the most difficult operations of war: a withdrawal under

pressure. This, even more than the stand of Messervy's division in the Arakan, would be the ultimate test of the rebuilt Indian Army.

It started very badly for XIV Army, with the Japanese encircling 17th Indian Division immediately and, almost simultaneously, cutting the road between Imphal and the railhead and supply base at Dimapur. The speed and ferocity of the Japanese assault resembled what had happened in Malaya and Burma in 1941–1942. The Japanese goal of acquiring abundant Churchill supplies seemed, briefly, attainable. Then the reality that confronted Hanaya in the Arakan asserted itself. This was a very different opponent.

7

A Difficult Beginning

I should have remembered that battles, at least the ones I had been engaged in, very rarely went quite according to plan.
—Field Marshal Sir William Slim, *Defeat Into Victory* (1956)

The Battle of Imphal opened on the Tiddim Road, the lifeline of Cowan's 17th Indian Division, whose history provides a microcosm of the Indian Army's experience since unlimited expansion became the order of the day in 1940. Part of the 1941 expansion program, the division had been raised by Major General J. G. "Jacky" Smyth, VC. Assessed late in that year by the Directorate of Military Training, it was, as we have seen, deemed unfit for combat without at least three more months of intensive training. At that point this did not seem to present a problem, since it was destined for the Middle East, where it would form part of the Levant-Caspian Front being built up in Iraq and Persia to guard against the possibility of a Russian collapse that would allow the Germans to attack the Middle East via the Caucasus. That front was covered by Lieutenant General E. P. Quinan's X Army, largely made up of newly raised Indian divisions, short of nearly everything. 17th Indian Division would join them, complete its training (which had of course been focused entirely on the Middle East), and perhaps even receive its full outfit of equipment before facing an opponent. Then came the Japanese attack. Two of its brigades were rushed to Singapore and lost there. The division headquarters and the third brigade went to Burma, where they were almost immediately in action. Although two brigades—one already in Burma, one taken from a division forming in India—were added to Smyth's command hurriedly to bring it up to strength, 17th Indian went to war a scratch formation, incompletely trained and equipped—and, as has been noted, with a sick commanding officer. Smyth was ill before he left India. Examined by army doctors shortly after reaching Burma, he was told that he needed at least two months' rest but, oddly, was not declared unfit to remain in command. However, conscious that he needed help, Smyth decided to commandeer the services of Brigadier D. T. Cowan (known in the army as "Punch" because of a supposed resemblance, hard to discern in his pictures, to the figure on the cover of the British humor magazine of that name). Cowan had been serving in the Military Training Directorate in Delhi and could have had no illusions about the combat readiness of the division. Sent out to replace a brigadier in the 1st Burma Division judged to have failed in the campaign's opening encounter, Cowan instead found himself drafted into the 17th Indian Division headquarters by Smyth as his Brigadier General Staff, an appointment not usually found at divisional level. In effect, he had been made the assistant division commander, a post not found in British or Indian divisions. However unusual the appointment, it was a very fortunate one. Shortly afterward, withdrawing across the Sittang River under heavy Japanese pressure, Smyth ordered the sole bridge over the river demolished, under the impression that the bulk of his division had crossed when in fact it was still on the far side. A result of both Smyth's debility and the proverbial fog of war, the Sittang disaster shattered the division, which mustered only some 3,500 men, with very little equipment, in its aftermath. It also shattered Smyth's career. The theater commander, General Sir Archibald Wavell, arriving in Burma shortly after the Sittang calamity, summarily sacked Smyth, ordered him back to India, reduced him in rank, and retired him—a brutal but not entirely unmerited end to a hitherto distinguished career. Cowan took over the remnants of the division, which he would command for the duration of the war.

17th Indian Division, patched back together after the Sittang debacle, fought all through the retreat, arriving in the Imphal Plain to confront a complete lack of quarters, replacements, supplies, and medical support—not to mention Irwin's disdain. There was no immediate possibility of sending anyone on leave, and the line of communications was in such a state of underdevelopment that the division was on half-rations for months. At one point a quarter of it was also down with malaria. The determination and leadership of Cowan held it together (the fact that Irwin quickly moved on to Eastern Army, to be replaced at IV Corps by Geoffrey Scoones, a fellow Gurkha officer, doubtless helped). Brigadier Ronnie Cameron of 48th Brigade (who had been in command of a Gurkha battalion at the Sittang, an experience that turned his hair white overnight) was given the job of writing a report on the organization, tactics, and equipment necessary to defeat the Japanese—an early example of the effort at unit level to reorient, reconfigure, and retrain the Indian Army for its new role, an effort that would be systematized and made army-wide in 1943. Cameron's report led to 17th Division becoming an Indian Light Division—basically a division stripped of the cumbersome "tail" of vehicles designed for the Middle East but a handicap in Malaya and Burma. Mules and jeeps became divisional transport. Gradually the division's health was restored, its training in new tactics undertaken, and its morale and cohesion vastly improved. The small-scale actions of 1943 in the Chin Hills had sharpened its fighting skills. By early 1944, it was a much different unit than it had been two years before. As a light division it had only two brigades, made up of five Gurkha battalions and one British battalion. Three more battalions remained under direct divisional command—two Indian and one British. Given that British battalions were at this point chronically understrength, the division was overwhelmingly Indian Army—in this prefiguring the future development of XIV Army as a whole. Dangling at the end of a 164-mile road from Imphal, much of which the division had built itself, it looked very vulnerable to the standard Japanese tactic of hooking behind the British, cutting their line of communications, and forcing them into disorderly retreat. The new 17th Division was unlikely to disintegrate as had the raw units in Malaya and Burma, but it was vulnerable to being cut off. Hence the crucial nature of the timing of Cowan's retirement.[1]

When Slim approved Scoones's change of plan he stipulated that the withdrawal order should only be issued by Scoones personally once it was absolutely certain that the Japanese offensive had begun. It is easy to see why Slim made this stipulation. A premature withdrawal would not only yield to the Japanese ground they would otherwise have to fight for, incurring losses but also lower the morale of the troops involved, and Slim, Cowan, and many others had spent eighteen months rebuilding the Indian Army's morale and fighting spirit. And unlike the situation in the Arakan, the troops on the Central Front had yet to experience the morale-enhancing effect of a major victory. However understandable the delegation of authority to Scoones, the man on the spot, Slim, in retrospect came to feel he had made a major error. Scoones was a very cautious soldier, given to clearing his mind on any subject by writing an analysis ("appreciation") of the issue. The result was that by the time he ordered 17th Division to fall back it was too late—the Japanese had already cut the road behind it.[2]

There had been warning signals. A Gurkha patrol had reported on 9 March a large Japanese force in the hills west of the Tiddim Road.

Spread over those hills were, in addition to V Force patrols, Barforce and Hasforce, made up of troops from the Bihar Regiment (a new Indian Army unit recruited from outside the martial-races family), the Chin Hills Battalion (a paramilitary unit), and the Chin Levies (lightly armed, British-led tribesmen). These were supposed to act as a tripwire—but all seem to have missed the Japanese. On 11 March Scoones finally learned, from V Force, that a Japanese column (in fact an infantry regiment, an artillery battalion, and some engineers) was in the hills to the west of the vital bridge where the Tiddim Road crossed the Manipur River. Once again, a Japanese offensive had opened with a tactical surprise.

As had been the case in the Arakan the previous month, a long-anticipated Japanese attack began with Japanese infantry and gunners moving faster than expected—even the retrained Indian Army still thought in terms of the time a British or Indian unit would take to move a certain distance. This misreading of Japanese mobility is curious. As far back as 1904, Lieutenant General Sir Ian Hamilton, acting as an official British observer of the Russo-Japanese War, had noted "the fact is that Japanese infantry, in mountains, has against other infantries some of the attributes of cavalry."[3] And there had been abundant recent validation of Hamilton's observation in Malaya and Burma—most recently in the Arakan the preceding month. The Japanese, despite carrying three weeks' worth of supplies, simply moved faster than expected.

The Japanese *33rd Division* was the first of Mutaguchi's divisions to attack, its mission not only to destroy 17th Indian Division but also to draw British reserves from the Imphal Plain south, thereby opening the vital base area there to attack by the Japanese *15th Division* moving toward it from the east and northeast. Initially it seemed that the Japanese design had been successful: not only was the road cut behind Cowan's division but Scoones's reserve (Ouvry Roberts's 23rd Indian Division) was ordered to commit two of its brigades to help extricate Cowan.[4]

Here the first of the controversies about the battle appears: the timing of Scoones's withdrawal order to 17th Division. Scoones ordered Cowan to retire to the Imphal Plain on 13 March, forty-eight hours after V Force alerted him that Cowan's right flank had already been turned. The official historians, while refraining from criticism of Scoones, claimed that 17th Indian Division had then delayed its withdrawal for a further twenty-four hours after Scoones's headquarters had transmitted the code word "moccasin," the signal for the retirement to begin. This had the effect of spreading the blame, but was in fact untrue. On 12 March, knowing

that the order to withdraw would come soon, Cowan had begun preliminary moves. At 11:30 PM that night, Scoones had sent a warning order to
Cowan that "moccasin" was now imminent. When that order was transmitted on the evening of 13 March, Cowan passed the order to his units
within the hour, and the anabasis of the 17th Division—16,000 march-
ing troops, 2,500 vehicles, and 3,500 mules—began.[5] Slim, however, was
certainly correct to assert, in retrospect, that Scoones's headquarters, su-
pervising the withdrawal of two widely separated divisions in the face of
Japanese thrusts coming from three different directions, should not have
been burdened with the task of deciding when the retreat should begin.[6]

The crucial issue, however, was how 17th Indian Division would handle the situation in which it now found itself, which by 15 March looked
extremely precarious. The road had been cut in no less than four places,
and three small detachments—one holding the Manipur Bridge, another
guarding a very large supply dump north of the bridge, and the third on
the road north of the dump—were isolated from one another and from
the main body of the division. Scoones, by now fully aware that he faced
a crisis, began reinforcing his right flank to aid Cowan's withdrawal. First
the corps machine-gun battalion was pushed down the Tiddim Road on
12 March (it quickly became two of the three isolated pods of troops on
the road). Then, on 13 March, 37th Brigade of his reserve division (23rd
Indian) was ordered to start down the road. On 14 March, his second
reserve brigade, 49th, followed. At this point, since 23rd Division's remaining brigade was screening the Imphal Plain from the east, Scoones
had only 254th Indian Tank Brigade left in reserve. But it was also at this
point that Cowan's division began to show the results of the rebuilding
process that had begun as soon as Burcorps staggered into Imphal. And as
Cowan's men methodically fought their way back up the Tiddim Road,
Slim began rebuilding Scoones's reserves—while at the highest level of
SEAC a nasty squabble erupted.

A week before Cowan was ordered to retire, Slim, knowing that a
Japanese attack would develop soon, ordered one of his reserve divisions,
25th Indian, to relieve Briggs's veteran 5th Indian in the Arakan. The
5th would then move to Scoones's command between mid-March and
mid-April. Giffard, the 11th Army Group commander, decided to use
the remaining two brigades of Wingate's Special Force (14th and 23rd),
held in reserve in India, to assist Scoones by mounting short-penetration
operations behind Mutaguchi's attacking divisions.

On 14 March Slim met the theater commander, Mountbatten, at
XIV Army headquarters. Scoones had already committed his reserves to

support Cowan. Slim told Mountbatten that it was now crucial to move 5th Division to Imphal rapidly. Mountbatten promised to provide the troop lift needed, even if it meant pulling cargo planes off the Hump airlift.[7] Washington had agreed to lending cargo squadrons from the Hump to Mountbatten to meet the Japanese Arakan offensive. Since the Japanese attack on the Central Front was part of a single Japanese plan (in which the Arakan attack was merely the opening gambit), Mountbatten construed that permission as still valid. Thus he procured the Dakotas (and the slightly larger C-46 Commandos) that would be absolutely vital to the development of Slim's plans. As the combat deepened on the Tiddim Road, Slim and Giffard were already moving a division to Scoones's support (with a second, Messervy's 7th Indian, due to follow). Two LRP brigades had been earmarked to support IV Corps. In addition, Giffard had alerted XXXIII Corps—training in India for amphibious operations—to be ready to move to XIV Army's support with at least one of its divisions, 2nd British (the only complete British Army division in the theater). Slim was assembling his pile driver. (Oddly, Mountbatten's rather waspish chief of staff, Lieutenant General Sir Henry Pownall, told his diary that Giffard and Slim were slow to respond to the situation developing on the Central Front. In fact, it is hard to see how they could have moved faster than they did.) It was at this moment, with the battle intensifying by the hour, that Mountbatten picked a quarrel with Giffard.

When Mountbatten was appointed to SEAC he had been given a trio of service commanders. Unfortunately, two were incompatible with "Dickie." Admiral Sir James Somerville, a very senior and vastly experienced officer, simply could not tolerate a junior officer of his own service—a forty-three-year-old substantive captain—as his superior, a situation that would eventually lead to his replacement in the autumn of 1944. More important for Slim and XIV Army, Giffard also disliked Mountbatten. Like Somerville he was much superior to the Supreme Commander in rank and, quiet and reserved himself, was repelled by the showmanship that was part of Mountbatten's personality.[8] Fully conscious of Giffard's attitude, the Supreme Commander chose this moment to write Giffard a letter accusing him of failing to grasp the seriousness of the situation during the week (7–14 March) when Mountbatten had been confined to hospital following an accident that temporarily blinded him. The accusation was not true (but is clearly reflected in Pownall's contemporaneous comments). Giffard, with Slim, had begun to move all the reinforcements that available air transport and the Assam line of communications could handle (rather more, in fact, as far as the Assam line of communication was concerned, as Auchinleck pointed out to Giffard when faced with the requirement to move XXXIII Corps forward). Slim, whose relations with Mountbatten were—and remained—good, would nevertheless go out of his way in his memoirs to praise Giffard, and the official historians would also point out that Mountbatten's complaint had no substance. While all this went on well above the heads of Scoones and his troops, it is nonetheless important to bear in mind that the atmosphere in which Slim operated was rather toxic: his immediate superior, the army group commander, was at daggers drawn with his ultimate superior, the theater commander. It is an interesting commentary on Slim himself that he retained the unstinting support of both.

Meanwhile, there was the retirement of Scoones's divisions to manage. Gracey's 20th Division (which had been part of Slim's XV Corps at Ranchi in 1942) had a reasonably smooth but certainly not uneventful withdrawal to its designated position blocking access to the Imphal Plain from the east.[9] The problems encountered, however, illustrated how far the Indian Army had come. Due to the type of disconnect all too common in complex withdrawal arrangements, a position astride the Tamu Road was prematurely evacuated. Two battalions forward of the position then found their withdrawal blocked by infiltrating Japanese. In 1942, this would have doomed them. Instead they adroitly sidestepped the block and continued their retirement. A tank-infantry patrol sent down the road to collect stragglers and wounded met six Japanese tanks and destroyed them all. Simultaneously, a Japanese column approaching Gracey's new position from another direction was effectively ambushed. By 20 March, 20th Indian Division was firmly settled into its new positions. By this time, however, a new crisis was developing on its left flank.

Northeast of the Imphal Plain, Scoones had positioned 49th Indian Infantry Brigade of Roberts's 23rd Division at the track junction of Ukhrul. (Apart from the roads on the plain itself and the Dimapur-Imphal Road, the only communications worthy of the name "road" were those built behind the advancing 17th and 20th Indian Divisions in 1943–1944. Everything else was "tracks," a few "motorable" in dry weather, but often mere footpaths, difficult for men and mules and barely negotiable even by the indomitable jeep.) Track junctions, in close and difficult country, were correspondingly important. When Roberts's 49th Brigade was pulled into the struggle on the Tiddim Road, it was replaced by 50th Indian Parachute Brigade, which had been under direct XIV Army command since December 1943. The 23rd Division, basically reduced briefly to one brigade, was back to three brigades by 20 March as the first Dakota loads of 123rd Indian Infantry Brigade from Briggs's 5th Indian Division began to deplane at Tulihal Airfield at the north end of the Imphal Plain. As it did so, Brigadier Maxwell Hope-Thompson's 50th Brigade clashed with an advancing Japanese column in what was to be one of the most important engagements of the Imphal battle.

Sangshak

Paratroop units were new everywhere in 1940. They featured dramatically in the stunning German conquest of the Low Countries, and Churchill was anxious to see comparable British formations. General Sir Robert Cassels, Commander-in-Chief, India, expressed an interest in creating an Indian parachute formation in October 1940. One actually took shape in January 1942. Its three battalions were made up of volunteers from British units in India, Indian Army infantry regiments, and the ten Gurkha regiments. The brigade then lost its British battalion to the Middle East and over the next two years gradually crept closer to the front, moving from India Command to 11th Army Group and then to XIV Army. There were discussions about using it to mount an assault on Akyab, but when it moved to Imphal, although highly trained, it had never been in combat. That move began on 10 February when Slim placed it at Scoones's disposal and ordered it to move to Imphal as rapidly as possible. It was to relieve Ouvry Roberts's 49th Indian Infantry Brigade in the Ukhrul area, where it was watching the northeastern approaches to Imphal and covering the Imphal-Kohima Road. This would allow Roberts's entire division to be concentrated on the Imphal Plain as Scoones's reserve. By the time Brigadier Hope-Thompson and his headquarters reached the area on 14 March, it had already been vacated by 49th Brigade, pulled south by the emerging crisis on the Tiddim Road. Roberts had left one of 49th Brigade's battalions behind to provide a screen that would at least alert IV Corps about any Japanese advance from the northeast. Hope-Thompson was told to take the battalion (4th/5th Mahrattas) under command, which at least brought his brigade up to strength, albeit with a unit with which it had neither trained nor previously worked. The following day the first of 50th Brigade's two battalions arrived and was positioned southeast Ukhrul, with the Mahrattas in reserve several miles behind them. That night, patrols from Gracey's division found that the Japanese were crossing the Chindwin on a wide front, threatening 20th Division's left flank, and on the following day V Force reported another large Japanese force crossing farther north, moving on Ukhrul from the east. 50th Indian Parachute Brigade was about to go into action.[10]

The savage battle that followed resembled the much better-known stand by the garrison of Kohima. There was, however, one important difference. Kohima has been widely written about and memorialized, while Sangshak is largely forgotten. Perhaps the reason is that whereas Kohima was held Sangshak was lost, although much of the surviving garrison slipped away. There is also the fact that while a key component of the Kohima garrison was a British infantry battalion, Sangshak was an exclusively Indian Army battle—and one fought by the 50th Indian Parachute Brigade with very little of the support that higher headquarters brought to the assistance of Kohima's tenacious defenders.

The root of the problem seems to have been an underestimation of the forces that the Japanese were likely to direct on Kohima. The British had consistently estimated that the Japanese could maintain only a brigade group across the wild hill country, known as the Naga Hills, between the Chindwin and the Imphal–Kohima–Dimapur Road. In fact, Mutaguchi committed an entire division (ironically, maintaining a much larger force had been facilitated by the work of 23rd Division's engineers in building a jeep track from the Chindwin to Kohima). East of the main road, it offered an axis of advance toward Kohima, especially to an army with even fewer vehicles than an Indian light division. The district commissioner for the Naga Hills area, Charles Pawsey, whose headquarters were at Kohima, evidently pointed this out, but as a civilian he carried little weight with the military. The assumption that the Japanese would use only a brigade group north of the Imphal Plain clearly made it easier for 23rd Division—and IV Corps— as the crisis developed on the Tiddim Road, and Gracey's division started its planned withdrawal from the Kabaw Valley—to feel comfortable that the arc of country north and northeast of the Imphal Plain, from Kohima through Ukhrul, whence an improved track ran directly to Imphal, was adequately covered. East of Kohima, the Assam Regiment (like the Bihar Regiment, another of the Indian Army's new non–martial races units) was deployed. The 50th Indian Parachute Brigade screened the northeastern approaches to the plain. The leading brigade (123rd) of Briggs's division was beginning to deplane at Tulihal Airfield, forty miles to the west, rebuilding IV Corps's reserve. However, what was approaching along the tracks from the Chindwin was not a Japanese regiment (the equivalent of a British brigade) but the entire Japanese *31st Division*, as well as the right wing of *15th Division* pressing around Gracey's left. If 17th Indian was at risk of being encircled on the Tiddim Road, the back door to the plain was in danger of being kicked off its hinges only forty miles from the absolutely vital airfields. It was this that the stand of the 50th Indian Parachute Brigade, for which the overworked adjective "heroic" is appropriate, averted.

Two regiments of the Japanese *31st Division* were directed toward Kohima, the third moved toward Ukhrul, and south of it the *Right Assault Unit* of the Japanese *15th Division*, another regiment, was moving toward a large British dump (Churchill supplies) at the northeastern end of the Imphal Plain. Neither was aiming at Sangshak. Both were drawn into a vicious battle there that cost them casualties—and, more important in the circumstances, time.

Brigadier Hope-Thompson first became aware that large Japanese forces were moving toward him on 19 March. Various intelligence reports that might have alerted him earlier had, although received by both IV Corps and 23rd Division, never been passed on to him. (Indeed, there seems to have been a certain amount of distraction and disorganization affecting both headquarters at this point, perhaps a result of the unexpected way the battle was opening.) Hope-Thompson immediately began collecting the widely scattered components of his brigade, aided by the time bought for him by a company of the Indian parachute battalion holding an outpost known as Point 7378 (the number indicates the height in feet of the "hill" the company held).

Although virtually the entire company was wiped out, it slowed the Japanese. Over the next six days the brigade bought more time, but at a very high cost. Hope-Thompson managed to get it assembled on a small, flat-topped hill—roughly 600 by 300 yards—just east of the village of Sangshak. There, until 26 March, the three battalions, two Indian and one Gurkha, supported by a battery of mountain guns (one of whose officers, Lieutenant O. P. Malhotra, would eventually become the chief of staff of the Indian Army after independence) plus a few machine guns and mortars, withstood attack after attack by growing numbers of Japanese. Requests for barbed wire with which to prepare the position went unheeded by higher headquarters during the brief window when it would have been possible to supply it. Aerial supply, which played a major role at Kohima and in the extrication of 17th Division, failed at Sangshak, where most of the drops fell outside 50th Brigade's perimeter. Some of this was doubtless the result of the small size of the position. Some of it, however, according to one of the brigade's officers, was the result of the aircrews' dropping in a way the brigade had warned against. The Japanese benefited from the airdrops more than Hope-Thompson's men. Water was in very short supply, as was sleep. At length, when it became clear that to hold longer would result in the total loss of the brigade, 23rd Division told Hope-Thompson to break out after dark on 26 March—*sending the message in clear*, thereby alerting any Japanese listeners. The breakout was nevertheless reasonably successful, most of the survivors making it back to Imphal, although the Indian parachute battalion lost 80 percent of its strength and the Gurkha 35 percent. Their sacrifice gained priceless time—but would not have, despite their valor, if the Japanese had not in effect cooperated.

Japanese infantry divisions had a unique command structure. A lieutenant general commanded the division while a major general commanded the division's infantry group, in effect the bulk of the division. In *31st Division*, that post was held by Major General Miyazaki Shigesaburu. He also commanded the southernmost of the division's three columns. Sangshak was not even within his division's boundaries. It was one of Miyazaki's battalions that "bumped" the Indian company at Point 7378, starting the battle. Perhaps deceived by the ferocious defense put up by the Indian paratroopers into believing that a strong British force lurked on his flank, Miyazaki brought most of his brigade across the interdivisional boundary to deal with it. The fight then drew in a regiment of *15th Division* (which was at this point only two regiments strong) as well. Thus large parts of two Japanese divisions were delayed for the best part of a week (and of course they only had three weeks to reach their objectives). During that week, the reinforcements Slim had arranged poured out of the (largely borrowed) Dakotas onto the Imphal Plain—and the road to the greatest prize of all, the sprawling Dimapur supply base, was effectively blocked.[11]

Kohima

Kohima was a small hill station, the administrative center for the Naga Hill Tracts. It stood at 4,700 feet elevation where a pass marked the summit of the road from Dimapur to Imphal. To the west were mountains up to 10,000 feet high, to the east stretching toward the Chindwin the Naga Hills (whose name belied their height, which reached 8,000 feet). Some of this wild country had never been completely mapped. The Naga and Kuki tribesmen scattered in small villages over this landscape, which only they knew intimately, were divided in their loyalties. The Nagas, their head-hunting habits nominally foresworn (many had been converted to Christianity by American Baptist missionaries), were almost without exception loyal to the British, often at great cost, supplying guides, porters, and intelligence. The other tribal group, the Kuki, were more ambivalent—something that would have significant consequences. Kohima itself, in addition to its civil functions, was the site of a collection of hospitals and depots, manned by rear-area supply and service units, none of them combatant formations. Security was provided by a battalion of the allied Nepalese Army, not a first-line formation, and by the Assam Rifles, a British-officered paramilitary force whose nominal duties were to patrol, under the direction of the civil administration, the tangled hill country. As the Japanese offensive opened, responsibility for the defense of this key point (which controlled not only the road but the approaches to the vital supply base at Dimapur) was passed rapidly from one headquarters to another, so that who exactly was in charge was not settled until it was almost too late.

Kohima was initially the responsibility of IV Corps. The assessment that the Japanese would direct a brigade group at most toward Kohima—the same assumption that had governed the deployment of 50th Indian Parachute Brigade—led to a battalion of the new Assam Regiment being spread out east of Kohima to cover the tracks leading toward the Chindwin, along which two-thirds of the Japanese *31st Division* was making its way toward Kohima. (The effect of the faulty assessment of the likely strength of a Japanese thrust toward Kohima was compounded when Kuki tribesmen betrayed the locations of some V Force outposts to the Japanese, thus temporarily blinding IV Corps intelligence.) Scoones named Colonel H. U. Richards commandant of Kohima on 22 March and told him to hold the place. Then a bewildering series of changes in which headquarters actually controlled Kohima set in.

Slim, conscious of the importance of Dimapur, flew into the base on 28 March accompanied by the XXXIII Corps commander, Lieutenant General Montagu Stopford, and put the commander of 202 Line of Communications Area, Major General R. P. L. Rankin (another Indian Army officer who wore a decoration for valor won on the Somme) in operational control of Kohima as well as the sprawling depot pending the arrival of XXXIII Corps. Slim then had what must have been a very worrying conversation with the brigadier commanding the Dimapur base, who told him that of the 45,000 men on the "ration strength" of the depot he could probably scrape together 500 who knew how to fire a rifle. To defend Dimapur at that moment, Rankin had one battalion of the Burma Regiment (hill tribesmen who had remained in their Burma Rifles units and followed Slim into Assam in May 1942). Just beginning to arrive was Brigadier D. F. W. Warren's 161st Indian Infantry Brigade (of Briggs's 5th Indian Division). On the way, but not expected for nearly a week, were 2nd British Division's leading brigade and one of the units of Wingate's Special Force, Brigadier

Lance Perowne's 23rd LRP Brigade, together with XXXIII Corps's main headquarters.[12] Stopford would assume command when his headquarters was complete. But, meanwhile, Rankin was left with his scratch force and firm orders from Slim to hold Kohima and Dimapur—the latter at all costs. The following day units of the Japanese *15th Division* cut the Imphal Road, which would not be reopened until June. Rankin, tasked to hold Kohima and Dimapur, positioned Warren's brigade east of Kohima in support of the forward positions held by the battalion of the Assam Regiment, already under heavy pressure. However, he was conscious of having Stopford at his elbow, outranking him and due to take command the minute his headquarters was complete. Stopford, when passing to Rankin written confirmation of Slim's verbal orders, made it clear that 161st Brigade was not to be split up and needed to be pulled back to a position covering Dimapur. At the same time, erroneous reports reached Rankin that Japanese columns were approaching the railway and depot that were his prime responsibility. Consequently, on 30 March he ordered Warren back to a position between Kohima and Dimapur. Warren protested that he was about to extricate the now very hard-pressed Assam Regiment, which his withdrawal would leave isolated and in serious jeopardy—but he complied and by the evening of 31 March 161st Brigade was back at Nichugard, north of Kohima and covering Dimapur. This left the Assam Regiment to fight its way out, its withdrawal delayed by a radio breakdown that prevented a message reaching the battalion commander that he was to fall back on Kohima. Eventually a messenger reached him with the retreat order, but by that time the Assam Regiment's two widely separated posts were encircled, and although the troops broke out, less than half the battalion reached Kohima.[13]

Later, both Slim and the official historians would blame Rankin for pulling back 161st Brigade (although Slim did acknowledge that Rankin's situation was difficult and the security of Dimapur the first priority). This criticism seems rather unfair. Rankin had virtually no combat units available to protect Dimapur, which both Slim and Stopford had told him must be held. Warren's brigade was therefore crucial to his mission—and he had been told it must not split up. Given the circumstances, and his orders, it is hard to see what else he could have done.[14] The real problem lay in the unexpected weight of the Japanese thrust toward Kohima and, it must be said, the hastily improvised command structure put in place on 28 March. A nonoperational line of communications headquarters was suddenly transformed into a combat command, and Rankin was given very precise orders from both Slim and Stopford that left him with little flexibility. The victims of all this were the Assam Regiment—and the defenders of Kohima.

From the time Scoones put Richards in command of Kohima he had been trying to put it in a defensible state while uncertain what forces would actually be available to him. The leading brigade of 5th Division was at first destined for Dimapur, but the worsening situation on the approaches to Imphal led Scoones to request that it be diverted to the plain. Its leading unit (2nd West Yorkshire) had, however, already landed at Dimapur. They moved to Kohima, but the minute the leading units of the next 5th Division brigade, Warren's 161st, began landing at Dimapur the 2 West Yorks continued down the road to Imphal to rejoin their brigade (being the last unit to travel the road before the Japanese cut it). Then 161st Brigade deployed to the east of Kohima and—from the point of view of Kohima's defenders—vanished as quickly as it came. The battalion of the Assam Regiment, expected to fall back on Kohima and form the core of its defense, arrived instead a tattered, exhausted remnant. With each turn of the kaleidoscope, Richards had to readjust his defense layout. Finally, on 2 April Stopford's headquarters opened and he assumed overall command—but left Dimapur and Kohima, together with 161st Brigade, under Rankin, who was now authorized to withdraw the Kohima garrison if it faced destruction. This seems an odd order. Kohima at that moment had only a scratch defense force facing what Stopford knew was the bulk of the Japanese *31st Division*. How could he have imagined that it was not in danger of destruction? In any case it was Rankin who took the crucial step of telling Stopford on 4 April that, with the arrival of 2nd British Division's leading brigade to thicken Dimapur's defenses, 161st Brigade could be told that it should push forward a battalion and some mountain guns to strengthen the defenders of Kohima. Early the following morning the British battalion of Warren's brigade, the 4th Royal West Kents, made it into Kohima just before the Japanese clamped an iron ring around it, beginning one of the war's memorable sieges.[15]

Finale on the Tiddim Road

Successful withdrawals under pressure are perhaps the most difficult of military maneuvers. Helmuth von Moltke, creator of the German General Staff, is supposed to have said that no one could be considered a great general who had not conducted a successful retreat. Some are epics— like Xenophon's. Some should be—like Burcorps's retreat in 1942. The withdrawal of 17th Indian Division up the Tiddim Road to Imphal certainly qualifies. Lieutenant General Yanagida Kenzo's *33rd Division*, with which 17th Division had contended since 1942, had planned and carried out a double-envelopment of 17th Division, with one regiment moving through the hills west of the Manipur River, while another, with supporting artillery, climbed the 8,000-foot Letha Range that separated the Kabaw Valley from that of the Manipur River. By the time the division began its 164-mile trek north, the Japanese pincers had closed on the road. Cowan's sappers had blown so many demolitions in the road they had slowly and painfully built that the Japanese force (which included artillery and armor) following up along it was delayed badly and played no substantial part in the ensuing three-week battle. Cowan leapfrogged his two brigades, which methodically cleared the Japanese roadblock south of the vital Manipur Bridge, then retook the supply depot north of the bridge, which the Japanese had briefly overrun, capturing enough (or so Japanese officers thought) to sustain a Japanese division for two months. However, the Japanese did not hold the depot long enough to remove more than a few of these Churchill supplies. Continuing remorselessly on, 17th Division smashed through another roadblock north of the depot. Meanwhile, 37th Brigade had been fighting its way south, hammering through two roadblocks while the Japanese inserted yet another behind them. On 28 March at Milestone 101, sixty miles south of Imphal, Cowan's 63rd Brigade linked up with Roberts's 37th Brigade and the whole force continued north, breaking the last Japanese roadblock at Milestone 72. By 5 April, Cowan's Division and Roberts's two brigades were back in the Imphal Plain, whose southern door they had firmly shut in Yanagida's face.

The three-week fighting withdrawal of 17th Indian Light Division was not only an impressive feat; it also provides, even more than the Arakan battle, a vivid picture of the transformation in the Indian Army after mid-1943. Cowan's was certainly the most battle-hardened division in XIV Army. It was also virtually an all-Indian army—or, rather, an all-Gurkha division. Five of the six battalions in 48th and 63rd Brigades were Gurkha. (The lone British battalion, the 9th Border, was, according to a British Royal Engineer officer with the division, "not too well commanded.") Roberts's 37th Brigade, which fought its way down the road, was also an all-Gurkha formation. The Japanese had lost none of their skill in rapid movement across very difficult terrain, nor their ability to quickly construct formidable defensive positions blocking roads. They still held those positions with the same tenacity. But the Indian Army had gotten very much better at dealing with them.[16]

Another dramatic change was in the logistics in this corner of the war. The enormous and complicated job of improvising the Assam line of communications had made it possible to build up, and sustain, IV Corps on the Imphal Plain. But once the Japanese offensive began, the key to the battle became the Dakotas. Mountbatten's great contribution was ensuring that enough C-47s were available to Slim. This in turn made it possible for Slim to quickly pour two brigades of the veteran 5th Indian Division onto the Imphal Plain, more than rebuilding Scoones's reserve while simultaneously covering Dimapur by shifting the division's third brigade there. The withdrawal of Cowan's division also depended on aerial supply. When it began, Cowan ordered all units to destroy surplus supplies: the division would depend on supply by C-47 until it reached Imphal. (A number of 17th Indian personnel, with vivid memories of 1942, were very uneasy about that particular order.) The Dakota pilots, however, came through (backed by British control of the skies), skillfully weaving their way along the narrow valleys edged by towering mountains through which the road ran, delivering everything needed onto the necessarily constricted drop zones.

The success of 17th Indian Light Division sounded the death knell for Mutaguchi's offensive design. The Japanese *33rd Division* was supposed to capture Imphal by mid-April and was provisioned on that assumption. On 25 March, however, most of the division had yet to cross the Manipur River, 120 miles south of the plain. By the time Yanagida closed up to the southern edge of the plain in early April, his division had already suffered some 2,000 casualties and its supplies were nearly exhausted. It was now obvious that the assumptions about the Indian Army on which Mutaguchi's plan was based were very wrong. *That* Indian Army no longer existed. Yanagida told Mutaguchi as much: taking Imphal before the onset of the rainy season was now impossible, because the Indian Army's organization and equipment (and, he might have added, fighting skills) had become so much better. If the rainy season caught Japan's *Fifteenth Army* locked in combat on the edge of the Imphal Plain, the result would be a "tragedy." Best to break off the offensive and fall back on a defensive line within the mountain jungles through which his division had just hacked, and fought, its way. Mutaguchi, at army headquarters in Maymo, the British hill station near Mandalay some 250 miles from Imphal, did not want to be told bad news. He ordered Yanagida to press on and began planning Yanagida's removal. He also took the astounding step of authorizing *33rd*'s senior staff officer to issue operational orders, thereby leaving the division with two commanders, one of whom had clearly lost his superior's trust. It would have been far better for his *Fifteenth Army* had its commander listened to Yanagida—because Slim was now preparing to introduce his pile driver.[17]

8

The Pile Driver

Retelling in his memoirs these events, Slim was, as so often, generous: "Thanks to my mistakes the battle had not started well." But certainly the battle about to unfold at Imphal did not open as he expected.[1] Punch Cowan's 17th Indian Division would have to shoot its way back to the Imphal Plain (but in doing so badly damaged Japanese *Fifteenth Army*'s *33rd Division*, disrupted its timetable, and broke the morale of its commander). This was largely down to IV Corps's delay in ordering Cowan back. (Slim was right that he left too much in Scoones's hands.) Scoones, as well as Roberts's 23rd Indian Division headquarters, had mishandled 50th Indian Parachute Brigade (although Roberts, like Scoones, was likewise focused on extricating Cowan). The errors at Kohima were more complex. As far back as November 1943—shortly after Slim had assumed command of XIV Army—Giffard's headquarters asked about the possibility of the Imphal-Kohima Road being cut by a Japanese raiding force. In reply, XIV Army agreed that it was possible and estimated that the Japanese could use a regiment (equivalent to a British brigade) in the direction of Kohima.[2] There the matter rested for the time being, but the idea that a brigade-sized force was all the Japanese could direct on Kohima, largely because of the poor communications across the Naga Hills, seems to have taken root. The realization that not a Japanese regiment but an entire division was descending on Kohima therefore took a while to dawn and seems largely to blame for the way the responsibility for its defense was tossed from one headquarters to another as the Japanese *31st Division* remorselessly bore down on Kohima. This in turn was responsible for both the failure to adequately support the withdrawal of the Assam Regiment and for the heterogeneous nature of Kohima's garrison. One thing seems clear: Major General

Rankin, of 202 Line of Communication Area, although criticized in a guarded manner by Slim and much more straightforwardly by the official historians, was the victim of the ever-changing command arrangements and guilty of nothing beyond carrying out orders given by the army commander in person.

The rocky beginning, however, had been salvaged by Slim's new army. Cowan got back to the plain; the door to the plain from the northeast was shut when the stand at Sangshak bought time for the Dakotas to bring in Briggs's men. At Kohima, the Assam Regiment also bought time, expensively, and just enough of a garrison was cobbled together to deny the Japanese *31st Division* its prize. Slim could begin to feel that his original plan had not been fundamentally dislocated and that it was time to begin to use the pile driver.

The following three-month struggle can only be described with any clarity by breaking it into its constituent components, but it is important to bear in mind that it was all happening simultaneously. And from Slim's point of view everything resolved itself into three key points: the Japanese were to be held by Scoones's IV Corps at the gateways to the Imphal Plain and, above all, the crucial airfields were to be protected; Stopford's XXXIII Corps was to reopen the Dimapur-Imphal Road; and, perhaps the most vital point of all, the availability of the Dakotas that were IV Corps's lifeline had to be guaranteed. As complex as all this was, Slim was very clear about one overriding consideration: the task of IV Corps was not to fight its way out of the besieged plain. It was the anvil. It was Stopford's XXXIII Corps that had the pile-driver role as it attacked from Kohima southward, crushing the Japanese *15th* and *31st Divisions* against that anvil.[3] Stopford, facing one Japanese division, had two divisions (2nd British and 7th Indian)—far less than the three-to-one superiority usually taken as necessary for offense to prevail over defense. Scoones, in contrast, had four divisions (5th, 17th, 20th, and 23rd Indian) plus a tank brigade to deploy against the two attacking the Imphal Plain. The geography of that area, however, meant that he had to spread his divisions over the four gateways, which meant that he, too, could not assemble a pulverizing superiority at any one point. That despite this, the pile-driver concept worked was due in part to the way in which the relentless Japanese commitment to the offensive played into Slim's hands. This is most apparent in the battle's most dramatic and best-known episode: the defense of Kohima.

As the official historians would later put it, "Kohima, unlike Imphal, was not a deliberately selected battleground."[4] Dimapur, with its depots sprawling for eleven miles along the railroad (and averaging a mile wide), was the point that had to be held. Stopford had even given Rankin permission to withdraw the Kohima garrison if necessary to avoid its destruction. That one of the most famous sieges in British military history occurred there was completely fortuitous. The Japanese drove faster and in greater strength than expected at Kohima. The delay imposed on that drive by the Assam Regiment's gallant delaying action allowed time for Colonel Hugh Richards to organize Kohima's defenses. When, as we have seen, Stopford told Ranking on 5 April to move Brigadier Warren's 161st Indian Infantry Brigade back to Kohima, Warren realized that there was simply not enough room on the narrow Kohima Ridge for his full brigade and, halting it at Jotsoma, about 2.5 miles northwest of Kohima, pushed an infantry battalion and a battery of four mountain guns into Kohima. This decision was crucial on two counts. Warren's British battalion (4th Royal West Kents) was to play a crucial role in the defense, and the 161st Brigade defensive box at Jotsoma provided enough ground to deploy the 25-pounder field guns that provided absolutely crucial fire support to Kohima's garrison. Kohima's own artillery, one 25-pounder and two guns of the mountain battery, were quickly silenced by Japanese gunners, and there were no good positions on the narrow ridge to deploy the remaining two mountain guns whose gunners thereafter served as spotters and a radio link to the guns at Jotsoma. On 7 April a company of the 4/7 Rajputs from Warren's brigade reached Kohima—the garrison's last reinforcements. The Japanese thereafter closed in, completing the encirclement of Kohima and also blocking the road to Dimapur behind 161st Brigade. The siege had begun.

The Kohima position was in fact several positions. The road from Dimapur winds around the Kohima Ridge and then continues south to Imphal. The ridge, steep and narrow, is crowned by several hills, named by the function the buildings installed on them served (e.g., Detail Issue Stores/DIS Hill or Jail Hill). The roughly 1,500-strong garrison was a very mixed lot. There was, of course, Lieutenant Colonel John Laverty's Royal West Kents, but they were outnumbered by Indians: roughly half the Assam Regiment had returned, as well as units of the paramilitary Assam Rifles, the company of the 4/7 Rajputs, a unit made up of muleteers from the Royal Indian Army Service Corps. And because Kohima was the site of various administrative installations, there were several composite companies of Indians and Gurkhas from a transit camp under a scratch assortment of officers. There were also bits and pieces—stray engineers, signalers, and even a few men of V Force. There were also still about 1,000 noncombatants, although most had been pulled out. In total a very heterogeneous, weak brigade faced Lieutenant General Sato Kotoko's on-coming division. Of course, if Sato had simply dropped enough troops to bottle up the garrison and headed for Dimapur, there would have been no battle at Kohima but instead a head-on clash with the arriving 2nd British Division and a very different story. Or, if Sato had decided to attack the Jotsoma box, held by 161st Brigade with a third of its infantry gone, he might well have deprived Kohima's defenders of any effective artillery support. (The Jotsoma box was seriously attacked only once—by a Japanese battalion—to no effect.) In the event, it was Sato's decision that focused the full efforts of his division on a position that Stopford had been prepared to abandon.

The siege of Kohima lasted only ten days (8–18 April) but involved some of the most intense infantry combat of the war for both the British and the Indian armies. The scratch garrison, assailed by an entire Japanese division—doing what the IJA did best, attacking relentlessly—was slowly but remorselessly compressed until its final positions (Garrison Hill and DC's Bungalow Spur) were bracing for a last stand. The defenders faced multiple problems besides the Japanese. There was, as noted, no good place to deploy any artillery—without the guns firing from 161st Brigade's box at Jotsoma the defenders would have almost certainly have been overwhelmed. The Japanese at an early stage overran the garrison's water source. Fortunately a spring was discovered on the north side of Garrison Hill whose flow was, however, weak. It improved with work by the engineers to barely adequate, but throughout the siege the water situation was critical, a problem exacerbated by the mounting number of casualties, for whom the outlook was particularly grim. Not only did the ridge afford no deployment room for artillery; it offered no secure place for the field hospital, which had to cope with heavy casualties while itself under fire. Wounded waiting on stretchers for treatment were re-wounded because they were lying in the open, there being no other place to put them. On one occasion, shells hitting the hospital area killed two doctors and wounded a third—a serious matter for the garrison's small, and shrinking, medical establishment.[5]

Resupply of the garrison posed another problem. Because Kohima had had a variety of depots, some categories of supplies were plentiful, but ammunition was not. As the perimeter contracted it became harder and harder to air-drop supplies—a task already complicated by the fact that to drop accurately the Dakotas had to come in very low. Japanese ground fire was thus added to the menace of the mists that swept unpredictably down from the peaks surrounding Kohima, blinding pilots on their approach to the drop zone. Not surprisingly, many drops, as at Sangshak, went astray. The Japanese, again as at Sangshak, benefited from Churchill supplies, air delivered. Since they had captured a number of British mortars, the ammunition was particularly welcome.[6]

On the morning of 18 April, as the exhausted defenders prepared to make a final stand in their now very compressed perimeter on Garrison Hill, vulnerable to overwhelming Japanese numbers on three sides, XXXIII Corps finally broke through to them. The 2nd Division's arrival now covering Dimapur adequately, Major General J. M. L. Grover pushed a brigade forward to relieve Warren at Jotsoma, freeing 161st Brigade, supported by its gunners, to push forward and relieve Richards's tattered garrison at, almost literally, the last moment. Two days later, Richards and his men were pulled out, the official historians later commenting that they "played a small but very vital part" in Slim's great victory.[7]

The fighting at Kohima did not end with the relief on 18 April. Stopford now had to retake Kohima Ridge as well as break through adjacent Japanese positions in the tangled, heavily forested hills and peaks on either side of the Kohima-Imphal Road, whose reopening was now his principal objective. Since the Japanese could be depended on to fight to the bitter end for the positions they held, they effectively fixed themselves in place for XXXIII Corps's pile driver. But by the time Stopford broke through—6 June 1944—the seven weeks of brutal fighting had taken a heavy toll not only on Sato's division (which was wrecked) but on 2nd Division as well. Grover lost all three of his infantry brigadiers (one dead and two severely wounded) as well as a fourth who had barely replaced his dead predecessor when he himself was killed. Grover himself became a casualty, sacked by Stopford for his division's repeated failures to take Japanese positions. Stopford in turn was under pressure to break through to Imphal because concern was mounting in the command stratosphere— at SEAC and in London—about the sustainability of the Imphal Plain's garrison. Only Slim, backed by Giffard, remained calm, certain he now had the battle in hand.

The problems and delays that beset XXXIII Corps's drive down the Imphal Road began with 2nd Division itself. A regular army unit, it had gone to France with the BEF in 1939, returning via Dunkirk. It was shipped east in 1942, and two of its brigades were drawn into the final stages of Irwin's muddled Arakan offensive. When the Japanese counterattacked, tumbling 14th Indian Division into precipitate retreat, 2nd Division's 6th Brigade was very badly cut up and lost its brigadier. Thereafter, 2nd Division was assigned to a potential "Indian Expeditionary Force" and spent most of the next year in southern India, training for amphibious warfare. Although some jungle training was done, when the force was rushed to Dimapur it had not fought as a division since 1940, and much of its recent training was largely irrelevant to the situation it now faced. It was, moreover, organized in the worst possible way for tackling the terrain it encountered. Fully mechanized, it arrived with masses of mechanical transport that completely clogged the narrow two-lane road from Dimapur to Kohima. (A fully equipped British division had some 3,000–4,000 vehicles and, if stretched out in column, would occupy 140 miles of road.) Since it was impossible to deploy this mass of transport anywhere off-road, the division had to be converted instantly to a different organizational structure. 2nd Division handed 1,400 vehicles over to the always needy Assam line of communications—and the surplus personnel, some 1,300 BORs, became available as infantry replacements, something the division would soon desperately need.[8] Transport and supply would henceforth depend on Royal Indian Army Service Corps mule companies, Naga porters, and aerial resupply by Dakota. However, 2nd Division had never trained for working with muleteers and porters (with whom, in any case, they had no common language)—or with the complexities of supply by air. Moreover, like all British units their training had emphasized strong artillery support for any infantry attack. The division had its full complement of guns (three field regiments) plus two 5.5-inch howitzers found at the Dimapur depot and three more brought from the Arakan. But deploying them was difficult due to terrain, and initially there was a shortage of shells for the 25-pounders of the field regiments. The tactical conundrum facing the division was that it had to attack on a frontage of 7,000 yards against well-prepared Japanese defenses anchored by the bunker complexes that had posed serious problems for the British since the First Arakan Campaign. Slim's preferred solution—tank-infantry teams supplemented by both artillery and tactical airpower—was hard to apply. Throughout April the gunners were short of shells. Worse, while tanks were available, and their 75mm guns at point-blank range could destroy the bunkers, getting them to the bunkers was a nightmare. The steep hillsides, heavy with vegetation and, as the premonsoon rains increased in intensity, slippery as well, presented daunting obstacles. Engineers had to build ramps to get the tanks up the slopes or use winches. In the face of all these problems, Grover adapted very straightforward tactics—perhaps, in the circumstances, the only course open to him. Pushing one of his brigades straight up the road axis, he tried repeatedly to outflank the Japanese positions by sending his other two brigades around both flanks. These attempts either failed or secured partial successes at a very high cost. With each failure, Stopford's patience with Grover shortened. 2nd British Division certainly did not lack for dour determination; one company of the 2nd Dorsets, initially 100 strong (and thus understrength), ended a five-day defense of a position it had taken over from some of the original Kohima garrison, with only three officers and twenty-nine BORs left.[9] The casualties among senior officers—the worst suffered by any British division during the war—speak for themselves. XXXIII Corps's advance began to gain traction, however, only when Stopford could deploy his second division, the very experienced 7th Indian, commanded by Frank Messervy, shifted from the Arakan piecemeal by Dakota over a period of nearly a month. Difficult as the situation in which 2nd Division found itself was, it may have added to its own problems by its attitude toward learning from Indian units with more—and more relevant—experience. A British officer of 268th Indian Infantry Brigade noted, "Some of the British, a few, seemed to look upon us as some sort of native levies, an attitude that annoyed me intensely. In this I detected something of the antipathy which went right back to the days of 'the Sepoy General.'"[10] Stopford's growing dissatisfaction with Grover, which would culminate in his replacement after the battle, was in turn driven by the need to re-open the road to Imphal before the monsoon's impact on aerial resupply had serious effects on IV Corps—something that, as noted, was causing ripples of concern not only at SEAC headquarters but as far away as London.

Slim, once the initial surprises on the Tiddim Road and at Kohima had been overcome and the situation on the Imphal Plain stabilized, had on 10 April ordered his divisions to take the offensive. Over the next six weeks, as XXXIII Corps ground up Sato's division, while making slow progress southward, and as the divisions on the Imphal Plain inflicted heavy damage on the Japanese *15th* and *33rd Divisions*, concern began to be expressed about the ability of IV Corps to hold out. Mountbatten's chief of staff, Lieutenant General Sir Henry Pownall, was in London for consultations and on 27 May signaled the Supreme Commander that the British Chiefs of Staff had criticized the delay in reopening the Dimapur-Kohima-Imphal Road. Mountbatten's reaction, as it had been at the beginning of the Japanese offensive in April, was to send a highly critical message to Giffard (whom, in any case, he had already decided to sack, something Pownall had told Giffard in mid-May). The message's conclusion—"I . . . really must ask you when you can start your offensive to the north"—is reminiscent of Irwin's handling of Slim in 1943, positioning a disliked subordinate to carry the burden of any failure. Slim, who was very careful not to criticize Mountbatten, did not discuss this episode directly in his memoirs but was clearly alluding to it when he wrote that visitors to headquarters "believed Imphal was starving" and needed to be relieved "before it was too late," adding, "neither General Giffard nor I was as anxious as they appeared about Imphal's power to hold out."[11] Slim remained firm that it was up to XXXIII Corps to open the road—and that it would be done by the third week in June, a month before IV Corps's supply situation would become critical. However calm Slim seemed—and later sounded in his memoirs—he fought the battle from mid-May conscious that his key ally, Giffard, was on borrowed time; that the soon to break monsoon would vastly complicate the supply situation on the plain; and that the most crucial element in his supply line—the Dakotas—belonged largely to his capricious US allies, a situation further complicated by the rather tepid support the British Chiefs of Staff lent to Mountbatten in his fight to be sure Slim had enough of them.

The fight over the availability of Dakotas went right to the top of the Anglo-American coalition—and right to the heart of its divergent aims in Southeast Asia. The Americans were only there to support the Chinese war effort. By 1944, the bombing of Japan by the B-29 bomber force they planned to establish in China had been added to this. The Dakota and Commando squadrons in the US Air Transport Command were there to support those purposes. (The Americans had even muscled themselves into running the Assam railway to improve the flow of supplies to the airlift.) To use transports from the airlift required reference to Stilwell—usually unavailable for quick consultation since he rarely left his headquarters in northern Burma, whereas SEAC had moved from Delhi to Kandy in Ceylon (Sri Lanka). Using transport aircraft from the Hump airlift also meant consulting the Chiefs of Staff in London, sometimes the

Combined Chiefs of Staff in Washington, and occasionally the president and prime minister. It is difficult to think of an arrangement less conducive to the rapid and flexible use of airpower in response to a swiftly evolving tactical situation. Mountbatten, in an attempt to speed matters up, had asked for the right to automatically draw on the airlift in an emergency—a right the Americans would not concede. Mountbatten's fallback position was to ask that Stilwell's authority be delegated to his deputy, Lieutenant General Daniel Sultan, who (unlike Stilwell) was available in Delhi and who (again unlike Stilwell) had consistently good relations with the British. This the Americans were willing to allow. However, even when Mountbatten had extracted as much as possible from the airlift, there was still a shortfall. More Dakotas simply had to be found from elsewhere. The Americans promised four more "combat cargo groups" (subsequently revised downward to two) of 100 Dakotas each. These, however, would take some time to arrive and become efficient in the theater. The obvious choice, suggested by the US Chiefs of Staff, was to draw on the resources of the Mediterranean theater. Here another of SEAC's problems suddenly surfaced. Just as China was the American lodestar, the Mediterranean was of paramount importance to the prime minister. It was a British-commanded theater. The preponderance of forces there were "British" (actually, Indian and Dominion formations plus the British-directed Polish Corps equaled the British formations deployed there). Churchill's favorite general, Sir Harold Alexander, commanded the armies in Italy and was about to mount a massive offensive (Operation Diadem) to finally take Cassino, relieve the besieged Anzio beachhead, and push on to Rome. Beyond that Churchill envisioned further operations to continue the push north toward the Po Valley, and he and the British Chiefs of Staff were fighting with Roosevelt and the US Joint Chiefs to prevent the momentum of Alexander's advance from being crippled by the diversion of resources to a landing in the south of France (Operation Anvil) intended to support the premier 1944 Operation Overlord. If the Americans had minimal interest in XIV Army's fight, so did London at that moment. In the end, some seventy-nine Dakotas, mostly US, were extracted from the Mediterranean—for a month. The fight now shifted to stretching that month. That struggle was so intense that, on 4 May, Giffard (supported by Slim) told the Supreme Commander that if the seventy-nine Dakotas left without replacement he would not answer for the consequences. Even if he was already resolved to rid himself of Giffard, Mountbatten could not ignore this. He promptly, on his own responsibility, ordered the aircraft on loan from the Mediterranean held. The prime minister, in one of his increasingly rare interventions in Burma operations, promptly backed him: "Let nothing go from the battle that you need for victory. I will not accept denial of this from any quarter."[12] Even so, it took another two weeks to nail down all the details. This is the background against which Slim fought—not until mid-May could he be sure that the essential minimum of air transport would be at his disposal until the battle was finally won.

However, the air-supply problems were not confined to the availability of Dakotas. Once available they had to be protected. The slow transports would have been easy targets for Japanese fighters—if they could have gotten to them. However, by the time the Imphal battle began, the Japanese *5th Air Division* had lost 40 percent of its strength recalled to Japan or transferred to other theaters. In late February 1944 the Allies' Third Tactical Air Force began a relentless offensive against the Japanese *5th Air Division*'s forward airfields, to which the bulk of its strength had been deployed to support Mutaguchi's attack. This had the effect of steadily reducing the Japanese air effort; between 10 March and 30 July *5th Air Division* flew about 1,750 sorties, while the RAF fighter squadrons of 3rd Tactical Air Force flew 18,860 and its USAAF squadrons another 10,800. These 30,000 sorties reduced *5th Air Division* to forty-nine aircraft by the end of July. This victory created the environment in which the Dakotas could operate.[13] But even if they were available in adequate numbers, and could fly under the umbrella of Allied air superiority, they had to have somewhere to land.

There were two all-weather airfields on the plain: Imphal and Palel. Tulihal, at the north end of the plain, was supposed to be made all-weather before the onset of the monsoon by surfacing it with "bithess"— long strips of jute sacking (known as "hessian" cloth) coated with bitumen (asphalt) to produce waterproof material that was then laid in overlapping strips to produce a temporary waterproof surface for roads and airfields, one of many imaginative solutions devised in a theater chronically short of everything.[14] Tulihal—where Briggs's arriving 5th Indian Division landed at the beginning of the battle—was duly weatherized when ten of the larger Commando aircraft flew in 368 tons of bithess 20–26 April. Although they got the material there, it was quickly discovered that the Commandos were too heavy for the surface of any of the airfields in the plain (they were already known to be unsuitable for supply-dropping). The value of the Dakotas therefore became even greater—only they could sustain XIV Army. Then, as the rains became more intense, the surfaces of both Tulihal and Palel began to break up. Only the single runway at Imphal was left. Congestion (and accidents) resulted, along with delays as loaded Dakotas circled, waiting to be called down. The situation was relieved somewhat when it was discovered that the fair-weather field at Kangla drained well enough that it could continue to be used, with delays (up to two days after the heaviest rain). Many Dakotas, as the monsoon season deepened, took off from their fields in eastern Bengal in clear weather with good conditions also reported over the plain, only to be turned back by towering masses of storm-laced cumulus clouds over the mountains that separated Bengal from Imphal. In such situations they would land at a field near Silchar in eastern Bengal, off-load, and return to base. When the weather improved, other aircraft would shuttle the loads the short distance on to Imphal. This saved precious hours of flying time. Dakotas, airfields, and arrangements for coping with monsoon weather were not the sum total of the problem to be overcome to keep Imphal supplied. Crucial to the whole operation was the efficiency of the combined RAF-army teams at the airfields that handled the loading and unloading of the Dakotas. That organization in turn had to be expanded quickly to support the new Dakota squadrons from the Middle East, and it would take some time for the new arrivals and their ground teams to develop maximum efficiency.

On 17 April, the day before the relief of Kohima, a conference was held at XIV Army headquarters at Comilla in eastern Bengal (which Slim described as a depressing place, "its walls mildewed and stained by past monsoons").[15] Representatives of XIV Army and 11th Army Group together with the two air headquarters (Eastern Air Command, which under the US Lieutenant General George Stratemeyer controlled all Allied air operations in Burma; and Air Vice Marshal John Baldwin's Third Tactical Air Force, which handled direct air support to XIV Army) worked out a plan to cover the entirety of air-supply operations in Burma. Its core was Operation Stamina, the support of IV Corps's 155,000 troops and 11,000 animals (mostly mules). The assumption was that the Dimapur Road would be reopened by the end of June (though Slim expected that the road would be open by the third week of the month—the actual date was 22 June). The Comilla conference's blueprint included provision for a two-week reserve of supplies to be available at Imphal if the road was not open by 1 July. The success of Stamina was fundamental to XIV Army's victory.[16]

Because of the complexity of the undertaking the margins were tight. Initially deliveries fell below targets. Scoones had already implemented a precautionary one-third reduction in rations on 9 April; in May a further cut of 14 percent for men and 21 percent for animals was imposed. Some ammunition shortages began to occur. On 1 May, however, Baldwin was placed in control of every aspect of the aerial supply of IV Corps, and after this simplification of the command structure the situation gradually improved and the Comilla conference targets began first to be met and then exceeded. Slim closed some of the admin boxes into which rear-area personnel had been gathered and shipped them back to India; Baldwin improved the airlift's efficiency; the new squadrons and their ground staff gained experience; and there was even a brief pause in the monsoon. The Dakotas flew in tirelessly with reinforcements and replacements (figured at 250 per day). They flew out with casualties and personnel either not needed or not needed enough to be kept on the plain consuming rations. "Even if the Imphal Road had not been reopened until the end of July," the official historians noted, "the corps supply position would have still been better than it had been at any time since the airlift began on the 18th of April."[17] Delivering 12,250 reinforcements and 18,800 tons of supplies, and flying out 13,000 sick and wounded and 43,000 noncombatants, Stamina's 7,500 sorties were absolutely essential to Slim's victory. The architecture of the battle was his; the tactical successes were won by the rebuilt Indian Army. But the Dakotas, their pilots (exhausted by the end of June), and the ground crews, working often in torrential rain to load and service them, were what made it all possible.

While Kohima was besieged and relieved, and 2nd British Division (soon joined by 7th Indian) began its battle to take the adjacent ridges and reopen the road to Imphal, the battle on the rim of the plain itself continued. Again for clarity's sake, each of IV Corps's divisions will be considered in turn moving clockwise around the plain and ending, where the battle began, with 17th Indian Division on the Tiddim Road.

When IV Corps had completed its withdrawal to the edge of the plain, it had four divisions spread along a ninety-mile arc from Dimapur Road in the north through Ukhrul track in the northeast to Shenam Pass in the east around to Tiddim Road in the south. Scoones laid out the tasks for his divisions on 5 April, and when Slim ordered the resumption of offensive operations on 10 April "the pattern of operations . . . for the next

two months" was set. Briggs's 5th Indian Division, which had flown into
Tulihal and Palel 19–26 March, was ordered to drive up Dimapur Road.[18]
To do this, it was necessary to clear the high ground bordering the road.
The first stage of Briggs's advance brought his division up against Nung-
shigum, a "hill" nearly 4,000 feet high from whose summit there was
excellent observation over the Imphal Airfield, six miles to the west—the
only field that, it turned out, was reliably available during the monsoon.
It was also only four miles from IV Corps headquarters. On 7 April the
Japanese had taken the summit of Nungshigum from a company of 9th
Indian Brigade's 3/9 Jat Regiment. The battalion, backed by air strikes
and artillery, quickly retook it (a VCO winning a posthumous Victoria
Cross in the process). On 11 April the Japanese, having recognized its
significance, once again stormed and took the summit. Since they could
not be allowed to retain it, a major attack was mounted on 13 April.
Dive-bombers and Hurricane fighter-bombers, together with Briggs's
gunners, pounded the Japanese positions for ninety minutes, after which
a fresh battalion (1/7 Dogras from Briggs's other brigade, 123rd) attacked,
supported by tanks that had to be winched up what Slim described as
"incredible slopes." Firing point-blank at the apertures of the inevitable
Japanese bunkers, the tanks of 254th Indian Tank Brigade's 3 Carabiniers
and the Dogras took the summit—and this time 5th Indian Division held
it. Slim noted in his memoirs: "casualties in this kind of fighting were
not light."[19] The Carabiniers, for example, went into action with open
turrets to allow the commanders to guide their tanks through the jungle
vegetation and lost five of them in action (the Carabiniers would thereafter consider Nungshigum their regimental anniversary). The Japanese
15th Division, facing remorseless pressure, recognized that it had lost the
initiative and went over to the defensive north of the plain on 19 April.

Briggs's plan was to loosen the Japanese hold on the Imphal-Dimapur
Road by moving north from Nungshigum, along the valley of a little
river, the Iril, east of the road, outflanking its Japanese defenders. However, in mid-May the monsoon took a hand, breaking early and flooding
the valley. Briggs thereupon switched one of his brigades, supported by
tanks, to the road itself while another moved through the hills east of the
road in a series of short outflanking hooks. Slowly 5th Indian Division
ground forward, retaking the (almost intact) supply depot at Kanglatongbi
in mid-May and pushing on steadily until in mid-June it was at Kang-
pokpi, a dozen miles farther. Looked at on a map this seems like a very
slow rate of advance, but as the official historians noted it was textbook

terrain for a delaying operation. The road ran alongside another small stream, the Imphal Turel, which a monsoon downpour would transform into an unfordable barrier. Beyond it, to the east, were a series of hills, each held by Japanese units willing to die where they stood, each having to be taken, each with slopes so precipitous that, after the frequent monsoon downpours, attacks had to be called off because they were simply unclimbable.

As 5th Indian Division inched up the Dimapur Road, Roberts's 23rd Indian Division also began to move forward, its target the track junction at Ukhrul, whose capture would, it was believed, cut the already inadequate supply lines of the Japanese *15th* and *31st Divisions*. Roberts's division had, of course, been nearly deconstructed at the beginning of the battle, with two brigades diverted to the Tiddim Road to support the withdrawal of 17th Indian Division. It was restored to full strength only gradually, taking one of Briggs's brigades under command temporarily, as well as Gracey's 32nd Brigade (designated, however, as corps reserve and so not available for immediate commitment). By the time Slim ordered IV Corps to resume the offensive, Roberts again had two of his own brigades, 1st and 37th (the latter another all-Gurkha brigade; the remaining brigade, also all-Indian Army, remained at the southern gate of the plain). Over the next few weeks, Roberts's brigades slowly cleared the Ukhrul Road, and the adjacent hills, to within fifteen miles of Ukhrul itself. In the process, 1st Brigade, operating away from any tracks on a pack-mule basis, nearly captured the headquarters of the Japanese *15th Division*, forcing its hasty relocation, leaving behind documents of considerable value to intelligence analysts. On 9 May Slim decided that 23rd Division would, one battalion at a time, swap roles with Gracey's 20th Indian Division, which since its successful withdrawal had held Shenam Pass, the eastern gate to Imphal.

At Shenam, Gracey held a front of about twenty-five miles, centering on the road from Palel to Tamu. He had been told that Shenam Pass had to be held at all costs, covering, as it did, the vital all-weather Palel Airfield (which no one yet realized would break up once the monsoon began in earnest). To do that, he had only two of his brigades, 80th and 100th, his third brigade (32nd) having rotated into corps reserve. Facing him was *Yamamoto Detachment*—initially four battalions of infantry and most of *Fifteenth Army*'s armor and artillery, plus an unusually high allotment of mechanical transport, led by Major General Yamamoto Tsunaru, the infantry group commander of *33rd Division*. The commitment of the armor and artillery to this line of advance had something to do with the availability of the road built by Gracey's division over the previous eighteen months, but also with the fact that the Tamu-Palel Road was the shortest approach to the heart of the Imphal Plain. The Japanese began probing the defenses of the pass on 26 March. As at Kohima, those defenses were anchored on a series of hills that lined the northern side of the road though the pass—Crete East, Crete West, Cyprus, Scraggy. At 20th Indian's positions, the Japanese threw attack after attack, with their usual unblinking determination and with far more artillery and tank support than usual. The official history remarked of the three-month struggle for the Shenam Pass: "There can have been few places during the war the possession of which, in proportion to their size, was more costly in human life."[20] Although the Japanese took Crete East, forcing the evacuation of Cyprus, and eventually Scraggy, which they overran on 9 June after what the official history describes as "perhaps the most intensive bombardment ever put down by the Japanese in Burma," that marked the high-water mark of the Japanese advance through Shenam Pass.[21] By the time the Japanese had given up at Shenam, after suffering very heavy casualties, another battle on the Tiddim Road had marked the finale of Mutaguchi's attempt to break into the plain.[22]

By late April, it was clear that the Japanese *Fifteenth Army*'s offensive had comprehensively failed. The threat to Dimapur had evaporated; Kohima had been relieved; Stopford's corps, like the mills of god, was slowly but surely fighting its way toward Imphal, grinding the Japanese *31st Division*—short of men, food, medicine, and ammunition—to bits. The 5th and 23rd Indian Divisions were pushing steadily north and northeast, imposing punishing attrition on the equally ill-supplied Japanese *15th Division*, while 20th Indian held Shenam Pass, against which *Yamamoto Detachment* was fruitlessly expending its strength. A reasonable assessment would have accepted failure and ordered retreat. (Indeed, the Japanese *33rd Division*'s commander had advised just that when Cowan's division successfully fought its way back to the plain.) Lieutenant General Yanagida paid for his realism with his job because the whole ethos of the Imperial Japanese Army was that willpower could trump reality and deliver success. Mutaguchi was a perfect exemplar of that mindset.[23] Therefore he was still planning to take Imphal even if not in time to present to the Emperor as a present on his birthday (29 April). To that end he shuffled his forces. Moving his tank regiment from *Yamamoto Detachment* at Shenam to support *33rd Division* (which required the tanks to retrace their steps down Kabaw Valley and then up the Tiddim Road, a journey of some 400 miles), he added artillery and antitank units plus the last two infantry battalions in his army reserve. *33rd Division* was to resume its offensive, driving straight up the Tiddim Road toward Bishenpur, a village only seventeen miles from Imphal, while also sending a column through the hills west of the road to outflank Bishenpur's defenders.[24] But IV Corps was also planning to resume the offensive on the Tiddim Road. The result was a series of battles stretching throughout May and into June that rang down the curtain on both *33rd Division* and Mutaguchi's offensive.

As the Tiddim Road debouches into the plain it passes through one last defile at Torbung, thirty-two miles south of Imphal. The road, although not hard-surfaced, had been built to be usable during the monsoon, now imminent. Although cut in many places by demolitions during Cowan's withdrawal, the Japanese had made it usable enough so that a trickle of supplies could make its way forward along it—some ten to fifteen tons a day, mostly ammunition. It was this trickle that Cowan now proposed to shut off. 48th Brigade, which had been in reserve on the plain, would leave its British battalion behind and advance across country, seize the 3,500-foot eminence overlooking the road from the east, then descend into the valley through which the road ran and establish a roadblock on it. The division's other brigade, the all-Gurkha 63rd, would then attack south from Bishenpur, crushing the Japanese against the block. The "Black Cats" would do to *33rd Division* what the Japanese had repeatedly done to the raw Indian Army divisions they encountered in Malaya and Burma in 1941–1942. In fact, Brigadier Cameron of 48th Brigade had foreseen in December 1942 something like the situation that he faced in May 1944. 48th Brigade was then encamped at the southern end of the plain, recuperating from its long retreat out of Burma. Positing a Japanese drive up the Tiddim Road if they decided on a further push westward from the Chindwin, Cameron planned an exercise in which his brigade, advancing cross-country, put a block on the track from Tiddim at Torbung. Although the exercise was, in the event, canceled, the ground over which 48th Brigade would operate had already been thoroughly reconnoitered.

On 13 May Cameron's Operation AYO began. The two Gurkha battalions, an Indian mountain battery, a field company of the Bengal Sappers and Miners, and two mule companies of the Royal Indian Army Service Corps moved out from the plain across the hills east of the Tiddim

Road and seized the commanding height above the Torbung defile. And on the night of 16–17 May, the 1/7 Gurkha Rifles blocked the road and fatally disrupted Mutaguchi's plan to launch *33rd Division* at Imphal from the south.

When the Gurkhas blocked the road, the reinforcements that Mutaguchi had scraped together for *33rd Division* were caught on the wrong side of the block—as was Lieutenant General Tanaka Nobuo, slated to replace the overly candid Yanagida. The Japanese hurled themselves and their tanks at the Gurkhas from both north and south of the block, inflicting casualties (as did an errant RAF strike) but incurring losses that cut the already battered tank regiment's strength nearly in half.[25] The two Japanese battalions involved were reduced to the effective strength of a company each.[26] The Torbung block, of course, was only part of Cowan's design: it was the anvil on which the hammer of 63rd Indian Brigade would pulverize much of the Japanese *33rd Division*. However, 63rd Brigade's drive south was cut short when the Japanese launched *their* drive toward Imphal—an offensive seriously handicapped by the interruption in the flow of supplies to units north of the Torbung block. (Some Japanese guns in a position to shell the Gurkhas at Torbung did not do so because of an ammunition shortage.)[27] With 63rd Brigade unable to fight its way south and with 48th Brigade, after holding its block for a week, under growing Japanese pressure (not to mention the environmental pressure produced by the many unburied Japanese dead around the block and the ninety-one dead mules inside it), Cowan approved Cameron's withdrawal. In a modern variant of the old British square, 48th Brigade fought its way back up the Tiddim Road, reuniting with the rest of the division by 30 May.[28] While the Torbung block had not, as hoped, led to the destruction of *33rd Division*, it had inflicted irreplaceable losses, disrupted the planned drive on Imphal from the south, and proved once again that, unit for unit, the Indian Army could no longer be outfought.

Before, during, and after the battle of the Torbung block, a confusing series of engagements had been waged in the hills west of Bishenpur. From Bishenpur, a track struck westward across the Lushai Hills (which, like most of the hills in the region, rose to nearly 6,000 feet) to Silchar in East Bengal (now Bangladesh). The British were concerned that the Japanese would infiltrate westward along this track, and a force—the Lushai Brigade of four Indian battalions—was hastily improvised to cover Silchar (which was not only a roadhead and pipeline terminus but had two all-weather airfields, vital to the Dakotas waiting for weather over the hills to clear during the monsoon). The Japanese had no designs on Silchar, but they in their turn mistakenly believed that it represented an important supply artery for the British, which it did not. Jeepable for its entire length, it featured a 330-foot suspension bridge over an eighty-foot gorge, with tricky road approaches at each end (doubtless the reason even XIV Army's enterprising logisticians decided not to rely on the Silchar track). A brilliant Japanese commando raid, mounted by *33rd Division*, dropped the suspension bridge into the gorge on 15 April. To ensure the Silchar track was cut, the Japanese had also sent half a battalion from the overstretched *15th Division* to attack the bridge from the north. Although the force turned back when *33rd Division* destroyed the suspension bridge, the mistaken focus on cutting the Silchar track deprived *15th Division* of some precious infantry at a critical moment.

The six weeks of fighting in the hills west of Bishenpur certainly confirms one historian's summary: "Imphal was an extremely untidy battle. . . . Hundreds of encounters, ambushes, attacks and desperate defenses occurred that cannot be charted and never will be."[29] It was a conflict of platoons, companies, and occasionally battalions. The brigade-sized Torbung battle was the exception, not the rule, at this stage of 17th Division's fight. It was also a struggle in which the better-supplied and reinforced Indian units, with artillery and air support, could remorselessly grind down their ill-supplied and barely reinforced opponents. But it took its toll of 17th Division and supporting units. On one occasion, a tank, trying to reach the crest of a Japanese-held hill, was defeated by the steepness of the feature, toppling over and rolling to the bottom (amazingly, all but one of the crew survived). After this prolonged attritional fighting, one Gurkha unit (1/4 Gurkha Rifles) had taken over 200 casualties and had only three British officers left. The Japanese were in far worse shape, however. The hill fighting had virtually erased a battalion, and its parent regiment could field only some 900 men, barely a quarter of its normal strength. The damage inflicted by 48th Brigade at Torbung has already been mentioned. The Japanese attack on 63rd Brigade at Bishenpur—which prevented its move south to Torbung—and on 17th Division's headquarters (a "box" a few miles farther north) presented the interesting spectacle of two opposing divisions simultaneously cutting each other's communications. The end result, however, was disastrous for the Japanese. Scoones reinforced Cowan with an improvised brigade, 17th Division's headquarters remained intact, and 63rd Brigade successfully fended off the Japanese attack on Bishenpur, while Cameron's 48th Brigade remorselessly chewed its way back up the road to rejoin its division. The Japanese regiment launched at Bishenpur, and Cowan's headquarters was ruined. One battalion had only twenty men left, another one forty. Incredibly, the regimental commander reinforced the surviving twenty with head-quarters personnel and ordered it to resume the attack, which it duly did. Repulsed, the survivors dug in and were annihilated by a 17th Division tank-infantry counterattack.[30]

The fighting around Bishenpur demonstrates the soundness of the analysis Slim had made in the aftermath of the withdrawal from Burma and had begun to put into practice when he took over XV Corps. Now—thanks to the systemization of his ideas army-wide under the auspices of Auchinleck and Savory in 1943—he had the well-trained, well-led infantry who were, for him, the foundation of everything else. The Dakotas—however precarious his hold on them at moments—had freed him from the paralysis that Japanese roadblocks had imposed on Indian units in Burma in 1942 (and in Malaya before that). For the rest, his design for the battle had been vindicated: on the perimeter of the Imphal Plain, the fighting power of his infantry (backed by artillery, tanks, and tactical air-power) had shredded Mutaguchi's divisions. (Of course, he was aided by the military lunacy that marked the Imperial Japanese Army's approach to combat, as demonstrated in the doomed assault by the last twenty survivors of a Japanese battalion, "reinforced" by headquarters clerks, on 63rd Brigade at Bishenpur.) Yanagida had told Mutaguchi when 17th Indian Division had eluded *33rd Division* on the Tiddim Road that U-Go had failed. By the end of May, that failure had been compounded many times over. The only question was when the Japanese command structure would acknowledge reality.

U-Go had been authorized by Tojo himself, and he had intervened in May to quash the growing doubts of staff officers at both *Burma Area Army* and Imperial General Headquarters. The *Burma Area Army* commander, Kawabe, despite telling Tokyo that he was determined to push on, was beginning to reflect the serious doubts of his staff. In mid-May he sent his chief of staff to tell Mutaguchi that he should focus his efforts on *Yamamoto Detachment*, the easiest part of *Fifteenth Army* to supply. Mutaguchi, taking advantage of the fact that Lieutenant General Naka Eitaro, suffering from dengue fever, was in no position to argue forcefully, persuaded him to back his own plan of reinforcing *33rd Division* at the expense of *Yamamoto Detachment*. Kawabe, as he had before, accepted Mutaguchi's fait accompli. And even though Mutaguchi was shielded by Tojo and could ignore Kawabe, he now faced a revolt by one of his divisional commanders. Sato's *31st Division*, by the end of May, was in dire straits. Facing both the British 2nd Division and now the more experienced 7th Indian Division, its supply line had virtually collapsed, and no reinforcements were reaching it.[31] Watching it remorselessly crushed by Slim's pile driver, Sato had asked Mutaguchi to allow him to pull back to a position where he could be supplied. Mutaguchi refused. It was the last straw for the exhausted divisional commander. Organizing a 600-man sacrificial rear guard with orders to block the Dimapur Road as long as possible, Sato ordered what was left of his division to withdraw across country to the Chindwin, informing Mutaguchi that his (i.e., Mutaguchi's) failure to adequately support *31st Division* dissolved any responsibility to follow *Fifteenth Army* orders. The Japanese withdrawal was more like a rout than a military maneuver. Mutaguchi sent his chief of staff forward to try to restore *Fifteenth Army*'s control of the situation. He was confronted by the mere remnants of a division—tired beyond endurance—starving and discarding weapons along the march while trying to move 1,500 stretcher cases with them. A Japanese document recorded that "the Chief of Staff of the Army was astonished at the amazing, and in the Japanese Army unprecedented, spectacle of headlong retreat."[32]

As the situation worsened, Mutaguchi moved his headquarters from Maymo to near Kaleymo on the Chindwin to exert tighter control. He even briefly opened an advanced headquarters near *33rd Division* during the Bishenpur-Torbung fighting, which can hardly have filled him with optimism. It was at his headquarters near Kaleymo that he met Kawabe on 5 June. Mutaguchi could not bring himself to tell Kawabe that U-Go had failed: he hoped Kawabe would understand from his attitude (he had tears in his eyes) what he could not say. Kawabe, who certainly knew perfectly well that *Fifteenth Army* faced disaster, was unwilling to accept responsibility for acknowledging that fact. The only result of the conference was that both *Yamamoto Detachment* at Shenam and *33rd Division* on the Tiddim Road were ordered to continue attacking—which both Mutaguchi and Kawabe must have known they were utterly incapable of doing.

At midmorning on 20 June 1944, a patrol of 1/7 Dogra Regiment, part of Briggs's 5th Indian Division, accompanied by tanks of 3rd Carabiniers/254th Indian Tank Brigade (the team that had secured Nungshigum) probing up the Dimapur Road, made contact with 2nd Durham Light Infantry and a troop of tanks leading Stopford's advance. That night the first truck convoy since April drove into Imphal, and two-way traffic resumed a few days later. On 26 June, with *Fifteenth Army*'s *15th* and *31st Divisions* wrecked and *33rd* reduced to a skeleton (although preserving cohesion and, incredibly, its willingness to fight), Mutaguchi asked Kawabe for permission to do what most of his army was already doing: retreat. Kawabe covered himself by referring the matter to *Southern Army*, and they in turn asked Tokyo. Not until 5 July was the Emperor's permission received. *33rd Division*, which had opened the U-Go offensive, fought the closing rearguard actions as well, even though its two regiments were down to 400 and 150 men each. Only one tank survived (and it would soon fall victim to the RAF). When the Japanese *215th Regiment* attempted a delaying action at a village just south of Bishenpur, Cowan put in an attack by the 2/5 Royal Gurkha Rifles of 48th Brigade (which had been at the Sittang) backed by three field regiments and a medium regiment of guns, which put 9,000 shells on the Japanese position in less than an hour. When the Gurkhas advanced into the obliterated village "the only apparent survivor was a single dazed man who climbed out of a ditch and staggered slowly off along the main road, apparently oblivious to the hail of bullets which finished him off."[33] It is an appropriate close to the Imphal battle: Slim had based his plans on well-trained infantry, firepower, and sound (if nerve-racking) logistics. The Japanese had gambled on the fighting spirit of their infantry to overcome everything. Slim had won—as he always planned to.

9

Vindication

The battle for Imphal was over. The main concern of the British commanders now was to turn the defeat inflicted on the 15th Army into disaster.
—from *The War Against Japan* (1958), the official British history

The disaster that now overtook Mutaguchi's army was due to the fighting qualities of XIV Army but was also the inevitable result of its dysfunctional command culture. Yanagida had given Mutaguchi very sound advice in the form of a warning: when 17th Indian Division escaped encirclement and destruction U-Go was hopelessly compromised. By persisting for another three months, Mutaguchi, Kawabe, and Imperial General Headquarters allowed XIV Army to inflict heavy casualties. As important, it also left the Japanese, at the beginning of July 1944, fixed in placed while sharply reduced in numbers, ill supplied, riddled with disease, facing superior forces and firepower using Slim's pile driver remorselessly. When permission to break off U-Go was finally given, it was far too late to save Mutaguchi's divisions.

North of the Imphal Plain, 20th Indian Division pressed toward the track junction at Ukhrul (a crucial point on *15th Division*'s supply line) from the south while two of Messervy's brigades closed in from the north and west and Perowne's 23rd Long Range Penetration Brigade continued to work its lonely way across the wild hill country to the east, severing all the tracks to the Chindwin—and escape. Lieutenant General Yamauchi Masafumi, *15th Division*'s commander, was by now mortally ill with malaria, dying soon after his relief on 3 July. The *31st Division* was a wraith, its commander in open rebellion and its remnants streaming in disorder back toward the Chindwin. Major General Miyazaki, commander of its rear guard, was promoted lieutenant general and put in command of the division, but it made no difference—both divisions continued to fall back in disorder. Messervy's brigades pressed on after them, "struggling through blinding rain . . . often hungry for there were periods when air supply was impossible . . . ascending and descending as much as 4,000 feet in a single march." Messervy's troops were also beginning to show the physical effects of campaigning in these conditions: "Dysentery, scrub typhus and skin diseases were rife and there was no shelter or comfort for the sick or wounded."[1] The pursuit was broken off by mid-July since it was clear there was little left to pursue. The survivors of the two Japanese divisions had died by the scores on the tracks leading to the Chindwin amid a litter of wrecked and abandoned equipment: "Many of the dead had been sick and wounded men, who had dropped and died of starvation or had been drowned in the ooze that filled every rut and pothole."[2] Messervy's tired men, their resistance low, were halted before entering this charnel house and withdrawn, as were 20th Indian and 23rd LRP Brigade. Two of Mutaguchi's three divisions were no longer coherent military formations.

As XIV Army swung into the exploitation phase, Slim rearranged corps responsibilities, with Stopford's XXXIII Corps taking control of operations against *15th* and *31st Divisions* while Scoones's IV Corps handled operations at Shenam and on the Tiddim Road. Giffard approved, but Mountbatten weighed in to complain bizarrely that IV Corps's role was "nonaggressive." Giffard simply brushed this aside, pointing out that it was Slim's decision with which he declined to interfere.

With *15th* and *31st Divisions* seen off, Slim then swung his focus to *Yamamoto Detachment* at Shenam and the battered but still coherent *33rd Division* on the Tiddim Road. Roberts's 23rd Indian Division (whose original ten battalions had included only one British unit) had held Shenam Pass with a powerful five-battalion brigade throughout June, under constant, futile, and costly attacks by Yamamoto.[3] Now going over to the attack, Roberts planned to envelop the Japanese with his other two brigades while the defenders of the pass, 37th Brigade, drove straight ahead along the Tamu Road. In the last week of July, Roberts's brigades moved—impeded by torrential monsoon downpours and the usual stubborn "last man, last round" Japanese resistance. By the end of the month, they stood at the head of the Kabaw Valley and the engineers began to repair the road, built (and then destroyed) by 20th Indian, repaired and destroyed again by the Japanese, and continually obstructed by monsoon-induced landslides. The performance of Roberts's division, like that of Slim's other Indian Army divisions, as the Imphal battle moved from defense to grinding offense and then to pursuit and exploitation, signaled its transformation from the improving army of the Admin Box fight to what two historians of Britain's war against Japan christened "a cold, efficient killing machine."[4] Or as Slim grimly put it: "We had learned how to kill Japanese."[5]

The qualities of Slim's army were fully on display in the exploitation phase of the Imphal battle—the "monsoon pursuit." The 1944 monsoon had broken in earnest on 25 May, and reference has already been made to the difficulties it imposed on movement, supply, and the resilience of the troops. Slim illuminated the monsoon's impact in three sentences extracted from the war diary of a brigade pushing toward the Chindwin: "Hill tracks in terrible state, either so slippery men can hardly walk or knee deep in mud. Half a company took ten hours to carry two stretcher cases four miles. A party of men without packs took seven hours to cover five miles."[6] Not surprisingly, monsoon season, like winter in Europe, was customarily a time of sharply reduced military activity. Nearly two months of the Imphal battle had taken place in monsoon conditions. Slim had decided that keeping up the momentum of his advance to and over the Chindwin would position XIV Army advantageously to launch the dry-weather campaign on which he had resolved—the reconquest of Burma, overland from the north. But first, XIV Army would have to do what had never been done: push a corps-sized force steadily forward in the worst climatic conditions imaginable. Of all that army's achievements, this was one of the most remarkable.[7]

A series of readjustments in Slim's army preceded the monsoon pursuit. Scoones and his corps headquarters, which had carried the burden of the battle from the beginning, returned to India, and Stopford's XXXIII Corps took over direction of the pursuit.[8] The Indian divisions—7th, 17th, 20th, and 23rd—that had fought the battle were pulled back to healthier areas either in the Imphal Plain or around Kohima. Transport difficulties made it impossible to rotate entire divisions back to India, but at least officers and men could be sent on leave.[9] The 2nd British Division was also withdrawn to a rest area south of Kohima, after one of its brigades, taking over from 23rd Indian Division, had followed up the Japanese withdrawal along the road to Tamu on the Chindwin, which it entered in late July, finding only a shambles of wrecked equipment and dead Japanese.

Under XXXIII Corps, the pursuit was conducted by 5th Indian Division on the Tiddim Road and by 11th East African Division moving down the Kabaw Valley as well as by two quite unusual formations,

268th Indian Infantry Brigade and Lushai Brigade. When the Black Cats were finally withdrawn, they had been in the front lines since December 1941—three years and eight months, "a record, I should think," as Slim mildly put it.[10] Briggs's division continued the push south. When Briggs returned to India and a well-merited rest, Geoffrey Evans, the defender of the Admin Box, took over. When he in turn fell ill, "Daddy" Warren, whose 161st Brigade box at Jotsoma had made a crucial contribution to the defense of Kohima, took over, and under his command 5th Indian finally reached the banks of the Chindwin in November. The division's tactics, whoever was in command, never varied from "ejecting Japanese rearguards from their positions by air strikes, flanking hooks and frontal attacks, bridging streams and clearing landslides."[11] In fact, so difficult was it to keep the road open behind 5th Indian that the attempt to do so was abandoned. The road was allowed to collapse behind the division, which was henceforth maintained by air supply. The Dakotas never failed—nor did Air Vice Marshal Stanley Vincent's 221 Group, flying close air support. Casualties could no longer be evacuated by road; geography precluded airstrip construction for air evacuations, so volunteers were sought—and found in abundance—from among XIV Army's nurses to accompany 5th Division down the Tiddim Road. By October, the division was clawing its way up the "Chocolate Staircase," just short of Tiddim. In a seven-mile stretch, the road climbed three thousand feet with thirty-eight hairpin turns and a 1:12 gradient. All the while, whole hillsides slid away, taking chunks of the road with them. Two miles a day was a good day, but nothing—neither the Japanese nor the monsoon—now stopped XIV Army.

As the Japanese *33rd Division* was driven back by 5th Division's remorseless advance, a threat to its left flank, rear, and communications suddenly materialized out of the wild, mist-shrouded Lushai Hills to the west: Brigadier P. C. Marindin's Lushai Brigade. The brigade had been hastily formed in late March to prevent Japanese infiltration westward through the 6,000-foot-high Lushai Hills that would threaten Silchar's vital airfields. Brigadier Marindin, who had commanded a battalion during the 1942 retreat, was given four battalions, two scraped up from line of communications duties and one, the 1st Bihar Regiment, from a brand-new non–martial races unit, plus some of the British-led Chin and Lushai Levies. The brigade had only improvised signals, with no artillery or engineers—not even a complete outfit of headquarters equipment (reportedly, only one map). At the beginning of the monsoon pursuit, it was in the heart of the roadless Lushai Hills about 100 miles southwest of Imphal. No longer needing it to cover Silchar, Slim decided to use it offensively. At the end of June he ordered it to operate against the Tiddim Road, deep in the rear of the Japanese *33rd Division*, adding that little air supply and no ground support would be available. The Lushai Brigade responded to this rather daunting charge with a remarkable performance. Closing on the road, sustained by porters and mules, three of Marindin's battalions, spread out well over a hundred miles of road, inflicted casualties, destroyed vehicles (from a rapidly diminishing Japanese transport stock), and forced the closure of sections of the road to vehicular traffic. Meanwhile, Bihar Regiment, accompanied by the Levies (and their families), struck across country into the Chin Hills south of Tiddim, restoring British control and rousing the tribesmen to take up arms against the Japanese.[12]

While 5th Indian squelched south along the Tiddim Road, aided by Marindin's brigade, another remarkable chapter in the monsoon pursuit was being written by 11th East African Division and 268th Indian Infantry Brigade in the dreadful, disease-ridden Kabaw Valley. To fight the war to which Churchill vowed Britain in May 1940, the fullest exploitation of all its imperial assets was necessary. India is the most obvious example of this, but to a degree now often forgotten Britain's African colonies were also mobilized.[13] Two West African divisions (81st and 82nd) fought in Burma, as did 11th East African, which had reached Ceylon in late 1943, relieving Gracey's 20th Indian to join XIV Army. In April 1944, it was ordered to Chittagong, behind the Arakan front, as part of Slim's army reserve. Before it could concentrate there, however, its destination changed again—this time to Palel on the Imphal Plain, where under XXXIII Corps command it would take over the push down the Kabaw Valley.[14]

The terrain over which Major General C. C. Fowkes's division was now to advance was bad even by the standards of XIV Army's battlefields. Highly malarial, it was assigned to 11th East African at least in part because of the African troops' "believed high resistance" (in the carefully chosen words of the official history) to that disease. With a slight note of defensiveness, Slim later wrote that, had he had a choice, he "would have fought the Japanese in the healthiest, and not the most disease-ridden, areas I could find. We entered the Kabaw Valley because it was the most practicable route for our purpose." Slim would also argue that the East African sickness rate was lower than either British or Indian units would have sustained. (Stopford's later dissent from the general belief that East

African malaria rates were lower than the XIV Army's average was recorded by the official historians in a footnote to an appendix.)[15] Disease,
however, was far from 11th East African's only problem. They had perhaps the worst of monsoon conditions to face. The tracks leading down
the valley were continually ankle- to knee-deep in mud; all wheeled and
tracked vehicles had been pulled back because they quickly became im-
mobile. The weather limited supply drops as well as casualty evacuation.
To ensure artillery support, the departing 17th Indian handed over its 3.7-
inch mountain guns, which, disassembled and carried by porters, could
be gotten forward. Scarcely had the division begun to move into the
valley when for ten days the monsoon returned with virulence, stopping
all movement. The Dakotas struggled through, but casualty evacuation
stopped. Slim's Brigadier General Staff, "Tubby" Lethbridge, on an in-
spection tour, got as far as Tamu, where he was told that the only way to
visit 11th East African's forward units was to parachute in—and remain
indefinitely. Even radio contact intermittently ceased, the weather and
the blanketing effect of the sodden vegetation on radio signals imposing a blackout. By October, with the approaching end of the monsoon,
the division again began moving forward—"inching" might be a better
term. Engineers began building a corduroy road (logs surfacing the track
down the valley). Unable to support heavy traffic and requiring continual upkeep, the improvised road made it possible for jeeps and small
four-wheel-drive trucks to reach the front, albeit very slowly; a convoy
that covered five miles in twenty-four hours was making excellent time.
When light tanks of 254th Indian Tank Brigade were sent forward, they
had to be winched from tree to tree, covering fifty-five miles in three
weeks. And, of course, there were the Japanese. Wrecked and staggering
back into Burma, 55,000 of its original 84,000 men lost, *Fifteenth Army*
dropped behind it rearguard parties, who usually had to be killed to the
last man in dozens of small, intense, largely unrecorded clashes.

As the East Africans moved down the Kabaw Valley, another formation, 268th Indian Infantry Brigade, was working its way south through
the hills to the east, guarding its flank against Japanese reinfiltration across
the Chindwin. Originally the motorized infantry brigade of an Indian
armored division cast adrift when the division was disbanded, Brigadier
Max Dyer's brigade became a very successful independent formation for
the balance of XIV Army's campaign. It lost all its regular Indian battalions in August 1944 and never had any British units. It thereafter operated
with an ever-shifting number of recently raised Indian battalions (some,

like the Chamar Battalion, wartime raisings from hitherto unrecruited groups), units of the allied Nepalese Army, paramilitary Assam Rifles, and bits of V Force. By October, it had taken over a bridgehead across the Chindwin originally seized by the East Africans and was patrolling vigorously eastward into Burma.

By early November, as the landscape dried out, 11th East African Division was closing in on Kaleymo on the Chindwin. On 13 November, an East African patrol met a patrol from 5th Indian and *askari*s and *jawan*s entered the Chindwin River port that the British had abandoned two and a half years before.[16] The monsoon pursuit was over; it had cost some 50,000 casualties (55 percent of the average strength of XXXIII Corps). Sickness accounted for over 90 percent of the toll.[17] But the momentum of the advance had been maintained as Slim intended, and now it began to accelerate. Indian sapper and miner units assembled a Bailey bridge—the longest in the world at that point—in a tributary of the Chindwin, then floated it into the main stream, and in twenty-eight hours it was in place complete with barrage balloons and antiaircraft defenses.[18] Over its 1,154-foot span, the East Africans streamed, carving out and rapidly expanding a bridgehead. On 13 December, Shwegyin on the east bank was seized, the point where Burcorps had abandoned its last tanks, trucks, and artillery pieces in May 1942. Slim revisited it almost immediately: "There . . . were the burnt-out and rusted tanks that I had so reluctantly destroyed. . . . As I walked among them . . . I could raise my head. Much had happened since then. Some of what we owed we had paid back. Now we were going to pay back the rest—with interest."[19]

10

Final Thoughts

This account has tried to tell one of the great—and now little remembered—stories from the British Empire's final great war. In 1907, the Committee of Imperial Defence had defined Britain as a "naval, Indian, and colonial" power. And in 1940 it was upon that triad that Britain fell back following the German conquest of Western Europe and the summary expulsion of the British Army from the continent. The full scope of India's mobilization and what it (and the rest of the Empire) contributed to Britain's survival and victory is only now beginning to be assessed and appreciated. The near disappearance of the Raj and its army from the story of Britain's war is due, first and foremost, to Winston Churchill's refusal to acknowledge it in his enormously influential memoirs, and secondarily to the disinterest until recently in the army that had served the Raj by both British and Indian historians.

When examined closely, it becomes apparent that the Indian Army's story is one of the war's most remarkable. A long-service regular force with a limited recruitment base, just beginning to modernize itself in 1939, it had to grow in eighteen months from under 200,000 to over a million and then keep on growing to over two million while simultaneously deploying and fighting from the Middle East to Malaya. It also had to absorb new equipment—but never enough of it—and therefore new training regimens and tactical doctrines. At the same time, it had to change in a fundamental way the composition of both its officer corps and its recruitment base. All this while in the background powerful political forces attacked the whole enterprise. The great surprise is not the resulting defeats in Malaya and Burma in 1941–1942, but that the hastily expanded, underequipped, irrelevantly trained, and clumsily led force did not totally collapse, taking the Raj with it, with potentially catastrophic effects on the entire British and Allied war effort.

But, battered and bleeding, it held together, and in that fact lay the seeds of a remarkable revival. The bedrock of the Indian Army was the regiment. Not the distant, almost mythical King-Emperor, but the regiment and its officers were central to the loyalties of the *jawan*s of the pre-1939 army. Expansion diluted that—almost to the vanishing point in some instances—but just enough remained to see 17th Indian Division through its long trek out of Burma, and just enough remained, on the morrow of the longest retreat in British military history (in fact, one of the longest successful withdrawals on record), to become the foundation for a turnaround remarkable for both its speed and completeness in the face of every conceivable obstacle posed not only by its enemies but by nature, its allies, and its own remote, skeptical, and often apparently disinterested masters in London.

The rebuilding of the Indian Army was internally driven. London, the British Chiefs of Staff, the War Office, and even the manic energies of the minister of defense himself were all too focused on matters much nearer to hand—and, from their perspective, much more important—to spend much energy on whatever the Commander-in-Chief, India, and his headquarters in Delhi might be doing in the matter of training and tactical doctrine. In any case, the governance of India and the management of its army had, historically, been left to the career specialists of the Indian Civil Service and the Indian Army, and there was simply neither time nor desire to change that tradition after 1940. It was fortunate that there was a very talented generation of Indian Army officers just rising to senior command levels when the war—and army expansion—began. Sir Claude Auchinleck, in two tours as Commander-in-Chief, India (1940–1941; 1943–1947), both set the tone and provided the weight to carry change through. Indianization became a major shaper of the new army; the Infantry Committee, appointed by Sir Archibald Wavell as he exited Army Headquarters, both summarized the piecemeal changes already under way (not least in Slim's XV Corps) and provided "the Auk" with a template that he, ably seconded by Reginald Savory, made the army-wide norm. Then there was "Bill" Slim, who had seen clearly after his experience with Burcorps what needed to be done. Surviving Noel Irwin's attempt to marginalize him, he emerged in the autumn of 1943 as the reshaped army's field commander and, aided by a group of very able subordinates—Scoones, Briggs, Cowan, Gracey, and Messervy—wielded the newly refurbished weapon to produce the limited but crucially important victory in the Arakan and the triumph at Imphal, which both wrecked much of the Japanese army in Burma and consolidated the rebuilding of the Indian Army. As he stood on the banks of the Chindwin, looking at the relics of his defeat two and a half years before, he had already in mind the next step: the reconquest of Burma. But over XIV Army hung a sword of Damocles: neither London nor SEAC really wanted an overland drive to Rangoon, and the Americans, who had insisted on the campaign, began to lose interest in it.

Neither Churchill nor the British Chiefs of Staff had ever wanted the Burma campaign. From the first discussions in the spring of 1942, as Burcorps made its way back to India, the course of action that most commended itself to London, and then to SEAC, when it came into existence a year later was maritime and amphibious: taking Akyab and then moving on to Rangoon and finally the reconquest of Singapore, rehoisting the Union Jack over the city whose calamitous fall had so shaken the Empire's prestige and whose recapture, Churchill felt sure, would refurbish it. It was a beguiling vision with only two flaws: the British lacked the resources while the European war lasted, and the Americans, the paymasters (and by 1943 the senior partners in the alliance), wanted the British to do something very different. Mesmerized by China—as an ally tying down most of the Imperial Japanese Army; as a potential platform for bombing the Japanese Home Islands; and as a potentially huge future market—Washington saw reopened access to China via Burma as crucial to the attainment of US goals there. Reestablishing US access to China was what US policy makers saw as the appropriate role for the British in the war against Japan, and they were in a position to enforce their priorities. This was what Stilwell's presence really meant. Churchill, "Dickie" Mountbatten, and the SEAC planners might dream of striking across the Indian Ocean, and the British Chiefs of Staff might fight desperately with Churchill in 1944 over a fantasy British Pacific strategy, but what really mattered was that the Americans would not let the British escape from Burma until US aims were achieved and a road once more connected them to China. They were willing to underwrite the British in support of that—particularly with Dakotas, which turned out to be the wonder weapon of the campaign. British military historian Correlli Barnett wrote of the British by the end of World War II serving as a "warrior satellite" of the United States—and the great campaign of XIV Army illustrates his point. The remarkable rebuilding of the Indian Army and Slim's enormous gifts as an army commander would never have been displayed as they were had the British been able to fight their war against Japan as

London wished—but it was US wishes that counted, and the British had to fight in northern Burma. Then the Japanese took a hand, launching offensives that allowed Slim first to field-test his new army and then to use it in a battle of almost indescribable complexity to shatter a large part of the Japanese *Burma Area Army*. Then he maintained, through the sodden monsoon pursuit, a momentum that, as the 1944–1945 dry season opened, was very hard to stop. This was almost certainly Slim's intention. His army was at the peak of its fighting power, his plans for reconquering Burma had been formulated, and he pushed ahead, in effect dragging the unwieldy SEAC command structure behind him. The Americans, having gotten what they wanted out of the campaign, were, however, losing interest—and they still owned the majority of the precious Dakotas. Even Slim's iron determination might not have been enough had not developments half a world away come to his assistance.

The outbreak of World War I gave Slim his chance for an officer's career; the coming of World War II opened the door to high command for him. Now the Wehrmacht's successful rally on the borders of the Reich, prolonging the European war into the spring of 1945, removed the last possibility that XIV Army would be braked. Without the resources for the campaign they wanted, SEAC and London committed to the campaign they had. Victory in Burma was better than no victory at all. XIV Army would roll on to a remarkable, annihilating final triumph. There is a deep irony in the fact that during Slim's final drive on Rangoon it was Churchill—who had never wanted the campaign and disliked the Indian Army—who faced down US Army Chief of Staff George Marshall to extract the Dakotas needed to maintain XIV Army's momentum—in a battle he insisted on seeing as Mountbatten's.

Perhaps the most quoted words about the victorious Burma campaign are John Masters's (of 4th Gurkha Rifles). As senior staff officer to Major General Pete Rees, commander of 19th Indian Infantry Division, he was an observer as the drive for Rangoon (Operation Extended Capital—known in XIV Army as "S.O.B.," short for Sea or Bust) jumped off: "This was the old Indian Army, going down to the attack, for the last time in history."[1] The war in Burma had been the Indian Army's from the beginning. Burcorps was overwhelmingly Indian, as were the units that fought in the Arakan and in the Imphal battle. It is no denigration of the British units that were part of XIV Army to point out that there were never many of them, that British manpower shortages made them a wasting asset, and that ultimately, in 1945, most of those remaining were swapped out of XIV Army divisions for Indian units whose casualties were easier to replace and whose demands on Slim's always precarious logistics were lighter. By the time Rangoon fell, only 13 percent of Slim's army was British—and they were outnumbered by Africans.[2] Burma was the Indian Army's war and its victory. It also marked the fundamental transformation of that army: its training, doctrine, and equipment were modernized with remarkable speed after 1940. The vexed question of the pace of Indianization was dealt with equally rapidly: it was necessary to do it and at speed. Auchinleck, and sheer necessity, settled the issue, although Auchinleck's corollary—equal treatment regardless of race for *all* officers—took much of the war to work out. In 1918, the Indian Army could revert, in large part, to its prewar structure and practices. In 1945, that was clearly impossible. The Raj itself was in a terminal state, the triumph of its army in Burma a final curtain call. The real significance of Slim's great campaign in long perspective is that it so changed the Indian Army as to make rapid postwar independence inevitable, even if a variety of other factors had not also been pushing hard in the same direction. The huge transformation wrought by the war in the Indian Army, and therefore in the life expectancy of the Raj, was signposted and consolidated by Imphal. Perhaps this is why Winston Churchill devoted so few words to it.

Appendix A

Churchill and the Indian Army

In the most accessible of his many books, his autobiography *My Early Life* (published in 1930), Churchill tells an interesting story from his childhood. Speaking of his extensive collection of toy soldiers, he explains that his "were all British, . . . an infantry division with a cavalry brigade." His younger brother, Jack, his opponent in mock battles, however, "was only allowed to have coloured troops; and they were not allowed to have artillery. Very important!"[1] Jack Churchill's army replicated the post-Mutiny structure of the Indian Army, which had been stripped of its gunners (except for the mountain batteries) after the Mutiny and would not have field artillery of its own again until 1935. Clearly, 1857 made an impression on the young Churchill, not surprisingly since he grew up at a time when Mutiny memories were fresh and decorated (British officer) veterans of that epic event were rising to senior positions in both Britain and India. His father, Lord Randolph Churchill (who served briefly as secretary of state for India), numbered Lord Roberts, the archpriest of the "martial races" school of thought, among his friends. Churchill's family had no direct connection with India—people of their class rarely did—and so it is no surprise that he both imbibed in his youth and carried with him into adulthood the commonplaces about the Indian Army in circulation in Britain as he grew up: the Indian Army depended on the virile (and largely Muslim) martial races; Hindus were "soft" and treacherous; the army's loyalty might falter without the presence at its side (and behind its back) of the indomitable British infantryman; and, just to be on the safe side, it ought not to be entrusted with the full range of modern weapons. More than half a century later these beliefs were still there. In an August 1941 conference at Chequers with the newly appointed Commander-in-Chief, Middle East, General Sir Claude Auchinleck (an Indian Army officer who had been Commander-in-Chief, India, before his posting to Cairo), Churchill responded to Auchinleck's request for more modern equipment for India's burgeoning army (especially tanks for its armored units) by asking: "How do you know they wouldn't turn and fire the wrong way?"[2] This astoundingly offensive remark indicates the depth and durability of Churchill's prejudices on this issue—a tribute, if that is the correct word, to the tenacity with which he held fast to ideas on the subject embedded in him as a child and young man.

Churchill, however, had been in India, as a subaltern in the 4th Hussars. Why did this exposure to Indian realities not at least modify his preconceptions? The answer is that his exposure to the Raj was as brief as he could make it, further shortened by home leave and time away to participate in (and chronicle) Lord Kitchener's final campaign against the Sudanese Dervishes. Moreover, when he was in India, he lived in the peculiar bubble that largely insulated British Army officers serving *in* India from much involvement *with* India, unless they made an effort to break out of it (which Churchill certainly didn't). British cavalry regiments were still officered largely from the landed classes. Many of those officers had little interest in a lengthy Indian tour (British regiments could spend a dozen or more years there). Therefore when India was in prospect, they "exchanged" with officers of home-based regiments who were willing to go to India. One of the attractions of Indian service for British Army officers was the enhanced pay and allowances (coupled with the much lower cost of living). This made India a good posting for junior officers from expensive regiments whose finances were strained—a good description of Lieutenant Churchill. But more than his bank balance drove Churchill. His ultimate objective was a seat in the House of Commons. His time in India, if he could see action, would burnish his résumé with a medal—and then home to the hustings. His self-education during the hot afternoons at Bangalore, where his regiment was based, is well known. Little, if any, of that reading dealt with India. The action he craved, he found—a frontier campaign he wrangled himself into by pulling every string he could get his hands on (and the grandson of one Duke of Marlborough and the nephew of another had plenty within reach). The "despatches" he sent to the *Daily Telegraph* were quickly recycled into his first—still quite readable—book. *The Malakand Field Force* (published in 1898) had perforce to say something about the Indian Army, but what he said were late Victorian commonplaces that he could have written without leaving Britain: the crucial role of the British officer, the gallantry of the Sikhs, the smiling lethality of the Gurkhas, etc., etc.[3] Beyond his venture to the North-West

Frontier, Churchill's Indian time was largely spent in garrison routine. (The government of India rarely deployed British units whose cost on active operations was much higher than that of a comparable Indian unit.) There was polo, of course. Many officers availed themselves of the abundant opportunities for shooting and other forms of sport—especially those placed at their disposal by the Indian rulers, clients of the Raj, who were (almost) social equals. Churchill visited the Viceregal court at Calcutta, where his name gave him favored entrée. He fell in love with Pamela Plowden, the daughter of a very senior member of the Indian Political Service (which managed the 500-plus client Indian rulers).[4] Otherwise he found the mostly middle-class British who ran the Raj largely beneath his notice (when he complained, in a letter to his mother, that there was nobody "interesting" in India, he was not referring to Indians). Indians—princes apart—he knew mainly as deferential servants. The one exception to this was the Indian moneylenders to whom he had recourse. (Even the more generous Indian scale of pay and allowances was not enough to keep the free-spending Churchill out of debt.) He discovered that, unlike British firms, Indian moneylenders did not allow the luster of a great name to moderate the exigency with which they collected on debts. This clearly annoyed Lieutenant Churchill, and the irritation peeps out in *My Early Life* three decades later.

When Churchill left India, he took with him confirmation of beliefs (prejudices, if you will) with which he had arrived, doubtless reinforced by the identical prejudices of the regimental mess. But he left with little realization of the complexity of either the Raj or its army. That gap in his knowledge would never be filled. Was Churchill therefore a racist? Many of his views would certainly merit that description today, but, for an upper-class Englishman born in 1874, they were more or less the norm. Indeed, in some respects, they were less than that norm—he never exhibited then-fashionable anti-Semitism, for example. Perhaps the best succinct verdict on that issue is Geoffrey Best's that in his youth "Churchill accepted unquestioningly, though without gloating or unkindness, the then prevalent notion of white superiority. He seems never subsequently to have thought differently."[5]

Over the four decades that separated Churchill's departure from India from his arrival at 10 Downing Street, little changed in Churchill's perceptions of India or his sense that its army depended on British leadership and could never, despite the acknowledged gallantry of the martial races, be fully trusted. One searches in vain the pages of his World War I memoir, *The World Crisis*, for any recognition that the Indian Army provided more troops to the imperial war effort than all the "white dominions" combined (or that 29th Indian Infantry Brigade, which fought at Gallipoli where Slim met it, had no British battalion). Churchill would invoke the martial races in his five-year struggle against the 1935 Government of India Act, but only to use them as a club to wield against that legislation, alleging that the "warrior races" would never tolerate the rule of the "Hindu priesthood" (a curious description of the lawyers, journalists, and businessmen who actually ran the Congress Party). Once he became prime minister, the crisis of May–June 1940 forced the huge expansion of the Indian Army, but Churchill's attitude toward it, as a long series of wartime remarks indicates, never changed: he distrusted and disdained it, even as he needed it since, once again, it outnumbered all the other Dominion and colonial contingents combined. Afterward, in the memoirs that shaped views of Britain's war for a generation (and which still condition much thinking about that war), he did his best to ignore it. He never acknowledged the dimensions of its contribution and used his "British-Indian" locution to underline the British contribution to its fighting power (even though, as we have seen, the British presence in Indian divisions was fading fast after 1942). He tried to sideline its role in Burma in 1943 and, in his memoirs, so scanted XIV Army that its British veterans became vocal and Slim took the matter up with Churchill personally. The resulting section on Burma in two chapters of *Triumph and Tragedy*, drafted by Churchill's military adviser, Lieutenant General Sir Henry Pownall, have a perfunctory air. XIV Army is still described as "British-Indian" despite the fact that, by the time Rangoon fell to it in May 1945, its British contingent was down to 13 percent and African troops outnumbered British within its ranks. There is, of course, no tribute to the Indian Army. That had to wait for the memoirs of its officers—like Slim and Masters—which, although eminently readable, were read far less widely than Churchill's.

In January 1942, Churchill wrote to the Australian prime minister, John Curtin, about the setbacks in northern Malaya, where the new, raw, understrength 11th Indian Infantry Division had been badly beaten by the Japanese. Explaining this defeat, the prime minister wrote: "so far the Japanese have had only two white battalions against them, the rest being Indian soldiers."[6] When reviewing this message for inclusion in his memoirs, Churchill's Syndicate of advisers persuaded him to drop the last five words (this was done, but in the published version there is no ellipsis to indicate any omission). They felt, they told Churchill, that the phrase might be taken as an adverse reflection on the Indian Army—which is, of course, exactly what it was.

It is possible to trace this thread in Churchill's career from the nursery onward, although it escaped the attention of both Churchill's meticulous official biographer and, indeed, most of those who have written about Churchill. But while the thread can be followed and suggestions offered as to its origins, its stubborn persistence still contains an element of mystery—about few other things did Churchill remain so obdurately wrong-headed. Clearly it was a visceral reaction. Churchill simply would not accept the obvious: the Indian Army was vital to the imperial war effort and alone made possible a British role in the war against Japan, albeit a role that Churchill did not want. And perhaps in that fact lies a clue: Britain's war in Asia ended, as far as the prime minister was concerned, disappointingly, a disappointment compounded by the rapid end of the Raj. For someone so dedicated to British greatness, it was perhaps too much to acknowledge generously the army that had made possible a victory whose fruits proved so quickly to be the apples of Sodom.

Appendix B

Wingate

When Orde Wingate emerged from the Trident Conference as a major general, he had been promised a "Special Force" of six LRP brigades. His original Chindit brigade (77th) had already been brought back up to strength by drafting three battalions to it, and a second LRP brigade (111th) that Wavell had ordered raised in February 1943 was in existence. Now four more brigades were to be created. The ultimate total of infantry battalions committed to Wingate—twenty-three—was the infantry strength of an army corps, normally a lieutenant general's command. To find this many men—and Wingate insisted his troops be British or Gurkha—Auchinleck had to break up 70th British Division, find two additional British infantry battalions, comb 600 men out of antiaircraft units, convert two armored units to infantry (which involved breaking up 251st Indian Armored Brigade), and call for volunteers from other British units in India. Even so, not enough British or Gurkha infantry could be made available (four battalions of Gurkhas became part of Special Force, but Gurkhas were in even shorter supply than British infantry). Wingate, therefore, having rejected Indian troops, had to accept 3rd (West African) Infantry Brigade, made up of Nigerian battalions. Wingate returned to India in mid-September 1943, lost several weeks when he fell ill with typhoid fever (brought on by impetuously quenching his thirst by drinking the water in a vase of flowers!), yet still had the initial wave of three LRP brigades ready to enter Burma by the end of February. Given how much had to be done to assemble, train, and prepare completely new formations at a time when the Indian Army was in a state of transformative flux, a new command structure—SEAC—was coming into existence and separating itself from India Command, and the machinery of the Raj, civil and military, was working overtime to build, staff, and maintain the infrastructure of Britain's war effort against Japan, that might be considered a very creditable achievement. Not, however, by Wingate. Convinced that his tactics alone offered the key to victory, contemptuous of conventional formations, seeing enemies and obstruction on all sides—and making liberal use of threats of either resignation or appeal to Churchill—Wingate bulldozed his way ahead, behaving, in the restrained words of the official historians, in a way that "tended to make enemies of those who were doing their best to co-operate with him."[1]

By October, Wingate's enlarged force was actively training (a fact that ought to disprove the allegations of sabotage that Wingate liberally flung about). But how, once ready, were they to be deployed? The Americans had invested very heavily in Wingate, believing that long-range penetration would facilitate Stilwell's advance. The plan, hammered out in tortuous interallied negotiations, for the 1943–1944 dry season called for Wingate to put three LRP brigades into northern Burma, while Stilwell, IV Corps, and the Chinese forces from Yunnan all moved forward. These operations would result in the clearance of northern Burma, with Special Force opening the way for main forces to follow up. No sooner was the design finalized than it began to fall apart in a fashion that would become the SEAC norm. Amphibious trooplift was recalled to Europe for use in Overlord and its Mediterranean counterpart Anvil. Without amphibious operations in the Bay of Bengal, Chiang refused to allow his forces in Yunnan to move forward. This in turn led to the scaling back of IV Corps's projected advance across the Chindwin. Suddenly, the design sketched out at Quadrant in September (and in which Special Force played a central role) had turned into something much more limited. There would be a forward movement to the Chindwin by IV Corps (soon canceled as Japanese offensive intentions became clear and Slim switched to a very different plan) and the slow crawl down the Hukawng Valley toward Myitkyina and its airfields by Stilwell's Chinese. But where did that leave Special Force and its ambitious commander?[2]

Slim had always understood that Wingate's force existed primarily to assist Stilwell's drive. He made this clear to Wingate at a conference held at XIV Army headquarters on 4 January 1944. It was on this basis that the deployment of 16th, 77th, and 111th LRP Brigades was planned. Bernard Fergusson's 16th Brigade would march in from Stilwell's Northern Combat Area—across some of the wildest, most difficult terrain in northern Burma. Michael Calvert's 77th Brigade was to be flown in, while W. D. A. Lentaigne's 111th Brigade, originally slated to march in from IV Corps's area, crossing the Chindwin with that corps's assistance, was in the event also flown in.[3] All three were to seize and develop defended airheads—"strongholds" in Wingate's parlance—that would contain an airstrip capable of handling Dakotas. From these bases they would focus their operations on the railway corridor—the north-south road and rail connection that ran from Rangoon to the terminus at Myitkyina and was the supply line of the Japanese *18th Division* that was very efficiently slowing down Stilwell's advance. This, however, was not the sort of mission Wingate had in mind for Special Force.

As the plans for the 1943–1944 dry weather season came apart— SEAC's amphibious plans canceled, the Chinese advance from Yunnan consequently dropped, and IV Corps shifting to a plan for a defensive battle—Wingate's plans for Operation Thursday (often called Chindit II) began to slip out of sync with those of XIV Army. Wingate's reaction was to lay down grander objectives for Special Force and demand more resources—in all probability a way of asserting the continued centrality of his operations to the theater despite the changing realities on the ground. This culminated in a pair of remarkable memos, sent to Mountbatten on 10 and 11 February 1944, in which Wingate proposed basically turning the army in India into a vast training machine to churn out LRP brigades with which he would not only reconquer Burma but move on to take Bangkok and Hanoi.[4] As Wingate's vaulting ambitions moved further from the reality facing XIV Army, a clash with Slim became inevitable.

In his memoirs, Slim remarked rather mildly that "it was impossible not to differ from a man who so fanatically pursued his own purposes without regard to any other consideration or person."[5] The tension came to a head over the use of 26th Indian Infantry Division. The division was Slim's XIV Army reserve formation. As Wingate elaborated his ideas for defended "strongholds" as bases for his brigades' operations, he developed a requirement for garrison battalions for them. Slim agreed to provide one from 26th Division and to train three more of that division's battalions for this purpose, but their commitment would rest with him. With Mutaguchi's offensive looming, it is easy to understand why Slim was very unwilling to commit 40 percent of his army reserve division unconditionally, but that is what Wingate affected to believe had been promised him. In a confrontation in Slim's office, Wingate invoked Churchill, pointing out that the prime minister had told him to communicate directly with 10 Downing Street if his plans were in any way obstructed. Slim merely "pushed a signal pad across my desk and told him to go and write the message. [Wingate] did not take the pad but he left the room. . . . That was the last I heard of his demand for the 26th Division."[6] Like many in the past (and a few in the future), Wingate discovered that it was very hard to best Bill Slim. It is an interesting footnote to this episode that Wingate, willing to threaten Slim over the provision of troops to garrison his strongholds, did not manage to produce a training memorandum on the subject of stronghold defense until a week before his operation launched.[7] This raises the interesting question of how effectively Wingate functioned as a senior officer.

One of Wingate's subordinates in Ethiopia remarked that his orders would be more sensible if he had ever commanded anything larger than a platoon.[8] In Chindit I, he had a brigade, which he handled none too deftly. Now he had been vaulted to, effectively, corps command. Between his return to India in September and the beginning of Operation Thursday in March, there were barely five months in which to assemble a headquarters, gather and train Special Force, and plan one of the most complex operations of the war to date. Planning and command were not aided by a trait noticed by Slim: "I do not think he ever confided his intentions or ambitions fully to anyone, certainly not to his own staff or his superior commanders."[9] On one occasion, he promised one of his brigade commanders the support of another LRP brigade for a major attack— then directed the second brigade to another objective without informing the commander to whom he had promised its support![10]

The pattern of episodes revealing that Wingate was really not prepared for high command continued. (Slim noted that he was "strangely naïve when it came to the business of actually fighting the Japanese.") On the eve of Thursday's launch, there was a scare that the Japanese knew at least one of its objectives. Wingate was so seriously rattled that Slim had to take the decision to proceed.[11] Once the operation was under way, columns from different brigades crisscrossed one another on their way to different objectives, and at one point Slim discovered that thirty-three of the precious Dakotas allotted to Special Force were standing idle and promptly diverted them, temporarily, to supply-dropping for XIV Army, which never had enough Dakotas at its disposal.[12] While this is not the place to analyze the unfolding of Thursday, it is plain, at minimum, that Wingate had not become comfortable as a senior commander.

Once Chindit II was actually launched, Wingate had little time to mature into his duties—he died in an air crash on 24 March. Slim promptly appointed as his successor Brigadier "Joe" Lentaigne of 111th LRP

Brigade, "the most balanced and experienced of Wingate's commanders." Three different officers (none of them Lentaigne) told Slim they
had been assured by Wingate that they were his designated successor—an
interesting indication of how Wingate managed his key subordinates.[13]
Slim ordered Lentaigne to focus Special Force on assisting Stilwell's advance on Myitkyina—he understood theater politics all too well and
realized that Special Force had come into being to support the US drive
to clear northern Burma. At this point, Special Force moves out of the
purview of an account focused on Imphal. One last matter, however, remains to be considered: How much did the Chindits contribute to XIV
Army's victory?

The Japanese had realized that a repeat of Chindit I was a possibility,
but the scale of Chindit II caught them by surprise. Neither Kawabe nor
Mutaguchi was prepared to delay their attack on Imphal. Kawabe simply
told Mutaguchi to put together an adequate force to mop up the Chindits.
Mutaguchi ordered *18th Division*, confronting Stilwell, and *56th Division*,
which was holding a front of several hundred miles along the Salween
River against the Yunnan Chinese (who enjoyed a ten-to-one superiority
over it), to each part with a battalion. His *15th Division* (already beginning U-Go minus its third regiment, delayed by the damage inflicted on
Burmese communications by Allied airpower) was also ordered to part
temporarily with a battalion. To this improvised force Mutaguchi added
some odds and ends (including two companies of convalescents). As the
scale of Chindit II became clearer to Kawabe, he added the four-battal-
ion *24th Independent Mixed Brigade*, a lower-category formation used for
occupation duties, and the equivalent of another infantry regiment assembled by grabbing battalions from a variety of units. By the end of March,
Major General Hayashi Yoshihide (in command of the hastily assembled
reaction force) had the infantry strength of a division but, of course, composed of units that had never worked together and without the supporting
arms and services that make a division a coherent fighting force. This
does not mean, however, that, but for the Chindits, Slim might well have
faced four Japanese divisions. Much of Hayashi's force was made up of
low-category occupation and logistic units; two of the three front-line
infantry battalions came from the heavily outnumbered divisions facing
Stilwell and the Yunnan Chinese (a good indication of how the Japanese
rated those antagonists!). None, with the exception of the single battalion
temporarily borrowed from *15th Division*, had ever been scheduled to be
part of the force assaulting Imphal, and that in any case was already as large

as the Japanese could hope to support (pending the expected capture of Churchill supplies).[14]

But if they did not divert troops from the Imphal attack, did the Chindits compromise the already precarious logistics of U-Go by disrupting *Fifteenth Army*'s communications? Slim was always clear that Special Force had come into existence with US support primarily to support Stilwell's advance. Wingate, however, as his ambitions for the future of Special Force soared—and a major Japanese offensive became imminent—began to focus on *Fifteenth Army*'s communications as a target. At his last meeting with Slim, on 21 March, at which Slim released to him Brigadier Tom Brodie's 14th LRP Brigade (placed at his disposal by Giffard earlier), Wingate proposed in conversation with Slim that the brigade be used to cut the communications of both the Japanese *15th* and *31st Divisions*. Slim rejected the idea, largely because changing the mission of Special Force would undoubtedly lead to a clash with Stilwell—the last thing Slim needed since the Americans controlled the Dakotas that were far more important to him than Special Force. In an action quite typical of his manner of proceeding, Wingate did not give either Slim or his staff a copy of his written appreciation laying out in detail his proposed plan for using Special Force against *Fifteenth Army*'s communications. Instead, he returned to his headquarters, ordered the 14th Brigade to begin its fly-in to Fergusson's "Aberdeen" stronghold immediately, and then gave Brodie written orders to operate against *Fifteenth Army*'s communications. (Fergusson, having been told by Wingate that Brodie would support his operations, was not informed of this change of plan.) A few days later, Wingate was dead and Lentaigne assumed command. He quickly discovered that neither Calvert nor Fergusson favored Wingate's final scheme and wanted to focus on the railway corridor. More important, perhaps, he discovered that the Japanese lines of communications were not where Wingate thought they were and therefore were less vulnerable to Special Force. On 9 April, Lentaigne met Slim and Mountbatten, and it was decided that the sole task henceforth of Special Force would be to assist Stilwell's advance. Although the LRP brigades discovered and destroyed some Japanese dumps as they crisscrossed the northern Burma landscape, their contribution to the logistic debacle that overtook *Fifteenth Army* was incidental. Bad Japanese planning did more damage to Mutaguchi's supply situation than did Special Force.[15]

In the end, it is hard not to agree with the verdict passed on Special Force by the official historians:

Special Force was a military misfit; as a guerilla force it was unnecessarily
large and, as an air-transported force, it was too lightly armed and equipped
either to capture strongly defended vital points or to hold them against
attacks by forces of all arms. . . . It must be remembered that, throughout
the whole period it was operating in Burma, Special Force never contained
more than about two-fifths of its own strength.[16]

Appendix C

Note on Chindit Historiography

When Wingate died, everyone, from Churchill down, said flattering things—with Special Force in the field, they had little choice. Afterward, however, dissent surfaced rapidly, and the argument between Wingate's critics and defenders rumbles on still. This note is not a comprehensive survey of that argument, but an indicator of some key publications.

First in the field, of course, was Churchill. The relevant volume of his memoirs, *Closing the Ring*, appeared in 1951. Considering the role Churchill played in giving Wingate Special Force, the interesting thing is how little he has to say about Chindit II—or Imphal, for that matter. It gets barely a page. Slim is never mentioned by name, nor is XIV Army. There is neither discussion nor assessment of Special Force. Churchill's "Syndicate" of assistants included two, Lieutenant General Sir Henry Pownall and Denis Kelly, who were sharp critics of Wingate. Pownall had, of course, been SEAC chief of staff in 1943–1944; Kelly was a wartime Indian Army officer. Perhaps Churchill himself had second thoughts about what he had set in motion at Quebec. But if Churchill was silent about both Chindit II and Imphal, both were covered impressively a few years later.

In 1956, Slim, by that time a field marshal and governor general of Australia, published his highly readable *Defeat Into Victory*. Slim wrote fluently and with a generosity and self-deprecating sense of humor that make *Defeat Into Victory* unique among the memoirs of senior military men. Slim also wrote it far from the records, but he had the invaluable assistance of Brigadier Michael Roberts, a fellow Gurkha officer who was a member of the team preparing the official histories. Roberts's papers, in the Churchill Archive Center at Churchill College, Cambridge, enable the researcher to track the writing of *Defeat Into Victory* as Roberts devilled for Slim, checking details, investigating contentious points (how many brigades did

Irwin cumber Lloyd with during the first Arakan offensive?), and generally doing for Slim what Churchill's Syndicate did for him. Slim was careful to acknowledge Wingate's strengths but was clearly critical of the whole Chindit enterprise: he referred to the creation of special-purpose forces as a "cult" and concluded that "such formations . . . were wasteful." In 1959, Wingate's official biography, *Orde Wingate: A Biography*, by Christopher Sykes, appeared. Sykes had never met Wingate but was a smooth, skillful writer and very well connected (his father was Sir Mark Sykes of the World War I Sykes-Picot Agreement). Sykes, although naturally seeing matters from Wingate's perspective, was smart enough not to tackle Slim—his tone in dealing with Slim's criticisms is one of hurt bewilderment. In 1962, Kirby and his team brought out the third volume of the official Cabinet Office history of Britain's war against Japan, which produced a sharp reaction among Wingate's partisans. Kirby, a retired major general, had been deputy chief of the general staff at Indian Army Headquarters in 1943 and had certainly experienced Wingate at his demanding worst. His principal assistant in telling the military side of the story was Brigadier Michael Roberts, a retired officer of the Indian Army that Wingate openly despised (and, as noted, a friend and collaborator of Slim's). Kirby had already, in his second volume, which devoted a chapter to Chindit I, been mildly critical, summing up the value of the operation thusly: "There was . . . , however, a possibility that much of the value of the lessons learnt would be lost if they were not kept in their proper perspective."[1] In volume three, Kirby gave Chindit II three full chapters (Imphal got six). While acknowledging Wingate's dynamism and ability to inspire, the general tone was carefully critical, ending with the summation already quoted. Read today, Kirby's verdict seems unremarkable. At the time, it enraged many of Wingate's devoted followers. Slim they may have been unprepared to openly challenge, but "official" criticisms of Wingate and the utility of the Chindit enterprise they were not prepared to allow to pass quietly.

Derek Tulloch was one of Wingate's oldest and closest friends, dating back to the time when they were both officer cadets at "the Shop"—the Royal Military Academy at Woolwich, where the British Army then trained its gunner and sapper officers (artillerymen and engineers). Wingate made him chief of staff to Special Force, a post he continued to hold under Lentaigne. In 1972, he published *Wingate in Peace and War*, and although he does not claim to be refuting the official history, he was clearly aiming to modify its verdict. Tulloch died shortly after publishing his memoir of Wingate, and the cudgels were taken up in the fight against Kirby's verdict by Brigadier Peter Mead, who had been a junior staff officer at Special Force. He was powerfully supported by Sir Robert Thompson, who had, as a junior RAF officer, been on both Chindit expeditions and then had won international fame as one of the architects of Britain's postwar counterinsurgency victory in Malaya. They were backed by the Chindits Old Comrades Association, a group of British veterans of Wingate's two Burma campaigns.[2] Their advocacy culminated in the delivery to the Cabinet Office of a lengthy defense of Wingate coupled with a request that a "working-party should be set up to review the relevant passages of Volume 3" of Kirby's history. (Kirby himself was by this time dead.) They claimed to have "serious doubts" about the objectivity of Kirby and his team and asked for action "to put the public record straight."[3] The Cabinet Office was unmoved. But Mead and Thompson were not done. Cold-shouldered by the Cabinet Office, Mead in 1987 published *Orde Wingate and the Historians* (with a foreword by Thompson) in which he took on not only Kirby but Slim, Slim's official biographer Ronald Lewin, and anyone else (like myself) who had ever written critically of Wingate.

Parallel with the argument over the judgment on Wingate and the value of the Chindit enterprise in the official histories, other accounts of the Chindit operations were appearing as participants wrote memoirs—which displayed a similarly wide range of assessments. Brigadier Michael "Mad Mike" Calvert was one of the first Chindits, a column commander in the 1943 raid, and commander of Wingate's original Chindit brigade, 77th LRP Brigade, in Chindit II. Some of Wingate's followers thought he, not Lentaigne, should have been named to command Special Force after Wingate's death. In 1952, he published *Prisoners of Hope*, an account of his brigade in Chindit II (reissued in 1971, with a foreword by Derek Tulloch). He followed this with a personal memoir, *Fighting Mad*, in 1961. In both, although recognizing that Wingate could be difficult and often made problems for himself, Calvert showed unshakeable loyalty to the man and a firm belief that the Chindit contribution to the 1944 victory had been decisive. Another 1943 column commander, who became an LRP brigade commander in 1944, displayed similar loyalty to Wingate (if with greater nuance and more literary polish). Bernard Fergusson was an officer of the Black Watch (and former aide-de-camp to Wavell). He escaped from a staff posting at Army Headquarters in Delhi to join Wingate in October 1942 as he assembled and trained 77th LRP Brigade. A column commander in Chindit I (about which he wrote a highly readable account, *Beyond the Chindwin*, first published in 1945), Fergusson led 16th LRP Brigade in Chindit II. In 1970, he published *The Trumpet in the Hall*, a very polished memoir that tells the reader a great deal not only about Wingate and the Chindits but also about the British Army of Fergusson's day. While more critical of Wingate—and more perceptive about him— than Calvert, Fergusson was equally certain that he had served under an extraordinary man "whose vision at the council table matched his genius in the field."[4] The perspective on Wingate changes sharply when one turns to the memoirs of the Indian Army officer who succeeded Lentaigne in command of 111th LRP Brigade, John Masters. From an Indian Army family, Masters joined 4th Prince of Wales Own Gurkha Rifles in 1934. In 1961, having moved to the United States and become a successful historical novelist, he published a war memoir, *The Road Past Mandalay* (having already written an account of peacetime soldiering in India, the very successful *Bugles and a Tiger*, published in 1956). Where Calvert and Fergusson saw Wingate's positives as outweighing his negatives, Masters, while acknowledging Wingate's manic drive and the sincerity with which he held his beliefs, laid out a long list of his negatives "because not enough has been said about it."[5] Heading the list were Wingate's scorn for the Indian Army and his criticisms of the Gurkha battalion that had served in Chindit I (and that Gurkha Rifles officers felt Wingate had badly mishandled).

One of the most interesting, but little noted, memoirs of Chindit II appeared in 1984: Terence O'Brien's *Out of the Blue: Pilot with the Chindits*. O'Brien, an Australian serving with the RAF, was one of the RAF liaison officers who served with the Chindits and whose role was crucial in arranging air support and supply-dropping. O'Brien's view of Wingate was skeptical: "He did not ask for help and he was not prepared to listen to gratuitous advice. He knew."

Inevitably, however, after participants, official biographers, and official historians had had their say, the moment would arrive when more dispassionate historians would tackle what Masters dubbed "the Wingate Problem." In 1979, Shelford Bidwell, a retired British Army officer who became an excellent military historian, published *The Chindit War*. Dedicated to Michael Calvert, and with an introduction by John Masters, Bidwell tried to strike a similar balance in his analysis. Recognizing, as all writers on the subject have, Wingate's ability to inspire, Bidwell was critical of both Wingate's skill as a commander of large formations and the return on the large investment of resources represented by Special Force. Although denounced by Brigadier Mead, Bidwell's study remains the best analysis to date. Many of the points made by Bidwell are echoed in two books by Julian Thompson: *The Imperial War Museum Book of War Behind Enemy Lines* (1998), and *The Imperial War Museum Book of the War in Burma, 1942–1945* (2002). Thompson, a retired Royal Marine major general who had led the Commando Brigade in the 1982 Falkland War, based his narrative on the unmatched collection of personal experience narratives and interviews held by the Imperial War Museum. His assessment of the Chindit venture is similar to Bidwell's, highlighting particularly failures in training and command.

Lest it be thought, however, that the judgment first rendered by Slim on Wingate has become the consensus view, there is David Rooney's *Wingate and the Chindits: Redressing the Balance* (1994). It picks up and carries forward the Mead-Thompson assault on Kirby (and everyone else seen as unfairly critical of Wingate). The latest entrant into the discussion is Simon Anglim, whose *Orde Wingate and the British Army, 1922–1944* (2010) is a very detailed and tightly focused academic monograph that concludes: "Rather than a 'maverick' Orde Wingate fitted into the British Army of his time."[6] He certainly fit into the pattern of regular British Army disdain for the Indian Army, which Anglim largely ignores despite the fact that the Indian Army is an unavoidable factor in the Burmese chapter of Wingate's career.

Even though Slim is finally receiving overdue recognition as the best British army commander since Wellington in such books as Robert Lyman's *Slim, Master of War* (2004), it seems clear that Wingate's odd, compelling personality (and perhaps the remarkable number of above-average memoirists among his Chindit officers) guarantees that writers will continue to be drawn to his brief, fiery, and controversial career.

Notes

Preface and Acknowledgments

1. The quote is from W. S. Slim, *Defeat Into Victory* (London: Cassell, 1956), p. 296.

2. The only recent attempt to come to grips with this sprawling battle is Robert Lyman, *Japan's Last Bid for Victory: The Invasion of India, 1944* (London: Praetorian Press, 2011).

Chapter 1. Monsoon, 1942

1. There is considerable literature on the 1942 withdrawal from Burma. The best summary is Alan Warren's *Burma 1942: The Road from Rangoon to Mandalay* (London: Continuum, 2011).

Chapter 2. The Indian Army

1. The best account of the Military Revolution and its impact is Geoffrey Parker, *The Military Revolution: Military Innovation and the Rise of the West, 1500–1800* (Cambridge, UK: Cambridge University Press, 1988), esp. chap. 4.

2. *Suttee* (or *sati*) was the practice of widows immolating themselves on their husbands' funeral pyres. British officials felt that such actions were often far from voluntary. While they were doubtless correct in many cases, they underestimated the impact on the minds of their Hindu subjects of their action.

3. John Pemble, *The Invasion of Nepal: John Company at War* (Oxford, UK: Clarendon Press, 1971), is an excellent study of the beginning of the Anglo-Gurkha relationship, which continues today in the form of the Royal Gurkha Rifles, a regular regiment of the British Army (not to mention the far more numerous Gurkha units in today's Indian Army).

151

4. One of the reasons Indian battalions remained so lightly officered was that the Company had chosen, for financial reasons, to hold down the number of European officers, substituting "Indian officers" who ranked above Non-Commissioned Officers but below the most junior European officer. They functioned both as a bridge between the British officers and the sepoys and as subalterns did in European armies. Promoted by seniority, they were often unfit when units took the field. After the post-Mutiny reorganization, they became known as Viceroy Commissioned Officers and, promoted now by seniority tempered by merit, became the backbone of the Indian Army. The senior VCO in an infantry battalion, the subhadar major, was the commanding officer's principal adviser on all matters pertaining to the sepoys' religion, traditions, morale, etc. Still junior to the most junior European officer, it would have been a very foolish British subaltern who challenged the subhadar major.

Given the fact that the Indian Army had so few British officers, and virtually no reserve of officers in 1914, replacing the very high officer casualties presented a huge challenge. It was met by a patchwork of expedients. These produced about 5,300 officers during the war. That the Indian Army continued to function effectively as its prewar regular officer corps dwindled is due largely to the VCOs. By 1939, the lessons of 1914–1918 had been assimilated, but World War II expansion so far outran prewar plans that it again had to cobble together an officer replacement system—the most important component of which was the granting of King's commissions to Indians, 15,540 of whom were commissioned during the war. The whole subject of officer recruitment and army training is definitively covered in Alan Jeffreys's forthcoming book on the subject: *Approach to Battle: Training the Indian Army During the Second World War* (London: Helion, 2017)

5. There are two excellent studies of the Indian Corps in France: Gordon Corrigan, *Sepoys in the Trenches: The Indian Corps on the Western Front, 1914–1915,* paper ed. (Stroud, Glos., UK: Spellmount, 2006); and George Morton-Jack, *The Indian Army on the Western Front: India's Expeditionary Force to France and Belgium in the First World War* (Cambridge, UK: Cambridge University Press, 2014). Morton-Jack points out that "old social tensions" between the two armies "resurfaced" in France and that Indian Army officers were "well aware" they were held in "low esteem" by British regulars. One striking exception to this was the commander of the Indian Corps, Lieutenant General Sir James Willcocks, a British regular but from a not very prestigious regiment who had spent most of his career overseas, largely in India. He spoke several Indian languages, understood the customs and traditions of his men, and would be sacked by Douglas Haig for trying to keep his corps from being consumed by Haig's passion for bootless frontal assaults. He retired to India and died there.

6. The Indian Army has attracted little scholarly attention until recently, and most of it has focused either on the 1857 Mutiny or on the two world wars. The Company's armies still await serious historical study. There is an excellent general account in Philip Mason's *A Matter of Honour: An Account of the Indian Army, Its Officers, and Men* (London: Jonathan Cape, 1974). Mason, a distinguished member

of the last generation of British officers of the Indian Civil Service, was secretary to the Indian Chiefs of Staff Committee during World War II. A born writer, Mason's account is the most readable extant, albeit heavily anecdotal and, perhaps inevitably, nostalgic. It can be usefully supplemented by T. A. Heathcote, *The Indian Army: The Garrison of British Imperial India, 1822–1922* (New York: Hippocrene Books, 1974); and, from an Indian perspective, S. L. Menezes, *Fidelity and Honour: The Indian Army from the Seventeenth to the Twenty-First Century*, paper ed. (New Delhi: Oxford, 2001). Menezes, who began his Indian Army career in the twilight of the Raj, retired a lieutenant general in the Indian Army. A recent effort to pull together existing scholarship on the subject is Daniel P. Marston and Chandar Sundaram (eds.), *A Military History of India and South Asia: From the East India Company to the Nuclear Era* (Westport, CT: Praeger, 2007). Two other studies of the Company's armies, addressing important aspects of their history, are Douglas Peers, *Between Mars and Mammon: Colonial Armies and the Garrison State in Early Nineteenth Century India, 1819–1835* (London: I. B. Tauris, 1995), and Raymond Callahan, *The East India Company and Army Reform, 1783–1798* (Cambridge, MA: Harvard University Press, 1972), which covers the confrontation between the Bengal officers, the Company, and London. On the new army that emerged from the Mutiny the best recent study is David Omissi's *The Sepoy and the Raj: The Indian Army, 1860–1940* (London: Palgrave Macmillan, 1994). There is a good recent biography of Roberts, whose views (and prejudices) did so much to shape the post-Mutiny army: Rodney Atwood, *The Life of Field Marshal Lord Roberts*, paper ed. (London: Bloomsbury, 2015). There is an excellent study of the impact of the Frontier on the Indian Army in Tim Moreman's *The Army in India and the Development of Frontier Warfare, 1849–1947* (London: Macmillan, 1998). The Indian Army during the two world wars is addressed in two recent collections: Kaushik Roy (ed.), *The Indian Army in the Two World Wars* (Leiden: Brill, 2012), and Alan Jeffreys and Patrick Rose (eds.), *The Indian Army, 1939–1947: Experience and Development* (Farnham, Surrey, UK: Ashgate, 2012). Daniel Marston's *The Indian Army and the End of the Raj* (Cambridge, UK: Cambridge University Press, 2014), is a definitive study of the last years of this remarkable institution.

Chapter 3. Slim

1. In contrast with the large number of books devoted to Montgomery and the desert war, Slim's life and career has remained underexplored by biographers and historians. This perhaps matters less than it might because he left two highly readable accounts that cover much of it. *Defeat Into Victory* (London: Cassell, 1956) is widely regarded as perhaps the best—and best-written—English-language general's memoir to come out of World War II (and perhaps the only British military memoir to compare to U. S. Grant's). Slim followed it up with *Unofficial History* (New York: David McKay, 1959), a series of vignettes ranging from the Mesopotamia campaign, through interwar soldiering in India, to his experiences

as a brigade and divisional commander in 1940–1941. (He never wrote about Gallipoli.) Some of the chapters, originally written between the wars, conflate several episodes into one or lightly fictionalize what is clearly autobiographical. But, written with verve and skill, they give an even better sense of the man than *Defeat Into Victory.* Shortly after Slim's death in 1970, Ronald Lewin produced an official biography, *Slim: The Standardbearer* (London: Leo Cooper, 1976). As polished a writer as his subject, Lewin won Britain's W. A. Smith Literary Award for the biography, something not common for official biographies of generals. A recent account, Russell Miller's *Uncle Bill: The Authorized Biography of Field Marshal Viscount Slim* (London: Weidenfeld & Nicolson, 2013), adds surprisingly little to Lewin's study. There are also two studies focused on the Burma campaign: Robert Lyman's *Slim: Master of War* (London: Constable, 2004); and Geoffrey Evans's *Slim as Military Commander* (London: Batsford, 1969). Evans commanded a division under Slim in Burma. Slim's notice in the standard British reference source, *The Dictionary of National Biography,* by Brigadier Michael Roberts (a fellow Gurkha officer and Slim's collaborator in the writing of *Defeat Into Victory*), was revised and enlarged by the current author when the dictionary itself was overhauled and republished as *The Oxford Dictionary of National Biography* (Oxford, UK: Oxford University Press, 2004). Slim's (surprisingly sparse) papers are in the Churchill Archive Center at Churchill College, Cambridge (some papers remain in family hands). There is clearly room for more work on Slim.

2. Since the decorations worn by some officers will figure in the text, some explanation is in order. The Victoria Cross is Britain's premier decoration for military valor, created during the Crimean War. The Distinguished Service Order (DSO) was created in 1886. During World War II it could be awarded either for gallant conduct by junior officers that did not quite rise to VC level or for distinguished leadership by senior officers. The Military Cross, created in 1914, was awarded during World War II to officers of the rank of major or below, as well as to warrant officers. Indians became eligible for the VC in 1911.

3. The "Mespot" campaign has attracted very little attention from military historians. A. J. Barker's *The Bastard War: The Mesopotamian Campaign of 1914–1918* (New York: Dial Press, 1969), by a professional soldier who served under Slim in Burma and long the standard secondary account, has recently been joined by Charles Townshend's arrestingly titled *When God Made Hell: The British Invasion of Mesopotamia and the Creation of Iraq, 1914–1921* (London: Faber & Faber, 2010). Readable and perceptive, it suffers, however, from the author's decision to ignore the Indian Army as an institution. "Indian Army" does not even figure in the index. The first three chapters of *Unofficial History*, written in the interwar years under the pseudonym "Anthony Mills," deal with the Mesopotamian campaign. In one of them, titled "The Incorrigible Rogue," Slim wrote this about Maude: "There was not a man in the Force who did not feel the renewed energy and hope that were vitalizing the whole army. To watch an army recovering its morale is enthralling; to feel the process working within oneself is an

unforgettable experience" (p. 42). It is an uncanny forecast of what Slim himself would do with XIV Army.

4. Slim, *Unofficial History,* chaps. 4, 5.

5. Pradeep Barua's *Gentlemen of the Raj: The Indian Army Officer Corps, 1817–1949* (Westport, CT: Praeger, 2003) is an excellent introduction to the complexities of "Indianization."

6. Brigadier Michael Roberts, on his relations with Slim, n.d., p. 1. Roberts Papers, MRBS 1/4, Churchill Archive Center, Churchill College, Cambridge (hereafter CAC).

7. During the interwar years Slim had honed another skill that would mark him as unusual among British senior officers in the ensuing conflict: he had turned himself into a good writer, with an easy, accessible style. He had always been interested in writing and had been practicing the craft while convalescing from his Gallipoli wounds. During the interwar years, he became a published author, under the pen name "Anthony Mills," satisfying his urge to write and at the same time earning some welcome additional income. (His appointments to Camberley and the Imperial Defence College had meant taking a substantial pay cut, Indian officers' salaries being reduced when posted home.) Slim's skill with his pen would enable him to chronicle his war in the most readable of British generals' memoirs, a story that is also, in many ways, an account of the old Indian Army's finale. The vote that carried his promotion was cast by a Gurkha Rifles officer.

8. Slim, *Unofficial History*, p. 148.

9. This essay is in the Slim Papers, 5/5/2. CAC.

10. Slim, *Defeat Into Victory*, p. 51. It should be noted that Stilwell's Chinese "armies" were less than they seemed. A Chinese "army" was smaller than a British or Indian division. Chinese units had no supply services. As a result they became an additional burden on scanty British resources. They tended to supplement their rations by pillaging the countryside. Their officers commandeered trains, forcing crews, at gunpoint, to operate them with no regard for safety considerations. Although, as Slim acknowledged, they could fight hard on occasion (even if Stilwell had to bribe commanders to attack), it is more than doubtful whether they retarded the speed of the Japanese advance appreciably.

11. The retreat from Burma is well covered in *Defeat Into Victory.* The British Official History was published in five volumes between 1957 and 1969. S. W. Kirby et al., *The War Against Japan, Volume 2: India's Most Dangerous Hour* (London: HMSO, 1958), is thorough, if discreet. There is also a (seldom-read) Indian official history: Bisheshwar Prasad (ed.), *The Retreat from Burma, 1941–1942* (Calcutta: Orient Longmans, 1954), which is heavily focused on the tactical level. A participant, Ian Lyall Grant, with a Japanese collaborator, Kazuo Tamayama, has produced an excellent account, drawing on material from both sides: *Burma 1942: The Japanese Invasion* (Chichester, West Sussex, UK: Zampi Press, 1999). Alan Warren's *Burma 1942: The Road from Rangoon to Mandalay* (London: Continuum,

2011) is an excellent overview, and there is a good "view from below" in Tony Mains's *Retreat from Burma,* paper ed. (London: New English Library, 1973). Mains, a Gurkha Rifles officer, was a junior intelligence officer during the retreat. There is a survey of the civil dimension of the retreat in Felicity Goodall's *Exodus Burma: The British Escape through the Jungles of Death, 1942* (Stroud, UK: Spellmount, 2011), which, despite the melodramatic title, is well done. There is also a scholarly study by Michael D. Leigh: *The Evacuation of Civilians from Burma: Analysing the 1942 Colonial Disaster* (London: Bloomsbury, 2014). Of course, the overwhelming majority of the refugees fleeing Burma were Indians, whose story, except for fleeting glimpses in British accounts, will never be fully chronicled. Chris Bayly and Tim Harper, *Forgotten Armies: The Fall of British Asia, 1941–1945* (London: Allen Lane, 2004), is essential to an understanding of the Burma campaign and much else besides. Despite its title it is not a tactical or operational history but rather an account of the wider political and social ramifications of Britain's war in Asia. Raymond Callahan, *Burma 1942–1945* (London: Davis Poynter, 1978), looks at the retreat through the prism of evolving Anglo-American theater strategy.

Chapter 4. Marking Time

1. It may seem surprising that Churchill, no admirer of the Indian Army, chose Auchinleck to command the vital Middle East theater. However, early in 1940 Auchinleck had been summoned home from India to assume command of an army corps. A rising star in the Indian Army and likely future commander in chief, there may have been a desire to bring him into closer touch with the regular British Army. His presence at home led to his involvement in the doomed Norwegian campaign, where his conduct made a favorable impression on Churchill. He then took over Southern Command in Britain, where he was responsible for the most likely invasion beaches. By the time he returned to India, late in 1940, to become commander in chief, Auchinleck was a known quantity in London—and Churchill placed high value on personal knowledge of those holding senior military appointments. Throughout the subsequent vicissitudes in their relationship, Churchill retained a regard for Auchinleck—if not for the army from which he came. Wavell's appointment as Commander-in-Chief, India, was not anomalous. British officers held senior appointments in India from the late eighteenth century, although sepoy battalions were always commanded by Indian Army officers. By the twentieth century, British and Indian Army officers alternated in the commander-in-chief position.

2. The official histories apart, there are few good overall accounts of the Burma campaign. Slim's has remained continuously in print, perhaps because it is so well written. Louis Allen, a Japanese-speaking XIV Army intelligence officer during the war, produced the best general account: *Burma: The Longest War* (London: J. M. Dent & Sons, 1984). Allen's command of Japanese allowed him to look at

the campaign from both sides. Raymond Callahan, in *Burma 1942–1945* (London: Davis Poynter, 1978), concentrates on alliance politics and theater strategy. Robert Lyman's *Slim, Master of War: Burma and the Birth of Modern Warfare* (London: Constable, 2004) studies the campaign through Slim's eyes. The Burmese Arakan is now known as Rakhine.

3. Reinforcing the Middle East and especially building up the Northern Front in Persia and Iraq in case the Red Army's defense of the Caucasus collapsed was a major concern of London until after the Russian Stalingrad offensive. There is more in Churchill's papers in August–September 1942, for instance, about this area than about Burma. A separate command, Persia and Iraq Command, was set up in August 1942 under General Sir Henry Maitland "Jumbo" Wilson. Its principal formation was Lieutenant General Edward Quinan's X Army—a largely Indian Army force.

4. There is an excellent account of the medical dimension of the Burma campaign in Mark Harrison, *Medicine and Victory* (Oxford, UK: Oxford University Press, 2004).

5. On the great panic that swept over India and was especially acute in the Madras Presidency, see Indivar Kamtekar, "The Shiver of 1942," in Kaushik Roy (ed.), *War and Society in Colonial India* (New Delhi: Oxford University Press, 2006), pp. 330–357. Madras, of course, is now Chennai.

6. A good brief account of the Cripps Mission is Robin Moore, *Churchill, Cripps, and India* (Oxford, UK: Clarendon Press, 1979).

7. The Congress Revolt has been rather overlooked by historians. A good brief account is in Lawrence James's *Raj: The Making and Unmaking of British India* (New York: St. Martin's Press, 1998), pp. 545–573. The Congress Revolt is central to Paul Scott's four novels known collectively as "The Raj Quartet" (1966–1975, subsequently adapted very successfully for television). However, Scott, a wartime officer in the Royal Indian Army Service Corps and hardly a supporter of the Raj, was not writing history, however realistic the novels may seem.

8. The one British battalion per Indian brigade rule had been breached in World War I. The 29th Indian Infantry Brigade, which landed on Gallipoli in April 1915 and remained there throughout the campaign (and whose 1/6 Gurkhas reached the summit of Sari Bair), was made up of Sikhs and Gurkhas. In 1939–1945, when the Indian Army grew to twice the strength of the World War I force, and while British manpower was even more severely stretched, all-Indian brigades became ever more common, and those British battalions that did serve in them became steadily more attenuated as the supply of replacements dried up. By 1945, only 13 percent of the "British" XIV Army was actually British.

Already in 1941, 9th Indian Division in Malaya (which had only two brigades) had no British units, while one of the independent brigades in Malaya Command also had no British battalion. The two Indian brigades in Burma in December 1941 had no British units. In January 1942, 17th Indian Division's two brigades were all Indian, while by February 1942 the division's three brigades had only one British battalion. It is true that some of the all-Indian brigades were in fact all-Gurkha brigades, like 48th Brigade in 17th Indian Division, and that Gurkhas topped the Raj's trustworthiness scale after 1857, but the mix of units in Indian brigades was driven primarily by British manpower problems (and the priority accorded to the European war). As this narrative proceeds it will be clear that the problem (from the viewpoint of traditionalists like the prime minister) only worsened in 1943–1944—and that it made no difference to the Indian Army's fighting qualities or reliability.

9. Kirby, *War Against Japan, Volume 2*, pp. 47–48.

10. The official history counted nine. Brigadier Michael Roberts, one of Kirby's team, told Slim he thought seven was more accurate. In any case there were too many units for a divisional headquarters to manage.

11. Perhaps unsurprisingly, the first Arakan offensive has not attracted much historical interest. Kirby, *War Against Japan, Volume 2*, chaps. 15, 19–20, lays out the story clearly. Slim's own account in *Defeat Into Victory*, pp. 147–167, is remarkably restrained. Robert Lyman's chapter on Irwin and the Arakan campaign in *The Generals* (London: Constable, 2008), pp. 143–186, is a clear, balanced account.

12. At this point, Wavell fades out of this story. Once considered an outstanding commander, his stature has diminished the longer—and harder—historians have looked at him. The first volume of the official biography by John Connell, *Wavell: Soldier and Scholar* (London: Collins, 1964) is hagiography. A second volume, which took the story to mid-1943 when Churchill relieved him—for the second time—was, after Connell's death, "completed and edited" by Brigadier Michael Roberts and published as *Wavell: Supreme Commander* (London: Collins, 1969). The best assessment to date of Wavell's military career is Ronald Lewin's *The Chief: Field Marshal Lord Wavell, Commander-in-Chief and Viceroy, 1939–1947* (New York: Farrar, Straus and Giroux, 1980). Wavell's time as Viceroy, where he may have made his greatest contribution, still awaits its historian. A very capable man with unusually broad intellectual interests for a British regular officer of his generation, he was, however, not the towering figure his admirers, then and later, imagined.

13. Churchill to Ismay, 24 July 1943. This document's citation when I first read it was PRO, PREM 3, 143/8. Britain's Public Record Office is now known as The National Archives; the series citation remains the same. Ismay was Lieutenant General Sir Hastings Ismay, chief staff officer to Churchill in his capacity as minister of defense and one of the key figures in wartime decisionmaking and also, incidentally, an Indian Army officer. His regiment, 21st Prince Albert Victor's Own Cavalry, was better known as Daly's Horse, one of the legendary Frontier Force regiments, first raised in 1849 by Lieutenant Henry Daly of the East India Company's Bombay Army. Despite this background, Ismay, who had long been away from Indian soldiering, apparently made no impact on Churchill's prejudices about the Indian Army. One wonders whether he even tried.

14. Ronald Lewin, *Slim: The Standardbearer* (London: Leo Cooper, 1976), p. 124. Irwin, after his relief, returned to Britain, where he was appointed to command the East Scotland District as a major general (his permanent rank). A

Gurkha Rifles officer later commented: "He was now safely back in Scotland commanding several thousand acres of heather and prisoners of war, but still vigorously blaming the Indian Army for the troubles he himself had brought upon it." Harry Seaman, *The Battle at Sangshak* (London: Leo Cooper, 1989), pp. 13–14.

15. Slim, *Defeat Into Victory*, p. 164.

16. SEAC's dysfunctional command arrangements had an unavowed purpose—they allowed Stilwell and the US Joint Chiefs of Staff to ignore the designation of SEAC as a British area of responsibility in which all communications from and to the Supreme Commander were channeled through the British Chiefs of Staff. Using the transparent excuse that they were communicating on American issues involving an American theater (the CBI), Stilwell and the Joint Chiefs created a private channel that Stilwell used to undercut and evade the official channel via London to the Anglo-American Combined Chiefs of Staff in Washington. It was an opportunity, needless to say, of which Stilwell took full advantage. Although aware of Stilwell's behavior, there was nothing Mountbatten could do about it.

17. On Orde Wingate, see appendix B in this volume and the works cited in appendix C.

18. The symbol chosen by Wingate for his brigade was the *chinthe*, a mythological beast that was the guardian of Burmese temples. Corrupted into "Chindit," it became the name by which Wingate's troops would be known to history.

19. Slim, *Defeat Into Victory*, pp. 162–163.

20. Alex Danchev and Daniel Todman (eds.), *War Diaries, 1939–1945: Field Marshal Lord Alan Brooke* (London: Weidenfeld & Nicolson, 2001), p. 436. The citation here is to Brooke's postwar "Notes on My Life," which he added to his wartime diaries as he reread them in the 1950s. There is no reason, however, to doubt that they reflected Brooke's contemporary realization that Churchill's motivations were essentially political.

21. The question of Churchill's attitude to the Indian Army (a subset of the question of his views on India) is discussed in appendix A.

22. Slim, *Defeat Into Victory*, p. 167.

Chapter 5. The Quiet Revolution

1. The officering of the Indian Army is a large, complex subject. There is a good introduction in Pradeep P. Barua, *Gentlemen of the Raj: The Indian Army Officer Corps, 1817–1949* (Westport, CT: Praeger, 2003). Daniel Marston, *Phoenix from the Ashes: The Indian Army in the Burma Campaign* (Westport, CT: Praeger, 2003); Alan Jeffreys, "Training the Indian Army, 1939–1945," in Alan Jeffreys and Patrick Rose (eds.), *The Indian Army, 1939–1947: Experience and Development* (Farnham, Surrey, UK: Ashgate, 2012); and Jeffreys's chapter titled "The Officer Corps and the Training of the Indian Army with Special Reference to

Lieutenant-General Francis Tuker," in Kaushik Roy (ed.), *The Indian Army in the Two World Wars* (Leiden: Brill, 2012), pp. 285–309, all discuss this issue with nuance on the basis of careful research. There is an excellent summary of all these issues connected with the expansion of the army—officer and rank-and-file recruitment, training, and Indianization—in Daniel Marston's *The Indian Army and the End of the Raj* (Cambridge, UK: Cambridge University Press, 2014), chap. 2. Alan Jeffreys's *Approach to Battle: Training the Indian Army During the Second World War* (London: Helion, 2017) has important material on officer training—and a great deal more.

2. John Masters, *Bugles and a Tiger*, paper ed. (London: Buchan & Enright, 1956) and *The Road Past Mandalay*, paper ed. (New York: Bantam, 1961). Both have been reprinted numerous times. There is an interesting sketch of Masters in Max Hastings, *Warriors*, paper ed. (London: Harper Perennial, 2005). It is useful to keep in mind when reading his memoirs that Masters, by the time he wrote them, had become a successful historical novelist.

3. There is a grassroots account of an ECO's wartime journey in Patrick Davis, *A Child at Arms*, paper ed. (London: Buchan & Enright, 1970). Davis served with the 8th Gurkha Rifles in Burma.

4. The "eight units" scheme, in addition to its discriminatory nature, had a logical flaw. Once Indian officers reached field grade and were eligible for non-regimental appointments, they would inevitably find themselves in postings with British subordinates. What then? World War II—and Auchinleck—saved the Indian Army from having to answer this embarrassing question.

5. There is a good, if dry and carefully neutral, summary of the multiple issues involved in army expansion in one of the volumes of the Indian official history: Sri Nadan Prasad, *Expansion of the Armed Forces and Defence Organisation* (Calcutta: Combined Inter-Services Historical Section (India & Pakistan), 1956). Alan Jeffreys's *Approach to Battle*, drawing on the papers of Lieutenant General Sir Francis Tuker, is definitive about the very complex process of turning a force of (largely) illiterate peasant soldiers into a modern, mechanized force.

6. The Bengal Famine of 1943 (which claimed about a million victims) is not, remarkably, directly germane to this account—it had very little impact on the Indian Army or the development of XIV Army's plans. It was a product of wartime dislocations, bad weather, the loss of imported food supplies from Burma, and the administrative ineptitude of the Bengal provincial government (a Muslim League administration, it had remained in office in 1939). The Army became involved only when Wavell succeeded Linlithgow as Viceroy in the autumn of 1943, visited the famine-stricken areas (a trip Linlithgow had never managed), and ordered the army to handle famine relief. There is a fascinating—and horrifying—account by an officer of 268th Indian Infantry Brigade, one of the units deployed: F. T. Burnett, *Keeping Up with the Hunt: The Story of the 268 Indian Infantry Brigade* (privately printed by Impress of Shrewsbury, UK, in 1983), pp. 22–33. There is a copy in the Imperial War Museum's Department of Documents. I am grateful to Alan Jeffreys for bringing this to my attention.

7. This information is from the obituary of Lieutenant Colonel John Maling, *Daily Telegraph* (London), 7 April 2009. Maling was with the unit from its raising and won a DSO commanding it in Burma in 1945.

8. S. W. Kirby et al., *The War Against Japan, Volume 2: India's Most Dangerous Hour* (London: HMSO, 1958), pp. 47–48.

9. Persia and Iraq Command and the overwhelmingly Indian X Army that was spread across it have largely disappeared from history, although at one point all, or part, of six divisions (four Indian) and an Indian motorized brigade were stationed there. Apart from one (anonymously authored) official account, *Paiforce: The Official Story of Persia and Iraq Command, 1941–1946* (London: Central Office of Information, 1948), no historian that I am aware of has taken an interest in this dead end of history, but in 1941–1942 it was a major concern for the Indian Army—and a very considerable commitment.

10. Lord Louis Mountbatten was a controversial figure during the war and became even more so for his conduct as the last Viceroy. His official biography by Philip Ziegler, *Mountbatten* (New York: Knopf, 1985), is careful but reasonably fair given the constraints of the genre. Adrian Smith's *Mountbatten: Apprentice Warlord* (London: I. B. Tauris, 2010) is well researched and devastatingly candid. Unfortunately, it takes the story only to the eve of Mountbatten's time at SEAC. A second volume is much to be hoped for.

11. Slim, *Defeat Into Victory* (London: Cassell, 1956), p. 139.

12. Ibid., p. 143.

13. The transformation of the Indian Army has fortunately been the subject of some excellent recent scholarship. Doctrinal development is covered by Tim Moreman, *The Jungle, the Japanese, and the British Commonwealth Armies at War, 1941–1945* (London: Frank Cass, 2005). Daniel Marston's 2003 account, *Phoenix from the Ashes*, covers every aspect of the Indian Army's transformation. Alan Jeffreys's contribution titled "Training the Indian Army, 1939–1945" in Jeffreys and Rose, *Indian Army, 1939–1947*, has been developed into a book, *The Approach to Battle: Training the Indian Army during the Second World War* (London: Helion, 2017). The history of the Indian Army's structural revolution during World War II is now more thoroughly studied than the wartime structural changes in the British Army itself.

It is an interesting reflection on the wartime evolution of both armies that in the Indian Army doctrinal uniformity was achieved, whereas in the British Army it never was. The British Army tradition that senior officers could develop their own approach to battle proved resistant to change even under the pressures of war. The closest thing to doctrinal uniformity in the British Army was Montgomery's success (backed by his patron, General Sir Alan Brooke, the chief of the Imperial General Staff) in imposing Monty's Eighth Army doctrine on the British units of Twenty-First Army Group prior to D-Day, a success that had very mixed results. See Timothy Harrison Place, *Military Training in the British Army, 1940–1944* (London: Frank Cass, 2000), for a full discussion. Montgomery's approach to battle, so very different from Slim's, is best understood in the context of the development of British Army thinking since 1918, brilliantly analyzed by Shelford Bidwell and Dominic Graham in *Fire-Power: British Army Weapons and Theories of War, 1904–1945* (London: Allen & Unwin, 1982), esp. pp. 244–247. The Montgomery style at its apogee is discussed by Stephen Hart in *Colossal Cracks: Montgomery's 21st Army Group in Northwest Europe, 1944–1945* (Mechanicsburg, PA: Stackpole Books, 2007). An Indian Army officer, Lieutenant General Sir Francis Tuker, whose 4th Indian Division served under Monty in the desert, Tunisia, and Italy, later dismissed him as being stuck in the year 1918. See Raymond Callahan, *Churchill and His Generals* (Lawrence: University Press of Kansas, 2007), p. 143. Monty's ponderous style owed much to the abundance of resources available to him; Slim, lacking abundance of anything but difficulties, had to be innovative to succeed and fortunately had the temperament to embrace innovation.

14. To do justice to the logistics of the Burma campaign would require a large book. There is a great deal of material in both the text and appendixes in two volumes of the British official history: Kirby, *War Against Japan, Volume 2*, chaps. 3, 11, and apps. 18, 24, 31; and S. W. Kirby et al., *War Against Japan, Volume 3: The Decisive Battles* (London: HMSO, 1962), chaps. 2, 22, and apps. 1, 4, 5, 23, 24, 25. Graham Dunlop's *Military Economics, Culture, and Logistics in the Burma Campaign, 1942–1945* (London: Pickering & Chatto, 2009) is an excellent monograph and, to date, the only significant study of this crucial subject. Yasmin Khan's *The Raj at War* (London: Allen Lane, 2015) is an excellent survey of the mobilization of Indian society by the Raj—and its costs. Raghu Karnad's *Farthest Field: An Indian Story of the Second World War* (New York: Norton, 2015) is a brilliant reconstruction of a single extended Indian family's experience in the Raj's last war.

15. Winston S. Churchill, *The River War*, paper ed. (London: Four Square Books, 1960). Chapter 8 in *The River War* ("The Desert Railway," pp. 157–176) ought to be carefully read by any student of Churchill and the Burma campaign. In it he describes a campaign with some very significant similarities to the war in Burma: waged in harsh and resource-poor country, against a determined enemy, and dependent utterly on the success of complex logistics. Churchill clearly acknowledged this: "On the day that the first troop train steamed into the fortified camp at the confluence of the Nile and Atbara Rivers the doom of the Dervishes was sealed" (p. 175). Unfortunately, in the four and a half decades that elapsed between the Sudan and Burma campaigns he had forgotten the importance of logistics he so clearly grasped in 1899.

Chapter 6. Curtain Raiser

1. The best history of the Imperial Japanese Army is Edward Drea's *Japan's Imperial Army: Its Rise and Fall, 1853–1945*, orig. ed. (Lawrence: University Press of Kansas, 2009).

2. There are two studies of Mutaguchi in English. Arthur Swinson's *Four Samurai: A Quartet of Japanese Army Commanders in the Second World War* (London:

Hutchinson, 1968) has an insightful essay. Louis Allen's "Mutaguchi and the Invasion of India" in Ian Nish and Mark Allen (eds.), *War, Conflict, and Security in Japan and Asia-Pacific, 1941–1952: The Writings of Louis Allen*, (Folkstone, UK: Global Oriental, 2011), pp. 243–266, is very instructive. Both Swinson and Allen served in Burma, Swinson with the 2nd British Division and Allen as a Japanese-speaking intelligence officer. The Indian National Army and Subhas Chandra Bose are treated by some Indian nationalists today as icons. The result has been a great deal of hagiography masquerading as history. The best brief treatment of the INA is Chandar Sundaram's "The Indian National Army, 1942–1946: A Circumstantial Force," in Daniel P. Marston and Chandar S. Sundaram (eds.), *A Military History of India and South Asia* (Westport, CT: Praeger, 2007), pp. 123–130. There was an additional problem that Mutaguchi was confronted with at the last minute. The timing of the two parts of his Operation: Ha-Go in the Arakan was supposed to draw in and tie down Slim's reserves. Its date, however, had to be advanced to forestall a pending XV Corps offensive. Then U-Go's start date had to be delayed due to the late arrival of *15th Division*, moving forward from Siam (as it then was). This delay was caused by the damage inflicted by Allied bombing on Japanese communications. When U-Go finally launched, a third of *15th Division*'s infantry had not yet reached the front. The net result was that the two attacks were not as tightly related as originally planned, affording XIV Army valuable breathing room.

The INA will not figure in the balance of this story. It proved a very damp squib. Ill equipped and supplied, and disdained by IJA officers, it made no impact on the battlefield and none on the loyalty of Indian soldiers. By the campaign's end, the Japanese were using its men as porters.

3. The persistence of plans for an offensive in the difficult terrain of the Arakan was due in large part to the continued yearning in London, especially by the prime minister, for an amphibious strategy that would bypass the messy complications of campaigning in northern Burma. Akyab Island, or rather the airstrips that could be built there, would be crucial for a seaborne assault on Rangoon. SEAC would plan ceaselessly for such an assault—and be as ceaselessly frustrated by lack of resources. This meant that Akyab remained an important objective that, in the absence of the ability to seize it from the sea, had to be taken by an overland advance.

4. Alan Stripp, *Code Breaker in the Far East*, paper ed. (Oxford, UK: Oxford University Press, 1989), is a fascinating account by a Bletchley Park veteran of British signals intelligence (Sigint) in the war against Japan. Of particular interest are Stripp's remarks (pp. 165–171) on Slim and Sigint.

5. XV Corps was planning to resume the offensive, something the Japanese realized. In order not to be forestalled, Hanaya brought forward the date of his own attack, something that may have helped him achieve tactical surprise.

6. Evans was a British Army officer who commanded a battalion in the desert, then, as a brigadier, the Indian Army Staff College at Quetta. He was serving as Brigadier General Staff (BGS) to Scoones at IV Corps when he was named to

command at 9th Indian Brigade. He would succeed Messervy as commander of 7th Indian Division and end the war as a corps commander.

7. Slim, *Defeat Into Victory,* p. 139.

8. Slim covered the Admin Box battle in *Defeat Into Victory*, pp. 223–247, in a chapter titled "Pattern for Victory." The official history—Kirby, *War Against Japan, Volume 3*, pp. 133–152—fills in details. Geoffrey Evans's own memoir, *The Desert and the Jungle* (London: William Kimber, 1959), pp. 123–167, adds more interesting detail. Louis Allen, *Burma: The Longest War* (London: J. M. Dent & Sons, 1984), pp. 170–188, has good description and analysis.

9. In January–February 1943, as part of the diversionary activities that helped to screen the passage of the first Chindit raid eastward across the Chindwin, units of Savory's 23rd Indian Division also crossed the river, patrolling into Burma proper, the first Indian Army units to do so since the withdrawal of Burcorps the previous May.

10. The Assam front in 1942–1943 is covered in Kirby, *War Against Japan, Volume 2*, pp. 405–406, and *Volume 3*, pp. 41–42, and, in rather more detail, in the Indian official history: S. N. Prasad, K. D. Bhargava, and P. N. Khera, *The Reconquest of Burma, Volume 1: June 1942–June 1944* (Calcutta: Orient Longmans, 1958), pp. 44–84, 149–173. The information about the 1st Northamptons is at page 167. The Indian Official History also includes a useful diagram of the standard Japanese bunker.

The whole question of British infantry replacements deserves a monograph to itself. By the end of 1942, both Churchill and the War Office saw a crisis approaching. Thereafter, keeping the British Army up to strength became a matter of expedients: combing out rearward services, substituting women for men as gun crews in Anti-Aircraft Command to release men for the infantry, and "cannibalization," the breaking up of whole formations to provide replacements for losses. From 1943 on, covering casualties in the infantry, where most of the losses were sustained, became increasingly problematic. The expedients employed produced many reluctant and unhappy infantrymen and contributed to the mutiny of 700 infantry replacements during the fighting at the Salerno beachhead. (Ignored by the official historians, this incident is fully treated in Dominick Graham and Shelford Bidwell, *Tug of War: The Battle for Italy, 1943–1945* [London: Hodder & Stoughton, 1986], pp. 92–94.) The basic fact is that Britain simply lacked enough men for the war it was fighting. As in everything else, priority went to European theaters. In Burma this meant that British units were chronically understrength by 1944.

11. The defense of Rorke's Drift, a supply depot, during the Zulu War (1879) is an iconic episode in Victorian military history. A small force of some 150 men, most from 24th Foot, fought off an attacking force numbering 3,000–4,000 Zulu warriors. Eleven Victoria Crosses were awarded for Rorke's Drift.

12. There is a good explanation by Slim of the plans he and Scoones made in a chapter titled "How It Was Planned" in *Defeat Into Victory*, pp. 285–295.

Chapter 7. A Difficult Beginning

1. Major General Ian Lyall Grant's books: *Burma 1942: The Japanese Invasion* (Chichester, UK: Zampi Press, 1993) and *Burma: The Turning Point* (Chichester, UK: Zampi Press, 1999). Although encompassing more than the story of the Black Cats, they constitute nonetheless a fine history of that division. Grant was a Royal Engineer who was posted to India in 1938, joining King George V's Own Bengal Sappers and Miners, which dated to the dawn of the Bengal Army under the Company. As part of the expansion process, he raised a new Bengal Sappers and Miners field company that went to Burma with 17th Indian Division. He, and it, served with the Black Cats throughout the withdrawal from Burma, the reconstruction process of 1942–1943, and the Battle of Imphal. The officers of Indian sapper units were often British Army officers serving on long attachment ("secondment") to their Indian unit—one of the many anomalies of the Raj.

2. Scoones, like all senior British and Indian Army officers, had served in World War I, winning both a Military Cross and a Distinguished Service Order—the latter on the Somme. Between the wars he commanded a Gurkha battalion on the ever active North-West Frontier and then, in 1939, became director of military intelligence and operations at Army Headquarters in Delhi. It was from his position that he moved to IV Corps command in 1942.

There are in this story a number of senior Indian Army officers with decorations won on the Somme in 1916—a battle in which only one Indian Army unit participated (and then only briefly). The explanation is that in 1914 Field Marshal Lord Kitchener became secretary of state for war and the dominant figure in the Cabinet on military matters. A former Commander-in-Chief, India, Kitchener knew that there were always a number of Indian Army officers enjoying home leave, something that they could do only infrequently. In the summer of 1914 there were over 400 "at home." Kitchener in effect confiscated 257 of them from the Indian Army and assigned them to his own "New Army" units, formations that would suffer appalling casualties on the Somme. At a stroke, "K" had deprived the Indian Army of 10 percent of its officer corps before a shot was fired. None of those officers—even if they survived—were returned to the Indian Army during the war. See George Morton-Jack, *The Indian Army on the Western Front: India's Expeditionary Force to France and Belgium in the First World War* (Cambridge, UK: Cambridge University Press, 2014), p. 116.

3. Quoted in Lyall Grant, *Turning Point*, p. 84.

4. Ouvry Roberts was not an Indian Army officer, but a British Army sapper—a Royal Engineer—but had had several key Indian Army appointments. He had been Deputy Director of Military Intelligence under Scoones and then had gone, in 1941, to Iraq as GSO I (in effect, chief of staff) to Slim's 10th Indian Division. During the pro-Axis Iraqi revolt he had been flown in to the besieged RAF training base at Habbaniyah, near Baghdad. Commanding a scratch force of British infantry and local paramilitaries (known as the Assyrian Levies) backed by

RAF training aircraft doubling as improvised bombers, Roberts held the indefensible air base until relieved—a brilliant feat for which he won the Distinguished Service Order. His next posting was to rejoin Scoones at IV Corps as his Brigadier, General Staff. If IV Corps and its component divisions were run by Gurkha Rifles officers, Roberts was at least an honorary member of that fraternity.

5. Lyall Grant, *Turning Point*, pp. 64–68, effectively demolishes the charge that Cowan delayed the beginning of the withdrawal, succinctly describing the official history's charge as "Rubbish!"

6. It has been pointed out, by a writer consistently critical of IV Corps, that Scoones's very able Brigadier General Staff, Geoffrey Evans (who had succeeded Ouvry Roberts), had been abruptly transferred in early February to brigade command in Briggs's 5th Indian Division (where, as we have seen, he became the defender of the Admin Box, a landmark in a career that would take him to lieutenant general's rank and a knighthood). His successor may not have had enough time to settle into his job before the crisis broke. Certainly Scoones's headquarters had some trouble juggling all its responsibilities in the opening phases of the battle.

It is very curious that in his memoir Evens recounts that, after being told it was urgent to get to Briggs's headquarters and arranging for an RAF friend to fly him part of the way, he arrived to be greeted by a surprised Briggs, asking why he had come. When told that he was to command 9th Indian Brigade, Briggs observed that he had already appointed a commander. The opening of the Japanese attack and Evens's immediate appointment to command the Admin Box solved the problem. What exactly was going on in Evens's transfer? Possibly only the confusion endemic to large organizations under pressure. Possibly an undisclosed personal issue, but if so there are no traces of it in Scoones's papers. Harry Seaman, *The Battle at Sangshak* (London: Leo Cooper, 1989), p. 43, notes the oddity of Evens's sudden removal from IV Corps. Evens's *The Desert and the Jungle* (London: Leo Cooper, 1959), pp. 123–124, recounts his arrival at Briggs's headquarters. If Evens thought there was anything odd about this sudden transfer, he never said so.

7. Cowan's withdrawal is discussed in S. W. Kirby, *War Against Japan, Volume 3: The Decisive Battles* (London: HMSO, 1962), chap. 13, and, in much greater detail, by Lyall Grant, *Turning Point*. Slim's moves to rebuild his reserves are also covered in the Kirby chapter cited. The complex alliance politics of the theater were reflected in the problem of finding enough Dakotas (or, rather, persuading the Americans to part with those readily available) to sustain XIV Army. Raymond Callahan, *Burma 1942–1945* (London: Davis Poynter, 1978), pp. 133–136, summarizes the constant Anglo-American struggle over transport aircraft that was the background music to the Imphal battle.

8. The theater air commander, Air Chief Marshal Sir Richard Pierse, was less of a problem—perhaps because, pursuing an affair with Auchinleck's wife, he did not have time to quarrel with his boss.

9. Gracey had raised the division and would command it throughout the war and well into the postwar period. He would then become commander-in-chief of Pakistan's army in succession to Frank Messervy.

10. It is interesting that Scoones had originally planned to use the crossing of the Chindwin by a large Japanese formation as the trigger for ordering the retirement of Cowan's Black Cats to the Imphal Plain. Lyall Grant, *Turning Point*, p. 57. His reasoning was that a crossing by a force of a battalion or more would meet Slim's criteria: be certain an offensive had begun before ordering 17th Indian to withdraw. By 15 March, of course, Scoones had already ordered Cowan and Gracey back. The weakness in Scoones's original idea was that most of the Japanese *33rd Division* and some supporting units were *already* west of the Chindwin before their offensive opened.

11. There was a controversial aftermath to Sangshak. Brigadier Hope-Thompson was relieved of command and sent back to the United Kingdom under a cloud, deemed to have mishandled his brigade and then suffered a nervous breakdown. (Actually, he was concussed by a fall during the breakout.) There were even rumors that some Gurkhas had fled the battlefield. An angry participant in the battle, Harry Seaman (a subaltern in the Gurkha battalion in 1944), published an account of the battle in 1989 in which he claimed that the shabby mistreatment of both Hope-Thompson and the brigade's reputation (and the misleading account of the battle in Scoones's official dispatch) were the work of Scoones's staff—and, by implication, of Scoones himself—covering up IV Corps's own failures. By the time Seaman published, Scoones was dead. He wrote no memoirs, and his papers, in the Imperial War Museum, are not very informative on anything—and say nothing about Sangshak. It is worth noting that the official history gave the battle rather full treatment and acknowledged its crucial importance, as did Slim in his memoirs. Nonetheless, unanswered questions remain about both Hope-Thompson's treatment and the swirl of rumors about battlefield misbehavior that almost instantly began to envelop the brigade after the engagement. Seaman, *Battle at Sangshak*; Slim, *Defeat Into Victory*, pp. 299–300; Kirby, *War Against Japan, Volume 3*, pp. 236–238.

12. Mountbatten's success in wrestling additional Dakotas from the Hump airlift eased the strain on the Assam line of communications just enough to make possible the immediate movement of XXXIII Corps, which Auchinleck had initially told Giffard was not feasible. Of all the units Giffard put at Slim's disposal, only Brigadier Tom Brodie's 14th Long Range Penetration Brigade did not fight in the main battle. It reverted to Wingate for his operations in Burma. See appendix B in this volume.

13. The stand by a battalion of the Assam Regiment at Jessami, east of Kohima, was a mini-Sangshak. This new battalion (which had detached a company to another outpost at Kharasom) withstood assaults from a Japanese regiment for five days before breaking out. The isolated company at Kharasom fought two Japanese battalions for four days before it, too, broke out. Some 260 survivors made

it back to Kohima. The stand of the Assam Regiment has been well described by Leslie Edwards, *Kohima: The Furthest Battle* (Stroud, UK: History Press, 2009), pp. 66–104 (which also includes a good description of the battle at Sangshak). Although a bit confusingly organized, Edwards's meticulous reconstruction is invaluable.

14. Stopford apparently agreed. Twenty years later, he told Arthur Swinson, who was writing a book on Kohima, that he felt that Rankin had been unfairly blamed, adding that if anyone was blameworthy it was himself. He admitted that he had been very anxious about Japanese infiltration into the Brahmaputra Valley, which would threaten the railroad and the Dimapur base. Stopford's papers are in the Imperial War Museum but sealed until 2040.

15. The preliminaries to the siege of Kohima can be followed in Kirby, *War Against Japan, Volume 3*, chap. 16; Slim, *Defeat Into Victory*, chaps. 13–14; Edwards, *Kohima*, chap. 3; and Fergal Keane, *Road of Bones: The Siege of Kohima, 1944* (London: Harper Press, 2010), chap. 14. Keane discusses Rankin's role on pp. 222–224. Stopford's sealed papers might be very illuminating on this issue.

16. It doubtless helped that Cowan and his subordinate commanders, nearly all Indian Army officers, were familiar with the tactics, perfected on the North-West Frontier, for moving a column along a road while controlling the flanking hills. Much of 17th Division's withdrawal took place in very similar circumstances— the hills were mountains, jungle-covered rather than rocky and sere, and the opponents far more deadly and tenacious than even the Pathan tribesmen—but the principle was the same. Kirby, *War Against Japan, Volume 3*, chaps. 12 and 16, cover Cowan's withdrawal; Lyall Grant, *Turning Point*, pp. 54–118, does so in much greater detail. (Grant is the source of the observation about 9th Borders, p. 103.) The Indian official history, S. N. Prasad, K. D. B. Barghava, and P. N. Khera, *The Reconquest of Burma, Volume 1: June 1942–June 1944* (Calcutta: Orient Longmans, 1958), pp. 187–198, has a great deal of detail.

17. Lyall Grant summarizes the beginnings of the slide of *Fifteenth Army*'s command structure into dysfunction in *Turning Point*, pp. 109–111.

Chapter 8. The Pile Driver

1. W. S. Slim, *Defeat Into Victory* (London: Cassell, 1956), p. 315.

2. S. N. Prasad, K. D. Bhargava, and P. N. Khera, *The Reconquest of Burma, Volume 1: June 1942–June 1944* (Calcutta: Orient Longmans, 1958), p. 163. The British official history does not mention this.

3. Slim discusses his design for the battle in *Defeat Into Victory*, pp. 332–333. See also Kirby, *The War Against Japan, Volume 3: The Decisive Battles* (London: HMSO, 1962), p. 351, n. 1.

4. Kirby, *War Against Japan, Volume 3*, p. 299.

5. Slim mentions (*Defeat Into Victory*, p. 316) an attempt to use inner tubes filled with water, which could be free-dropped, in an attempt to deliver water to

Kohima's defenders. The official history does not mention this, but it is typical of the improvisatory logistics that became one of XIV Army's trademarks.

6. Churchill supplies, except for the errant air drops at Sangshak and Kohima, proved to be a mirage for the Japanese. As we have seen, when they briefly captured a large supply depot on the Tiddim Road, 17th Indian Division retook it almost intact. Facing pressure from the Japanese *15th Division*, Scoones ordered a sprawling base area at Kanglatongbi on the northern edge of the Imphal Plain to be cleared and evacuated. When it was abandoned on 8 April, only a quarter of its 4,000 tons of stores had been backloaded. When it was retaken on 20 May, the abandoned stores were found largely intact. Despite planning on the basis of Churchill supplies, the Imperial Japanese Army's logisticians proved singularly inept in utilizing them when some actually fell into their hands—a striking example of the logistic weaknesses that were endemic in the IJA.

7. Kirby, *War Against Japan, Volume 3*, p. 306. It is interesting that only one VC was awarded for the defense of Kohima, posthumously, to a lance corporal of the Royal West Kents. The defense of Rorke's Drift (1879), to which Kohima is often compared, was recognized by eleven. Of course, the standards for the award had tightened in the intervening six decades, but the paucity of awards for what was an astounding feat of courage and determination by the whole garrison may also be due to the improvised, heterogeneous nature of the mostly Indian force. Put shortly: the Royal West Kents, an established British unit, were in a better position to put forward recommendations. The siege of Kohima has attracted more historical writing than any other part of the Imphal campaign. The best accounts are Fergal Keane's *Road of Bones: The Siege of Kohima, 1944* (London: Harper Press, 2010) and Leslie Edwards's *Kohima: The Furthest Battle* (Stroud, UK: History Press, 2009).

8. Kirby, *War Against Japan, Volume 3*, p. 346.

9. Ibid., p. 336.

10. F. T. Burnett, *Keeping Up with the Hunt: The Story of 268 Indian Infantry Brigade* (privately printed by Impress of Shrewsbury, UK, 1983), p. 67. The "sepoy general" reference is, of course, to the condescension by British Army officers toward Indian units and the British officers who commanded them. It is interesting that in his recent study of the Indian Corps that fought on the Western Front in 1914–1915 Gordon Corrigan (a former Gurkha Rifles officer) says this: "Some . . . officers of the British Army looked upon Indian [Army] officers as colonial curiosities and their men as colonial cannon fodder." *Sepoys in the Trenches: The Indian Corps on the Western Front, 1914–1915* (London: Cambridge University Press, 2015), p. 97. Clearly British Army attitudes toward the Indian Army were remarkably consistent over time.

268th Indian Brigade, an all-Indian brigade, had originally been formed as the lorried (i.e., motorized) infantry brigade of 44th Indian Armoured Division. When that formation was disbanded, it became an independent formation whose tireless commander, Brigadier Max Dyer, managed to keep continuously employed in XIV Army from March 1944 until the end of the campaign. Slim would refer to it in *Defeat Into Victory* as "that most useful maid-of-all-work" (p. 488).

Burnett has some interesting reflections (pp. 66–67) on the relationship between the last generation of British officers to serve in the Indian Army and the men they commanded, concluding, "I was glad I was not in the British Army. The Indian Army was more imaginative and more tolerant of individual initiative," which is a good description of the XIV Army.

11. *Defeat Into Victory*, pp. 332–333. Slim mentions being urged by a staff officer "not on my headquarters" to rush an armored column, escorting supply trucks, down the road to Imphal, on the analogy of resupply convoys the Royal Navy ran into Malta in 1940–1942. The suggestion betrays a truly remarkable ignorance of the actual situation on the ground, as well as a curious unawareness of the dreadful losses sustained by the Malta convoys and the relatively meager amount those expensive ventures actually delivered. Slim's recounting this story in *Defeat Into Victory* is as close as he ever came to criticizing Mountbatten. Mountbatten's message to Giffard is in Kirby, *War Against Japan, Volume 3*, p. 351. A cautious footnote indicates that the message was based on a misunderstanding of Slim's plan. Everyone was careful, it would seem, about criticizing "Dickie."

12. The "high politics" of Dakota availability can be tracked in the official histories: John Ehrman, *Grand Strategy: Volume 5, August 1943–September 1944* (London: HMSO, 1956), pp. 405–415; and Kirby, *War Against Japan, Volume 3*, chaps. 12, 16, 21–25, passim. Callahan, *Burma, 1942–1945*, pp. 134–137, summarizes the argument. Churchill printed his message to Mountbatten in *Closing the Ring* (Boston: Houghton Mifflin, 1951), p. 568.

13. Kirby, *War Against Japan, Volume 3*, pp. 385–390.

14. In more lavishly supported theaters the speedy creation of all-weather airfields was made possible by supplies of pierced steel planking that enabled engineers to rapidly turn flat space into working airfields. Pierced planking was not something XIV Army had, so, like the jute parachutes for cargo drops that were their answer to shortages of parachute silk, they improvised.

15. Slim, *Defeat Into Victory*, p. 200.

16. By the time of the Comilla conference, the Dakotas, all from either Troop Carrier Command or the Hump airlift, had been flying flat-out for a month. The four RAF squadrons and four USAAF squadrons (152 Dakotas) had moved 5th Indian Division to Imphal from the Arakan (less 161st Brigade, which was flown to Dimapur). A separate battalion, designated for the defense of IV Corps headquarters, was also flown into Imphal, and part of XXXIII Corps headquarters to Dimapur. These flights, beginning on 19 March and lasting until 31 March, meant twelve days of nonstop operations. The exhaustion of men and machines then enforced a four-day pause. From 5–15 April, the lead brigades of 7th Indian and 2nd British Division were flown into Dimapur. The Dakotas had as well numerous other commitments: supply-dropping to forces in the Chin and Lushai Hills, Wingate's Special Force in Burma, 17th Indian Division as it withdrew up the Tiddim Road, the Sino-American forces in Stilwell's Northern Combat Area

Command, the Chinese forces probing gingerly into Burma from the Chinese province of Yunnan, and, finally, the isolated garrison at Fort Hertz in far northern Burma where the British had maintained themselves since the 1942 retreat. The reinforcing squadrons from the Mediterranean did not begin to play a role until the beginning of Stamina in mid-April.

17. Kirby, *War Against Japan, Volume 3*, p. 327. The number of Dakotas increased, with the arrival of the Mediterranean squadrons (all USAAF) to 232. Kirby, *War Against Japan, Volume 3*, apps. 25 and 26, pp. 511–516, prints an exhaustive statistical summary of air supply and movement of units from the beginning of the Japanese attack in the Arakan (February) to the end of the pursuit phase of the Imphal battle in August. Curiously, there are no figures for Dakotas lost, either in the text or appendices. The relevant volume of the RAF's own history—Hilary St. G. Saunders, *Royal Air Force, 1939–1945, Volume 3: The Fight Is Won* (London: HMSO, 1954), pp. 323–331—is similarly uninformative. This seems an odd omission. Air Commodore Henry Probert, a former head of the RAF's Air Historical Branch, in *The Forgotten Air Force: The Royal Air Force in the War Against Japan* (London: Brassey, 1995), p. 194, gives three Dakotas lost to enemy action and thirty-two lost in total. Clearly, monsoon flying conditions were more dangerous than the Japanese air force. The relevant volume of the US official history of Army Air Forces operations in World War II, Wesley Frank Craven and James Lea Cate, *The Army Air Forces in World War II, Volume IV: The Pacific: Guadalcanal to Saipan, August 1942 to July 1944* (Chicago: University of Chicago Press, 1950), pp. 507–509, summarizes Stamina but, again, gives no figures for losses. There are some interesting reminiscences of Dakota pilots and ground crews in Roger Annett's *Drop Zone Burma: Adventures in Allied Air Supply, 1943–1945* (Barnsley, UK: Pen & Sword, 2008).

18. Briggs had only two brigades, his third—161st Brigade—having been diverted to Dimapur, where it came under the command of 2nd British Division and then 7th Indian. Briggs was brought up to strength with a brigade of Messervy's 7th Indian, which, however, could not be shifted from the Arakan until early May, a move much impeded by weather.

19. Slim, *Defeat Into Victory*, p. 324.

20. Kirby, *War Against Japan, Volume 3*, p. 310.

21. By the time Yamamoto took Scraggy, the switchover from Gracey's 20th Division to Roberts's 23rd was complete, and Scraggy was held by detachments of the 3/3rd Gurkhas from Roberts's all-Gurkha 37 Indian Infantry Brigade. The 3/3rd suffered some 200 casualties in their attempt to hold Scraggy. Pictures of the contested ground in the Shenam Pass resemble those of World War I battlefields (as do pictures of Kohima—with the addition of shattered trees draped with parachutes from supply drops).

22. Because of both the terrain and the ratio of force to space, there was no question of a continuous line around the Imphal Plain. Japanese forces could and did infiltrate. A battalion-sized force attacked—unsuccessfully—a box in the plain on 29 April. The garrison of the box, the 4/3 Madras Regiment, was an

example of how Indian Army expansion had drawn back into its ranks groups that had once been its backbone, then gradually excluded by the "martial races" doctrine, only to be rediscovered by wartime necessity.

23. It was not only at *Fifteenth Army* that wishful thinking overcame reality. Early in May, the assistant chief of staff at Imperial General Headquarters made a tour of *Southern Army*'s area of responsibility. When he visited *Burma Area Army*'s headquarters at Rangoon, Kawabe reiterated that he would take Imphal. However, lower-ranking officers made it clear to Lieutenant General Hata and his staff that *Fifteenth Army*'s logistic situation was precarious (an understatement), and Hata returned to Tokyo prepared to brief against the continuation of the operation. The chief of staff (Tojo)—who, of course, headed the army faction to which Mutaguchi belonged and who had signed off on his plan—however, had a message direct from Field Marshal Count Terauchi at *Southern Army* claiming that Imphal could be taken providing the attack was pursued with "determination." The result was that when Hata began a briefing on 15 May advising that there was "little chance" of success at Imphal Tojo cut him off and moved on to a new topic. Kirby, *War Against Japan, Volume 3*, p. 353–354.

24. When the Japanese *14th Tank Regiment* crossed the Chindwin at the beginning of the offensive it had sixty tanks. When it was ordered to move to *33rd Division* it had forty left after supporting the attacks on the Shenam Pass. The 400-mile journey from Shenam to Kaleymo at the bottom of the Kabaw Valley and then back up the Tiddim Road, climbing at one point to 8,000 feet, could only, thanks to the RAF, be made at night with stops every twenty minutes to allow tracks and bearings to cool (Lyall Grant, *Turning Point*, p. 186).

25. It is a tribute to Japanese determination that the tanks got as far as Torbung. The Japanese tanks were not terribly formidable in any case. As the block was being emplaced one Gurkha rifleman knocked out two light tanks with a Projector Infantry Anti-Tank (PIAT) weapon, the British equivalent of the American bazooka, designed by Major Millis Jefferis, who, sponsored by Churchill, developed a number of innovative weapons during the war. The Japanese light tank, according to the British official history, could not move off the road, lacking the weight and engine power to force its way through the dense, seven-foot-high "tiger grass" (Kirby, *War Against Japan, Volume 3*, p. 347, n. 2).

26. One incident illustrates why Japanese casualties were so punishingly high: early on 24 April, a single officer emerged from behind one of the burned-out Japanese lorries that littered the approaches to the 1/7 Gurkhas block and, with a bayonet fixed to a light machine gun, charged. He was immediately shot down (Lyall Grant, *Turning Point*, p. 149). This brave, if pointless, act was quite typical of the IJA.

27. In addition to lacking ammunition, *33rd Division* lacked a commander. Tanaka, stuck on the wrong side of the Torbung block, had a strenuous hike over rugged hills to reach his new headquarters, something that could have done little for the division's management of its battle.

28. On the evening of the day 48th Brigade linked up with its division, Punch Cowan told Cameron he was due for a rest and was to be posted to a training school in India. Lyall Grant strongly hints that this was an unpopular decision. Cameron, who had commanded the brigade since taking over in the aftermath of the Sittang disaster, was clearly both fearless and effective, and the timing of this command change does seem odd. Cowan, after all, who took over the division after the Sittang battle, commanded it though to the end of war.

29. Jon Latimer, *Burma: The Forgotten War* (London: John Murray, 2004), p. 272.

30. The fighting around Bishenpur can be followed—with difficulty—in Kirby, *War Against Japan, Volume 3*, chaps. 24, 25, passim, and much more clearly in Lyall Grant, *Turning Point*, pp. 119–201.

31. When Giffard assembled reinforcements for Slim at the beginning of the Japanese offensive, he included Brigadier Lance Perowne's 23rd Long Range Penetration Brigade, one of the reserve formations of Orde Wingate's Special Force. Departing from the Assam railway, the brigade worked its way across the wild, trackless Naga Hills, subsisting on air supply (another task for the Dakotas) and cutting across such supply lines as *31st Division* had. As far as I am aware, no account of this brigade's operations has ever been published—a truly forgotten part of the Imphal campaign. Yet 23rd LRP Brigade made a more substantial contribution to wrecking *Fifteenth Army*'s supply system than the main body of Special Force operating in Burma proper.

32. A Japanese account quoted in Kirby, *War Against Japan, Volume 3*, p. 359.

33. Lyall Grant, *Turning Point*, p. 209.

Chapter 9. Vindication

1. Ian Lyall Grant, *Burma: The Turning Point* (Chichester, UK: Zampi Press, 1999), p. 363.

2. Ibid., p. 364.

3. The weakness of British infantry units was a continual concern in XIV Army. By 1944, the British Army faced an unresolvable manpower crisis: Britain simply did not have enough men for the huge war it was waging. (There is a very good discussion of the British Army's manpower crisis in Allan Allport, *Browned Off and Bloody-Minded: The British Soldier Goes To War* [New Haven, CT: Yale University Press, 2015], pp. 203–220). In the run-up to Overlord, the War Office told Montgomery that it could only cover Twenty-First Army Group's expected "wastage" until July; after that, units had to be cannibalized to keep other units up to strength. Eighth Army in Italy had to comb out rearward services, antiaircraft units, etc., to fill the gaps in its infantry battalions—a process that all too often yielded reluctant infantrymen. The problem was at its worst in SEAC, which was at the end of the line for British infantry reinforcements as

for everything else. When Slim talked to Mountbatten on 2 July, he pressed the Supreme Commander to find reinforcements for his anemic British battalions. Mountbatten promised to try to comb out 4,000–5,000 men from now surplus antiaircraft units. It was, however, a losing battle. The British battalions that had been part of every Indian infantry brigade since the 1857 Mutiny were now a fading presence—17th Indian had had only one, as had 23rd. It made no difference. Slim's divisions won anyway.

4. Christopher Bayly and Tim Harper, *Forgotten Armies: The Fall of British Asia, 1941–1945* (London: Allen Lane, 2004), p. 388.

5. Slim, *Defeat Into Victory*, 3rd unabridged ed. (London: Cassell, 1972), p. 369.

6. Quoted in Slim, *Defeat Into Victory*, p. 349.

7. Mountbatten, who had an incurable tendency to annex any successful idea or operation to his own credit, later claimed that the monsoon pursuit was his idea, a claim then put forward in his official biography: Philip Ziegler, *Mountbatten* (New York: Knopf, 1985), pp. 250–251. In fact, there can be little doubt that the idea was Slim's, which *his* official biographer pointed out to Mountbatten in 1975. On all this see Robert Lyman, *Slim: Master of War* (London: Constable, 2004), p. 134.

8. Scoones was posted to Central Command in India—an administrative and training command. He then returned to Britain to become the last occupant of the position of Military Secretary to the India Office, the principal military adviser to the government department that supervised the Indian Empire. IV Corps would return to Burma for the 1944–1945 campaign under the command of Messervy, who had commanded 7th Indian Division in the Arakan and at Imphal.

9. The 23rd Division did rotate back to India, leaving 14th Army permanently. Roberts, promoted to lieutenant general, took over XXXIV Indian Corps, which would eventually mount SEAC's only amphibious operation (Zipper) in September 1945, shortly after Japan's surrender.

10. Slim, *Defeat Into Victory*, p. 357. For all but three months of that time, Cowan had commanded it, as he would continue to do until Rangoon fell in 1945.

11. Ibid., p. 360.

12. Ibid., pp. 359–360, pays generous tribute to Lushai Brigade. The official history accords their activities only brief, passing mention.

13. African formations had also been mobilized in 1914–1918 but were employed exclusively in Africa, largely in the long series of East African campaigns. The bulk of the mobilized African manpower was not, in fact, embodied in fighting formations but used as porters who constituted the logistic support for the campaign. On this see Hew Strahan, *The First World War, Volume 1: To Arms* (Oxford, UK: Oxford University Press, 2001), pp. 569–643. Total British combatant losses over the four years of fighting in East Africa were about 10,000, more than two-thirds from disease, compared to some 100,000 African porters who died.

14. The division was made up primarily of units of the King's African Rifles, recruited in Kenya, Uganda, and Tanganika. The King's African Rifles, like the

Indian Army, had expanded exponentially to meet the demands of the imperial war effort.

15. The "believed resistance" of the Africans to malaria is in S. W. Kirby, et al., *The War Against Japan, Volume 4: The Reconquest of Burma* (London: HMSO, 1965), p. 40, n. 1. Slim's remarks on the issue are in *Defeat Into Victory,* pp. 354–355. (The quotation is from page 354.) Stopford's dissent is mentioned in Kirby, *War Against Japan, Volume 4*, app. 14, p. 481, n. 1. Despite the belief in African resistance to malaria, all troops were on mepacrine and dustings of DDT were liberally applied.

16. Slim, *Defeat Into Victory,* p. 356, records the linkup, but then adds a clear criticism: "In hard fact it would have been better had the 11th Division reached Kaleymo while the Japanese were still locked with the 5th Division on the Tiddim Road." He then quickly adds that climate and terrain precluded a more rapid advance, concluding, "Their advance was a great achievement, which almost a year before would almost universally have been proclaimed impossible." This rather grudging praise, when taken together with Slim's criticisms of the structure of the African divisions in XIV Army (pp. 165–166, 353), raises the question of Slim's attitude toward African troops. John A. L. Hamilton, who served with 81st West African Division in the Arakan, wrote the only full-scale history of any of the African divisions: *War Bush: 81 (West African) Division in Burma, 1943–1945* (London: Michael Russell, 2001). He argues that Slim and his fellow "sepoy generals" had a poor opinion of African units and scanted their achievements both at the time and in retrospect, an attitude that in turn colored the views of the official historians. It is clear from *Defeat Into Victory* that Slim had reservations about the way his African formations were organized and officered. Clearly, he did not rate them as highly as his Indian Army divisions. His fundamental generosity of spirit, however, produced a clear acknowledgment of what "Fluffy" Fowkes and his division did during the monsoon pursuit. It is ironic that the disdain British officers of African units, like Hamilton, felt in Indian Army attitudes to them mirrored the condescension Indian Army officers felt in British Army views of their service.

While there is little writing on the African soldiers who served in Burma, there are two fascinating accounts of what it was like to leave a Nigerian village to fight in Burma. Barnaby Phillips, *Another Man's War: The Story of a Burma Boy in Britain's Forgotten African Army* (London: One World Publications, 2014), chronicles the experience of Isaac Fedoyebo, who served with 81st West African Division in the Arakan. Biyi Bandele's *Burma Boy* (London: Jonathan Cape, 2007), while a novel in form, is based on the experiences of his father and other African veterans who served in Chindit II. "Burma boy" was a colloquialism applied in West Africa to Africans who served in XIV Army.

17. Kirby, *War Against Japan, Volume 4*, app. 13, p. 461, prints a summary of the human cost of the monsoon campaign. The average weekly strength of XXXIII Corps for 22 June–16 November was 88,578. Less than half of this number were engaged in the monsoon pursuit. This portion of the corps suffered 47,098

casualties from sickness, the largest number falling to "malaria and other fevers." More than half of those who fell ill had to be evacuated from XXXIII Corps area and took no further part in the monsoon campaign. Battle casualties amounted to 3,289, of which only 372 were killed in action. It was in a footnote to this appendix that the official historians recorded Stopford's conclusion that evidence did not support the belief in greater African resistance to malaria.

18. The Bailey bridge was the brainchild of Donald Bailey, a War Office civil servant whose hobby was building model bridges. Quickly developed in 1941–1942, it was extensively used by British forces from 1942 onward—over 3,000 were built in Italy alone. A modular, prefabricated bridge that could be put together without either special tools or heavy equipment, it was obviously a godsend to XIV Army, where special tools and heavy equipment were hard to come by. Many Bailey bridges remained in service for decades.

19. Slim, *Defeat Into Victory*, p. 369. By the time Slim walked through the Shwegyn Basin, he was Sir William. His knighthood, as a Knight Commander of the Order of the Bath, had been "gazetted" (i.e., announced) in September 1944. He was actually "dubbed" on the Imphal Plain on 14 December 1944 by the Viceroy, Field Marshal Lord Wavell, acting for the King-Emperor. His three corps commanders—Scoones, Stopford, and Christison—were knighted at the same time. At this point, Slim (with IV Corps), XXXIII Corps, his old XV Corps, and numerous independent formations commanded the largest single army on the Allied side.

Chapter 10. Final Thoughts

1. John Masters, *The Road Past Mandalay*, paper ed. (New York: Bantam, 1961), pp. 306–307.

2. There is another point seldom mentioned about British units serving with XIV Army. There was concern about their morale as the European war drew to a close. Wavell had noted that, once Germany was beaten, British troops in India would want to go home. By 1944, many British units in India and SEAC had been overseas for years. In September 1944, the War Office, recognizing this, reduced the time overseas necessary to qualify for return home from five years to three years, eight months. That stripped 5,700 men from SEAC's British units, which were already 30,000 men short of establishment (10,000 of those vacancies were in XIV Army, mostly in infantry battalions). When Rangoon fell—just as, in Europe, Germany surrendered—British units in SEAC not only were understrength but also expected an early return home. It is a commonplace that in the July 1945 General Election the service vote went heavily for Labour. It was the opinion of British officers of XIV Army with whom I spoke that the Labour vote there was overwhelming. It was of course a vote for repatriation at the earliest moment. Had the Japanese war gone on into 1946, and had the British government continued to seek the largest possible role in it, they would have found themselves utterly

dependent on the Indian Army. Alan Allport, in his otherwise excellent *Browned Off and Bloody-Minded,* remarks oddly (p. 216) that "Mountbatten's Army" might not "have kept fighting at all without a massive—and politically controversial—resupply of troops from Europe." This rather misses the point that Slim's army had never had more than a minority—and by the end a very small minority—of British infantry. After the Japanese surrender XIV Army's units continued to perform well in combat in both French Indochina and the Netherlands East Indies in 1945–1946, as described well by Daniel Marston in *The Indian Army and the End of the Raj* (Cambridge, UK: Cambridge University Press, 2014), pp. 151–199. By that time, British combat units were very rare indeed.

Appendix A: Churchill and the Indian Army

1. Winston S. Churchill, *My Early Life,* paper ed. (London: Collins Fontana, 1959), p. 27. The American publisher's title is *Thoughts and Adventures.*

2. John Connell, *Auchinleck: A Critical Biography* (London: Cassell, 1959), p. 274, n. 1. It is interesting how little impact this bigoted remark, about an army that fought and died for Britain in every theater except Northwest Europe, has had on assessments of Churchill by his admirers.

3. Churchill's war reportage is reprinted in Frederick Woods (ed.), *Young Winston's Wars: The Original Despatches of Winston S. Churchill War Correspondent, 1897–1900* (New York: Viking Press, 1973). Churchill's *The Story of the Malakand Field Force: An Episode of Frontier War,* originally published in 1898, has been reprinted many times.

4. She turned him down but remained a lifelong friend.

5. Geoffrey Best, *Churchill: A Study in Greatness* (New York: Hambledon & London, 2001), p. 24. This is the best analysis of Churchill's career yet written.

6. Churchill to Curtin, 11 January 1942. The full message (and the Syndicate advice) is in the Churchill Papers, 4/235 A, f. 128, Churchill Archive Center, Churchill College, Cambridge. The published version is in Winston S. Churchill, *The Hinge of Fate* (Boston: Houghton Mifflin, 1950), p. 11.

Appendix B: Wingate

1. Kirby, *The War Against Japan, Volume 3: The Decisive Battles* (London: HMSO, 1962), p. 37. One of those so alienated was Kirby himself, in 1943 Deputy Chief of the General Staff at Army Headquarters, India.

2. The operations planned, then modified or canceled, in SEAC after Quadrant are a bewildering story. There is a summary in Raymond Callahan, *Burma 1942–1945* (London: Davis Poynter, 1978), pp. 69–114. Much more detail can be found in John Ehrman, *Grand Strategy, Volume 5: August 1943–September 1944* (London: HMSO, 1956), chaps. 3–5, and in Kirby, *War Against Japan, Volume 3,*

chaps. 1, 2, 5, and passim. In general, it is a good rule of thumb to remember that the only plans in SEAC that consistently worked out were Slim's.

The Chinese forces in Yunnan ("Yokeforce" to the Allies) flit through Anglo-American plans for nearly a year. Chiang dangled them in front of his allies, offering their participation in return for more supplies, extensive Allied operations (mostly amphibious and therefore impracticable), and, at one point, a huge cash subvention. The Japanese, who had gotten rather good at assessing Chinese units, rated the ten divisions in Yunnan (which, even at full strength, would have amounted to about two British or Indian divisions) as unready and of low quality. Certainly, when they finally crossed the Salween River into Burma, one understrength Japanese division contained them quite easily.

3. Brigadier W. D. A. "Joe" Lentaigne, unlike Calvert and Fergusson, was not an original Chindit. When, following the first Chindit expedition, Wavell had sanctioned the raising of a second Chindit brigade, he named Lentaigne to command it. Lentaigne, who came from an Irish family that had settled in Burma, belonged, like so many Indian Army officers who filled prominent positions under Slim, to the Gurkha Rifles, in his case 4th Gurkhas. He was not a true believer in Wingate's gospel, which may be why Slim picked him to succeed Wingate in command of Special Force. He oversaw the later stages of Chindit II and after Indian independence remained on in the Indian Army until 1956, commanding the Indian Defence College. Unlike Calvert and Fergusson, he left no memoir, but there are two interesting accounts of him commanding 111th Brigade: Frank Baines, *Chindit Affair: A Memoir of the War in Burma* (London: Pen & Sword, 2011), and John Masters, *The Road Past Mandalay*, paper ed. (New York: Bantam, 1961). Masters, a fellow Gurkha Rifles officer, was Lentaigne's brigade major (second in command) and took over 111th Brigade when Slim moved Lentaigne up to replace Wingate. Baines's account, written in the 1980s, was published posthumously.

4. These memos are reproduced as appendixes 17–18 in Kirby, *War Against Japan, Volume 3*, pp. 486–492. One suspects these documents were printed to support the critical evaluation of Wingate in the text, which Kirby and his team must have known would be badly received by Wingate's partisans (as it was).

5. W. S. Slim, *Defeat Into Victory,* unabridged ed. (London: Cassell, 1972), p. 216. Max Hastings, in *Warriors,* paper ed. (London: Harper, 2006), p. 202, was far more blunt, describing Wingate as a person "in whose make up there was much of the charlatan." One has the sense that Slim felt the same way (certainly in a private postwar letter he complained that no one would tell the truth about Wingate). However, he showed discretion—and generosity—in his memoirs.

6. Slim, *Defeat Into Victory,* p. 219. Perhaps the best commentary on Wingate's threats to invoke Churchill came from Mountbatten's chief of staff, Lieutenant General Sir Henry Pownall, who told his diary, "I don't doubt the P.M. has invited him to do so, he does it to many people, including myself in the past.

But Wingate, being abnormal, doesn't see that he cannot go about cracking that whip." Brian Bond (ed.), *Chief of Staff: The Diaries of Lieutenant General Sir Henry Pownall, Volume 2: 1940–1944* (Hamden, CT: Archan Books, 1974), p. 112.

7. Kirby, *War Against Japan, Volume 3*, p. 171, n. 1. There is in fact quite a bit of evidence that there were serious gaps in the training program for Special Force, which reflect on Wingate and his hastily assembled headquarters. Antimalarial discipline was weak—mepacrine was not routinely taken and field hygiene was ignored, as Wingate felt it was unnecessary for fast-moving columns. All this contributed to the very high levels of sickness in Special Force. Julian Thompson, *The Imperial War Museum Book of War Behind Enemy Lines* (Washington, DC: Brassey, 1998), app. B, pp. 426–431, is very illuminating about this aspect of Wingate's operations.

8. Wilfred Thesiger, *The Life of My Choice* (London: Collins, 1987), p. 334. The officer in question was Colonel Hugh Boustead, a veteran of World War I. Thesiger's memoir provides a very interesting view of Wingate in Ethiopia (or Abyssinia, as it then was usually called)—an underexamined chapter in his stormy career. Although Thesiger found Wingate "inspiring," he saw very clearly the character defects that ultimately made him as hated by many as he was admired by some: "Wingate seemed to take pleasure in provoking people, and was often deliberately rude and aggressive." He added that Wingate was "ruthlessly ambitious" (pp. 320, 350).

9. Slim, *Defeat Into Victory*, p. 217.

10. Kirby, *War Against Japan, Volume 3*, p. 208.

11. Slim's "strangely naïve" comment is in *Defeat Into Victory*, p. 218. Slim described the dramatic moments on the airfield at Hailakandi, with the Dakotas and the gliders they would tow ready to go, when aerial reconnaissance photographs showed one of the designated airheads (Piccadilly) obstructed by logs, which might indicate Japanese foreknowledge of the plan (it didn't—merely activity by Burmese foresters). *Defeat Into Victory*, pp. 259–262. See also Kirby, *War Against Japan, Volume 3*, pp. 178–180. Wingate's partisans resented the suggestion that he had panicked and abdicated decisionmaking to Slim, but the evidence is that, temporarily rattled, that is just what he did. See Shelford Bidwell, *The Chindit War* (New York: Macmillan, 1980), pp. 105–106, for a dispassionate analysis. Slim, in any case, as army commander, bore the final responsibility, so the ultimate decision had to be his.

12. Kirby, *War Against Japan, Volume 3*, p. 213, n. 1, 2.

13. Slim, *Defeat Into Victory*, pp. 269–270.

14. Kirby, *War Against Japan, Volume 3*, pp. 185–186, details the assembly of the Japanese force intended to deal with the Chindits. The battalion surrendered by *15th Division* was returned to its parent formation when Hayashi's force was completely assembled.

15. Kirby, *War Against Japan, Volume 3*, pp. 209, 212, 281, discusses Wingate's attempt to focus Special Force on *Fifteenth Army*'s communications. Special Force

did, of course, constrict the supply lines of *18th Division* facing Stilwell—but not enough to prevent it holding out in Myitkyina until August.

16. Kirby, *War Against Japan, Volume 3*, p. 445.

Appendix C: Note on Chindit Historiography

1. S. W. Kirby et al., *The War Against Japan, Volume 2: India's Most Dangerous Hour* (London: HMSO, 1958), p. 327. It is interesting that the Indian official history (in volume 1) devotes eight chapters to the Chindits, four on each Chindit operation. Its summary is more dismissive than anything Kirby's team wrote: "The estimate that the Force paid only a five percent dividend is not perhaps far from the truth" (p. 402).

2. The major group of British veterans of the Burma Campaign was the Burma Star Association, with which Slim was closely associated.

3. Titled "Paper by Sir Robert Thompson, KBE GMG DSO MC and Brigadier P. W. Mead, CBE, on behalf of the Chindits Old Comrades Association and others, *Official History of the Second World War—The War Against Japan—Volume III—by S. Woodburn Kirby and others. Judgment of Major General O. C. Wingate, DSO.*" This forty-five-page typescript, dated 28 April 1977, was delivered, according to Mead, "at the back door of the Cabinet Office." A copy is in the Imperial War Museum's Department of Documents, Ref. No. D/Docs. W. The quoted material is at page 35.

4. Bernard Fergusson, *The Trumpet in the Hall* (London: Collins, 1970), p. 191.

5. John Masters, *The Road Past Mandalay*, paper ed. (New York: Bantam, 1961), p. 135.

6. Simon Anglim, *Orde Wingate and the British Army, 1922–1944* (London: Pickering & Chatto, 2010), p. 218.

Note on Further Reading

This is a work of synthesis aimed at those who will probably not bring to it great familiarity with either the Indian Army of the British Raj, Slim, or the long Burma campaign. Accordingly, I have not only cited specific sources in the endnotes but also tried to flag reliable and, where possible, recent titles that will in their turn lead the interested reader further and deeper into the subject. For a comprehensive bibliography, London University's School of Oriental and African Studies (SOAS) hosts the Burma Campaign Memorial Library (https://www .soas.ac.uk/library/archives/collections/rare_books/bcml/), which has assembled a comprehensive collection of printed materials and other resources.

Index